GW01339159

SUPPLIED BY
MARITIME BOOKS
LISKEARD PL14 4EL
TEL: (01579) 343663
*Specialist Naval Booksellers
& Publishers*

THE HAND-ME-DOWN SHIPS

The Hand-me-down
SHIPS

KEN REED

This is the true account of the World War II exploits of ten ex-American Coast Guard cutters and the Officers and men of the Royal Navy who served in them.

Published 1993 by Ken Reed
Fleet Hargate,
Spalding, Lincolnshire.

Copyright © Ken Reed 1993

All rights reserved. No part of this publication may be reproduced in any form without the prior permission of the publisher.

British Library Cataloguing-in-Publication Data.
A Catalogue record for this book is available from the British Library.

ISBN 0 9522387 0 5

Printed in Great Britain by AbbeyPrint Ltd.,
Benner Road, Pinchbeck, Spalding, Lincolnshire.

This book is dedicated to all who served in the coast guard cutters and to the memory of those shipmates who were lost. It includes also my children whose encouragement proved invaluable during the researching of it.

ACKNOWLEDGEMENTS

This tribute to the cutters and the Royal Navy men who served in them, would not have been possible without the generous assistance given by the surviving members of their crews. The author offers his sincere appreciation for the countless contributions of first-hand accounts and photographs supplied from personal collections far too many to acknowledge individually.

This gratitude is extended also to all the other sources who provided valuable help during the long period of research:

Department of the Navy, United States of America; The United States Coast Guard; The Public Records Office; Royal Naval Historical Branch, Ministry of Defence; The Royal Naval Association; Navy News; U-Boat Archives, Germany; Charlie Chester 'Radio Soapbox'; City of Glasgow District Council; Guildhall Library, London; Royal Naval College, Greenwich; Imperial War Museum; The 'Telegraph', Official Organ of NUMAST; Office of the City Clerk, Vancouver, Canada; The 'Evening Telegraph', St. John's, Newfoundland, Canada; The Italian Embassy, London; The French Embassy, London; The Polish Embassy, London; Mr. David Thomas; Captain J. Baker-Cresswell, RN., Lt.Cdr. James D'Arcy Nesbitt RNR (Rtd); Vice Admiral Thomas R. Sargent III USCG (Rtd); Captain Oscar C.B. Wev USCG (Rtd); Captain Robert F. Barber USCG (Rtd); and Rear Admiral E.C. Allen Jnr. USCG (Rtd).

CONTENTS

	Page
INTRODUCTION	IX

CHAPTER ONE
    Assignment to the Royal Navy 1

CHAPTER TWO
    First impressions 10

CHAPTER THREE
    HMS 'Culver' — the first casualty 19

CHAPTER FOUR
    HMS 'Walney' and HMS 'Hartland' — suicide mission   33

CHAPTER FIVE
    HMS 'Landguard' — (1) 54

CHAPTER SIX
    HMS 'Landguard' — (2) 65

CHAPTER SEVEN
    HMS 'Lulworth' — U-boat Kill 74

CHAPTER EIGHT
    HMS 'Lulworth' — foreign commission 83

CHAPTER NINE
    HMS 'Totland' — from civvy to sailor 94

CHAPTER TEN
    HMS 'Totland' — first Caribbean Convoy 104

CHAPTER ELEVEN
    HMS 'Gorleston' — errands of mercy 120

CHAPTER TWELVE
    HMS 'Gorleston' — leads last assault of the war 128

CHAPTER THIRTEEN
    HMS 'Sennen' 145

CHAPTER FOURTEEN
    HMS 'Banff' and HMS 'Fishguard' 155

CHAPTER FIFTEEN
    Author's conclusions 170

Cutter's captains and technical data 174

End Piece 177

Index 178

Introduction

The maritime aspect of World War II, appropriately designated the 'War at Sea', has been the subject of countless books and films. The output will doubtless continue as more stories are uncovered about the ships and men who braved the rigors of war on the high seas, in order to keep open the shipping lanes, upon which Great Britain depended so much during the greatest world-wide conflict of all time.

Deeds of heroism during the clashes with enemy submarines, surface ships and air attack, were common-place, as were the victories and the tragic losses of ships and men, as the tide of the war flowed first one way, then the other. Encounters between the big ships, which spewed out their messages of death and destruction at long range, invariably made the headlines, as did the activities of the cruisers and dashing destroyers which were usually in attendance. Many of these exploits earned a place in the annals of naval history, and deservedly so, but for every one thus honoured, a great many more were destined to anonymity.

Since attention was usually centred around the 'main events' it is not surprising that the day-to-day activities of the small fry, whose contribution was no less important, attracted less attention. Their war was fought, often at close range, in the cat and mouse contest with enemy U-boats, the silent enemy, whose targets were the merchant ships and tankers which carried equipment and supplies vital to the war effort and Britain's survival. The accounts of their accomplishments are, in so many cases, tucked away in archives and the now failing memories of the diminishing band of survivors who endured the war at sea.

Among those little-remembered ships were ten ex-American Coast Guard cutters, offered to Great Britain in 1941, under the terms of the Lend-Lease Agreement. The offer was gratefully accepted at a

INTRODUCTION

time when British escort vessels were being hard pressed, and a particular need existed for long-range seaworthy ships for the Atlantic convoy routes.

The gravity of the situation at that time is evidenced in shipping losses for May 1941, when no fewer than 144 ships, totalling some 400,000 tons were sunk, the highest monthly losses since the outbreak of hostilities.

The cutters were additional to 50 ageing destroyers handed over by the Americans in 1940, in return for which, Britain ceded to the United States, sovereign rights for 99 years over sites for Naval, Military and Air bases in the Bahamas, Jamaica, Antigua, St. Lucia, Trinidad and British Guianna.

Since the cutters were extremely active on convoy escorts and countless other operations during their five years service with the Royal Navy, many of which featured action against the enemy, it is not possible to detail all of them in this volume. A selected cross-section of highlights from their individual careers will no doubt suffice to illustrate just how wide-ranging their operations were.

Ken Reed
Spalding, Lincolnshire.

Chapter One
Assignment to the Royal Navy

On 31st December 1940, with the fight against the Axis powers in its second year, most national newspapers carried the story of a German bombing raid on London. The resulting inferno was of such proportions that one paper described it as 'The Second Great Fire'. In that single assault on the Capital, on Sunday 29th, it was estimated that over 10,000 incendiary bombs were dropped, destroying many historically famous landmarks and causing casualties among the population. Miraculously, in the middle of the devastation, St. Paul's Cathedral survived.

The newspapers expressed not only their admiration, but that of the rest of the nation, for the courage and fortitude of the City's population, for whom this experience was to become all too familiar as the war progressed.

The good news in the newspapers of that date, was the annoucement that the United States of America was to step up its aid to Britain. The President, Franklin D. Roosevelt, was reported to have said in a speech to the American people:

"We must make America the great arsenal for democracy. We have furnished Britain with great material support and will furnish far more in the future."

It was further announced, the same day, that the United States Defence Commission had approved arms contracts valued at £2,500,000,000. There was an almost immediate boost to America's production to fulfil both American and British orders for a vast range of equipment, which included 50,000 planes, 9,000 tanks and 380 naval vessels. Such an output and accumulation of the machinery of war was evidence enough that whilst the Americans were not yet engaged in the fighting, they were aware that the defence of the

United Kingdom was vital to the defence of the United States, and intended to divert much of its considerable production capacity towards helping Britain sustain her effort.

Additional to the American's extensive production programme, aid was provided in many other forms, perhaps the most acceptable of which, was the supply of ships suitable for convoy escort duties. British escorts were already over-stretched, largely due to the increasing number of enemy submarines prowling the convoy routes, and the casualties suffered in the battle to ensure the safe passage of merchant ships and their vital cargoes to and from the United Kingdom. Further to filling the gaps in escort strength, the Lend-Lease ships provided valuable breathing space whilst the construction programme for a fleet of 'Flower Class' Corvettes was completed.

On the 5th April 1941, the President of the United States put his signature to Transfer Directive No. D-27-T, and in so doing, assigned to Great Britain, ten U.S. Coast Guard cutters. This Directive to the Secretary of the United States Treasury, with instructions — 'to arrange with the Chairman of the British Supply Council in North America for the time, method and other details of the disposition,' — was put into immediate effect. The ships assigned were the cutters *Cayuga*', *Tahoe*', *Champlain*', *Chelan*', *Itasca*', *Mendota*', *Saranac*', *Pontchartrain*', *Shoshone*' and *Sebago*'. All named after American lakes, and whilst appropriately designated the 'Lake' Class, they were popularly known as the '250 footers' and most of them were on operational duties immediately prior to their recall for transfer to the Royal Navy.

The decision to hand over ten of the best and most modern ships of the Coast Guard fleet, did not receive unanimous approval in some American quarters. Rear Admiral R.R. Waesche, Commandant of the U.S. Coast Guard, would have preferred that more ageing ships be transferred instead, whilst the Chief of U.S. Naval Operations, Admiral Harold Stark USN., is said to have expressed his desire for four of them for service with the U.S. Navy in the Caribbean.

The reluntance of Commandant Waesche to part with the cutters is understandable. First commissioned between 1928 and 1932, they embodied the results of the Coast Guard's one-hundred-and-fifty years experience in good sea ships. Not only were they designed by the Coast Guard, but one of their officers, Captain Q.B. Newman, was responsible for the design of the cutters' innovative turbo-electric-drive power plant.

Waesche's high regard for the cutters was shared by the men who served in them, from Admirals to blue-jackets, whilst Coast Guard veterans still speak of them with an affection born of the seaworthiness of the ships, affinity for the sea, and a fraternal relationship forged from the sharing of a common experience.

Rear Admiral E.C. Allen Jn. USCG (Rtd) served in the *'Cayuga'* in 1935, *'Mendota'* in 1938, and *'Sebago'* in 1939. He remained with the latter until May 1941, and on her being de-commissioned for transfer to Great Britain, was assigned to the U.S. Navy vessel *'Alexander Hamilton'*, which was torpedoed and sunk off Iceland on 29th January 1942. Of the 'Lake' Class cutters he said:

"They were the most seaworthy vessels in which I served. The hull design of 250ft, 42ft beam and 16ft draft, propelled by a deep four-bladed single screw, favoured by a severe flare forward and a high freeboard of 15ft, unaffected by much superstructure or top hamper, all combined to produce a vessel worthy of riding out any kind of sea and with the weather deck relatively dry. I sailed in them in all kinds of weather, including hurricanes. They could take it."

The most outstanding feature of the cutters was their endurance, which made them very desirable for convoy duties. The storage capacity for fuel, about 90,000 gallons, was sufficient for them to remain at sea for periods in excess of 21 days. They had a similar capacity for the storage of provisions. Shaft Horse Power ranged from 3200 to 3350, and their endurance of 6/7,000 miles at an economical 9 knots was superior to many RN ships of similar size.

In appearance, and throughout, they bore little resemblance to warships, if one makes comparisons with destroyers, corvettes, sloops and frigates of the time. The superstructore was located in a central position fore and aft, taking up about one third of the vessel's overall length. The bridge was located above a large wheelhouse (or lower bridge), the latter being fronted by windows along the entire width, affording excellent forward visibility. The wings of the lower bridge extended on port and starboard sides to the full width of the ship. Below the wooden caulked deck, the forward and after sections were linked by the portside passageway, which was flanked by offices and cabins on the outboard side. Accommodation was superb throughout by any standards. The large wardroom, to which entrance was by an imposing staircase, was surrounded by a bannistered gallery, off which opened the officers' cabins and the Captain's harbour accommodation. This area was later decked off to reduce the ships' vulnerability to damage. Sleeping facilities were bunks all round, which gave no assurance of a sound night's sleep in ships which had an uneviable reputation for rolling. The bunks were later removed and the British Naval ratings reverted to the more familiar hammocks.

On the debit side, the cutters had one rather disturbing feature, their minimal sub-division, which made them prone to sink very quickly if holed beneath the waterline. This disadvantage was made disastrously obvious when one of them sank in under one minute after being torpedoed in the Atlantic in 1942, and all but thirteen of the crew were lost.

In spite of their indisputable seaworthiness, their suitability for all-out warfare was viewed with some scepticism by some U.S. Naval and Coast Guard officers, among them Vice-Admiral Thomas R. Sargent USCG (Rtd), who had served his cadetship in cutters in the 30's, and some forty years later, became Vice-Commandant of the US Coast Guard (1970-1974):

"Most of us had grave misgivings of the cutters' suitability for all-out warfare. The ships were well armed and could be coverted into fine fighting ships, but the watertight integrity and wooden decks made them vulnerable to damage. The magnificent wardroom with the staircase, was very attractive but hardly suited to wartime service. However, they were outstanding vessels and would live through any storm, and they served us well and faithfully for years."

Some of the deficiencies to which Vice-Admiral Sargent referred were later rectified during a series of conversion refits, although very little could be done about the sub-division.

The cutters' complement comprised eight commissioned officers, four warrant officers and eighty-five enlisted men. That figure was increased substantially when the ships went into service with the Royal Navy.

In order to appreciate the way in which the ships perpetuated their good name during World War II, it is necessary to explain something of their activities whilst in the service of the US Coast Guard. They were constantly engaged on what their crews might casually describe as 'routine operations'. In fact, these 'routine operations' were often so naturally hazardous as to imperil both ships and crews alike. They were well known for their International Ice Patrol duties, keeping track of the movements of the ice and icebergs in Northern waters, often in conditions which tested the durability of the ships and the courage of their crews to the limit.

Such was the variety of tasks they were called upon to perform that volumes could be written on that subject alone. However, it will suffice to concentrate on a few selected operations in order to illustrate just how versatile the ships were.

In 1937, 'Itasca' was at the centre of one of the most puzzling events in aviation history; the disappearance of Amelia Earhart and her navigator Fred Noonan, during their attempted round-the-world flight in a Lockheed Electra aircraft. The cutter's involvement concerned the New Guinea to Honolulu leg of the flight and in anticipation of Earhart's departure from New Guinea, 'Itasca' was despatched from Los Angeles on 10th June, to arrive Honolulu on the 15th. From then on she was fully occupied in a number of activities relative to the flight. Three days after her arrival at Honolulu, 'Itasca' was despatched to Howland Island, a mere pin-prick in the vastness of the Pacific Ocean, carrying a large number of temporary personnel, including Army and Navy officers, Department of the Interior employees and two newspapermen.

On arrival, she landed her passengers, together with stores and equipment. She then stood off Howland until the 30th waiting for the news that Earhart had departed New Guinea, whilst the Department of The Interior personnel together with technical aides, set about the task of preparing runways.

On the 1st July, verification came from San Francisco that the Earhart plane had departed Lea, in New Guinea, and was headed for Howland Island, a flight of some two and a half thousand miles. At 0224 the following day, 'Itasca' was in radio contact with the plane. Three and a half hour laters, it's position was given as 200 miles out of Howland. With the plane in such close proximity, the cutter commenced laying a smoke screen to assist the fliers in identifying the island. At 0645 came the report that the plane was 100 miles off Howland, but a further report an hour later gave cause for concern, when Earhart indicated that the fuel supply was critically low. Although radio contact was maintained until 0900, there were no sightings, and an hour later, with no further communications it was considered that the worst had happened.

'Itasca' was despatched at full speed to make a search. This continued throughout the day and into the night of 2nd/3rd with searchlights. Extra lookouts were posted and the whole ship's company put on alert as the cutter scoured the ocean northward of Howland Island. Meanwhile, on the suggestion of 'Itasca's' Captain, a Navy plane was despatched from Pearl Harbour at 0723 on 3rd July, to assist in the search. However, due to bad flying conditions, the plane was forced to return to base without having taken an active part in the operation. The same day, San Francisco reported that four Radio Stations had received the Earhart position as 179°W with 1° 6' N, about 150 miles west of Howland. 'Itasca' stood west of the position for the purpose of proving or disproving the reports.

For twelve days, the cutter continued the search, which took her as far west as Tarawa Island, as far north as 5° 6', and as far south as Arorai, in a crescent-shaped search, spanning some 700 miles. At 0242 on 5th July, a message was intercepted by the Naval radio station at Wailupe, which prompted 'Itasca' to switch her search, and at the same time, advise all steamships in the vicinity to keep a lookout for the plane and the missing aviators. Lights with the appearance of flares were sighted at 2100, but upon investigation, these were finally attributed to a meteorological shower. This coincided with the findings of USS 'Swan'. By this time, the cutter was running low on fuel and on the 6th, rendezvoused with USS 'Colorado' to replenish her tanks before continuing the search on the 7th, south and west of Baker Island.

On 11th July, she proceeded under orders on a tour of adjacent Islands, when her officers went ashore in search of information on possible sightings of the plane. The calls took in Arorai, Taman, Nonouti, Kuria and Tarawa, none of which produced any evidence of the plane having been spotted, nor sightings of wreckage. On 16th July, 'Itasca' was relieved of further search duty. She returned to Honolulu on the 24th.

What happened to Amelia Earhart and Fred Noonan remains a mystery, in spite of the discovery in 1991 of fragments of wreckage and footwear on the small island of Nikumaroro, thought to have been evidence of the plane having come down there.

The experience of 'Cayuga' a year earlier, is equally typical of the wide-ranging activities of the cutters. In July 1936, after a spell of ice-breaking duty in Buzzard's Bay, off the eastern coastline of Massachusettes, she was despatched on a cadet cruise, one of many in her nine years duty with the US Coast Guard. To all intents and purposes, it was intended to be much the same as any other. There was certainly no knowledge among the crew that the ship was to become involved in the Spanish Civil War.

It was on 23rd July, whilst off Havre, France, that she was suddenly placed under the jurisdiction of the Navy Department and ordered to report to the Commanding Officer of USS 'Oklahoma'. There was nothing unusual about this transfer of command, since an Act of Congress approved January 28th 1915 provides that — 'the Coast Guard shall constitute a part of the military forces of the United States and shall operate as a part of the Navy, subject to the orders of the Secretary of the Navy, in time of war or when the President shall so direct'.

'Itasca's' first duty was to proceed to San Sebastian, where her

Captain was to confer with American Embassy Officials. On arrival, he was warned of the hazards of his assignment by officers from the British destroyer *'Veteran'*, who reported to him, that only the previous afternoon, a Government torpedo boat had been seen in action against rebel forces, incurring some damage to ships in the harbour. He was also advised that manouvering in the harbour was extremely difficult. Nonetheless *'Cayuga'* despatched one of her officers to a meeting of US Embassy Officials. In the meantime, a body of armed men, with machine guns aimed threateningly at the cutter's surf boats, demanded they leave the harbour. It was only after a long drawn out discussion that the ship was allowed to stay.

On the 25th, the cutter was ordered to proceed to Feunterrabia and there to make contact with Claude S. Bowers, the American Ambassador. Since conditions were seen to be reasonably quiet, the Ambassador saw no reason to leave. The cutter then returned to San Sebastian where she landed a representative to report to the Councillor of Embassy, Hallett Johnson. In the boat's absence, *'Cayuga'* suddenly found herself dangerously close to the line of fire from a Spanish torpedo boat and two other vessels, all flying the Spanish Ensign. Their target was a rebel stronghold, which they bombarded for about an hour before withdrawing westward.

The following morning and into the afternoon, sixty-one Embassy Officials of varying nationalities, and refugees, together with baggage, were ferried out to *'Cayuga'* in trying weather conditions. At 1620, she moved out, bound for Jean de Luz. Her next port of call was Bilbao, where she arrived on the 29th with Embassy codes and files on board. On the same day, the cadets on board were transferred to the USS *'Wyoming'* for transportation back to the United States.

A potentially dangerous situation had been averted on the 26th, when the German battleship *'Deutschland'* attempted to land an armed party at San Sebastian.

The fortunate location of the cutter at the outbreak of hostilities, and her prompt despatch to San Sebastian, were considered important factors in assuring the safety of American and other diplomats, whose situation was critical in the light of the lack of communications, and the fact that the coastal towns were hemmed in by rebels occupying the surrounding hills. *'Cayuga'* was commended for the efficient accomplishment of an extremely delicate mission.

Few ships can lay claim to such a variety of tasks as the US Coast Guard cutters. Anti-smuggling operations, and the destruction of derelicts were also activities which consumed much of their operational time. No less important was rescue, and in the period 30th June 1936 to 31st March 1941, the 'Lake' class cutters were engaged in no fewer than 500 rescue operations, when a total of more than 800 lives were saved. In a five year period up to March 1941, they cruised in excess of one million nautical miles, during over 119,000 hours under way.

These then were the ships the Royal Navy took over in May 1941. As we shall see later, they more than lived up to their reputation for versatility and endurance during World War II.

Chapter Two

First Impressions

The handing over of the cutters was preceded, and accompanied by a mountain of paperwork, as one might expect from such a transaction. There was also considerable equipment and stores, all of which had to be catalogued in detail and invoices prepared, how else, but in quintuplicate. Sets of clearly defined instructions were issued to all Commanding Officers, with the accent on delivery to Brooklyn Navy Yard: — 'as early as is practicable consistent with the readiness of the vessels and the availability of the relieving personnel.' The actual transfer of each ship was to be on a date designated by the Commander of the New York District, with the mutual agreement of the relieving British Officer. Each cutter was required to be fuelled to capacity, with an adequate supply of lubricants aboard, and fresh water tanks filled to the brim.

By April 9th 1941, all machinery for the transfer had been set in motion and by that date, four of the ships, *'Saranac', 'Tahoe', 'Pontchartrain'* and *'Mendota',* were being painted in the Royal Navy's war colours. Meanwhile others were being called in from operational duties, to prepare for the unfamiliar and testing times ahead.

Captain Robert F. Barber USCG (Rtd), was serving in *'Cayuga'* at the time, and recalls the imminent take-over:

" *'Cayuga'* had been despatched from Boston in March 1941 to Greenland, carrying on board a survey party of officers from several different US services and agencies, for the purpose of locating and deciding upon suitable sites in Greenland to be used for the 'transmission of aircraft' to Europe. While we were lying in Skibshavn and while the survey party was absent and about Greenland in a smaller Danish vessel, news suddenly came that we were to return

FIRST IMPRESSIONS

to Boston without delay, to be painted grey and fitted with certain naval equipment in Boston and Norfolk Navy yards, so that the vessel could be turned over to the British Navy."

'Cayuga' was not the only cutter to be involved in that operation. The bases established as a result of the surveys, were to prove of strategic importance to the war effort.

Captain R.W. Dempwolf, U.S. Coast Guard Commander in New York, was charged with the responsibility of handing over the ships on behalf of the United States Government, whilst Captain A.F.E. Palliser DSO., RN., Commanding Officer in the battleship 'Malaya' was to receive them on behalf of the Royal Navy. In a letter to Commandant Waesche, dated 24th April 1941, Captain Palliser indicated his near-readiness to proceed with the transfer;

"In reply to your verbal question, the transfer of the Coast Guard cutters is proceeding satisfactorily, and subject to the success of sea trials now in progress, I anticipate being ready to take over the first four next Wednesday, 30th April."

Two Coast Guard officers, Lt.Cdr. H.E. Grogan and Lt. J.P. German, Commanding Officer and Engineer Officer respectively in 'Pontchartrain', were designated to liaise with the Commanding Officers of the cutters and the relieving British Commanders.

The transfer was preceded by a twenty-four hour period of sea trials which, having proved satisfactory, were followed by approximately two weeks of instruction and indoctrination, carried out in Long Island Sound, to help acquaint the British crews with these unfamiliar ships. There was much to learn about the machinery and equipment, much of which bore little resemblance to that hitherto experienced in HM Ships.

Approximately 1500 officers and ratings were mustered to form the passage crews. Many were shipped out from Britain, but the majority were drawn from two of Britain's most illustrious battleships, 'Resolution' and 'Malaya', then undergoing lengthy repairs in Philadelphia Navy Yards, and the aircraft carrier 'Illustrious', refitting in Norfolk, Virginia. 'Malaya', the first British warship to refit in the United States, had taken a torpedo in her port side whilst escorting a north-bound convoy off Cape Verdi Islands on 20th March. *'Illustrious'* had suffered damage in the Mediterranean and was sent to the United States for refit and repairs.

Among the first British ratings to be drafted to the cutters was H.V. Emmins:

"I was a young Able Seaman in *'Resolution'* when she was torpedoed. We had limped into an American Navy Yard for repairs, which were obviously going to take a long time. Our prolonged stay there meant that there was little use for our services. We were subsequently drafted to the cutters and despatched to New York by train. Imagine our surprise when we discovered the ships were still manned by Americans, who showed no signs of leaving. Each morning we put to sea and the Americans put us through our paces. The conditions on board were a bit cramped, but they slept in their bunks whilst we slung our hammocks wherever we could."

Mervyn Roberts, an Able Seaman in the *'Malaya'*, was assigned to *'Tahoe'* and discounts the work-up in few words:

"During our couple of weeks with the American crew there was coffee on tap all day, but no 'tot' of rum, a hardship which did not go down too well with the men of the Royal Navy."

Prior to joining *'Pontchartrain'*, Ken Slater had undergone a period of special training at a radio school in Miami:

"The work-up was an interesting experience as was the American victuals, but eventually the good life came to an end. After the transfer, we went from pork chops, chicken, ham, eggs, apple pie and ice-cream, crashing back to reality with corned beef and mash . . . plus 'tot'."

On the 30th April, in a short ceremony attended by Rear Admiral Waesche, Admiral A. Andrews and Captain H.V. McKittrick of the US Navy, Captain Palliser accepted the first four cutters from Captain R.W. Dempwolf. The ships were given their new names, appropriately chosen from Coast Guard stations around the coast of Great Britain, and their pennant numbers. It is ironic, that residents of some of the named towns, were never aware that ships had been named after them. The new identities were as follows: *'Saranac' (HMS Banff) Y43;*

FIRST IMPRESSIONS

'Tahoe' (HMS Fishguard) Y59; 'Pontchartrain' (HMS Hartland) Y00; and 'Mendota' (HMS Culver) Y87. 'Chelan' (HMS Lulworth) Y60 was handed over three days later. Three more, *'Sebago' (HMS Walney) Y04; 'Cayuga' (HMS Totland) Y88; 'Champlain' (HMS Sennen) Y21*, were commissioned on 12th May in the presence of the Honorable Herbert E. Goston, Assistant Secretary to the Treasury; the Honorable William R. Johnson, Commissioner for Customs; and Captain H.V. McKittrick US Navy. The cutters *'Shoshone' (HMS Landguard) Y56*, and *'Itasca' (HMS Gorleston) Y92*, were handed over on 20th and 21st May respectively.

(From hereon all the cutters are referred to by their adopted names).

Geoff George was drafted from *'Resolution'* to *'Totland'* where he remained for about three years;

"After the ceremony, rum was served on the fo'cstle to anybody wishing to partake. Several of the Americans had more than one tot, and some left the ship the worse for it. The ship was well-stocked with stores. The large 'freezer' on the mess-deck was crammed with ice-cream and the cold store was full of meat. You can imagine our surprise when we discovered that the ship had a laundry, something we had not encountered on British ships, and a massive, exceptionally well-equipped galley."

J.O.C. Willson, a Sub. Lieutenant at the time, was assigned to *'Sennen';*

"Our British First Lieutenant had been to the States before, to pick up one of the old four-stacker destroyers. One of the lessons he had learned was not to declare all the provisions taken over in the ship. The American seamen appeared to live better than the Royal Navy chaps, judging by the tins of chicken and other goodies in the store. However, when we got to Halifax, Nova Scotia, the N.S.O. came aboard, and most of the foodstuffs went ashore. So when *'Sennen'* arrived there, a considerable amount of canned food, including condensed milk, was safely stowed away in the magazine."

One of the first British Naval Officers to be transferred to the cutters was Lt.Cdr. Russell Linsell RN. He was assigned from the *'Malaya'* as a T/Lt. (E) to act as liaison Engineer Officer, to assist the new intake of Engineering Staff in their familiarisation with the cutters' turbo-electric drive. A young Electrical Engineering Graduate, he was a good choice for the task. He later joined *'Gorleston'* as Engineer Officer and remained with the ship for two-and-a-half years.

Unfortunately, not all the Royal Navy Engineer Officers drafted to the cutters, had the benefit of his knowledge and know-how. Many of those who joined after the take-over, had to fathom things out for themselves. One such Officer is Lt. (E) K.M. Macleod DSC., RN., who had survived the sinking of the *'Cossack'* in October 1941. He was assigned to *'Landguard'*, and whilst his first impressions were not very complimentary, he developed a long-lasting affection for the ship:

" *'Landguard'* was a ship I had never heard of and which did not appear in our 1939 edition of Janes Fighting Ships. I found her lying alongside the quay at Londonderry. She was a strange looking warship with a profile like an overgrown tug. When I first visited the engine-room I was appalled. My weakest engineering subject had always been electricity and *'Landguard's'* machinery spaces looked like a generating power station. Everything was spotless, from the shining stainless steel chequer plates to the snow-white deckhead, but all around were black panels covered in warning lights and switch gear.

"There was a large electric motor driving the single propeller shaft and an assortment of steam turbine driven alternators. The ships in which I had served and done my training, in all, had geared turbine machinery, three Yarrow boilers, and electricity (all DC) was used for auxilliary purposes only. This ship had complex AC systems for everything, including main propulsion and the boilers were a Babcock & Wilcox type of which I had no experience at all.

"I had a sleepless night and then went ashore to see the Senior Engineer on the Commodore's Staff. An elderly Captain (E), he listened sympathetically to my story and then said he would like to see this new type of ship. We walked to *'Landguard'* and he wandered around the engine-room asking questions about her equipment, which was obviously just as strange to him as to me. We returned to his office, where he told me that he agreed with everything I had said, but pointed out that every other RN officer would be just as ignorant as I about this unusual machinery, indeed that my experience with AC motors as an apprentice at Mathers & Platts, gave me a small edge over the competition. He said he would appoint me an additional and very experienced electrical artificer to the ship and added that he relied on me to master her intricacies by the end of the first voyage."

Obviously Lt. Macleod fulfilled that requirement since he remained with *'Landguard'* until June 1943. The many engine-room refinements, not found in HM ships at the time, could have bred some complacency among the engine-room personel, as Lt. Macleod recounts:

"On my second night in *'Landguard'* I was plagued with sleeplessness and so dressed and visited the machinery spaces. It was the Middle Watch. All was well in the engine-room, but the boiler-room seemed totally unmanned and was filled with a strong smell of bacon and sausages. I found the Petty Officer and his stokers in a small space behind the boilers, squatting happily around an electric grill. The Petty Officer explained that there were automatic devices which controlled water and fuel supplies to the boilers, and implied that he and his crew were really superfluous. The next day the automatic devices were removed, as were the cooking appliances and steps were taken to ensure that standard RN boiler-room practices were followed."

Undoubtedly the most unpleasant tendency of the cutters was their prolonged roll, particularly in a cross sea. Not surprisingly it was designated the 'cutter roll' and many ex-cutter men have good reason to remember it. Mervyn Robins, in *'Fishguard'* recalls:

"I often wondered during the work-up, why the Americans dismantled the mess-deck tables and stowed them away after meals. Once we got to sea I discovered why. We got into a cross sea and the ship decided to do her party piece. The tables collapsed and tin gear and gash buckets started flying all over the place. This cutter habit was responsible for one of our many near disasters. The Electrical workshop was located in the engine-room behind the main switchboard, which was protected at the back by a very open-type grill. One of the articifers, who had joined us at Greenock, decided to repair a domestic pressing iron. At lunchtime, he left the workshop leaving the dissembled parts of the iron on the bench. In his absence there was a change of course accompanied by a heavy roll and the components of the iron flew off the bench and into the back of the switchboard, shorting out the main circulating pump. The result was that everything had to be shut down, while we laboured in torchlight trying to trace and remedy the fault. The remainder of the ship's company were on the upper deck, keeping an eye out for U-boats! It took a couple of hours to sort everything out and raise steam again, much to everyone's relief."

The experience of Able Seaman F.E. Lever, who joined *'Gorleston'* from the minesweeper *'Gossamer'* in 1941, was no less disturbing;

"My Action Station was depth-charge crew. One wet and very black night, we were attacking a confirmed submarine contact and it was necessary to release the ready-use charges so that we could replenish the racks from ready-use charges stowed on the deck. Suddenly the ship took a violent change of course into a beam sea. The depth-charges broke loose and rolled across the deck as we rolled heavily. There were six charges rolling wildly from side to side, while the hands leapt for safety. When the ship came back on course, we eventually managed to get the situation under control. Fortunately there were no broken bones."

'Banff' crew member Steve Stephenson, has his memory of this cutter phenomenon:

"How can one forget their unpredictable behaviour. I am not alone when I say I held my breath when *'Banff'* rolled until the wings of the bridge were skimming the waves. Then we started to roll back and we were, most of us, convinced she was going over. Each time we returned from convoy duty we had to count the breakages. Having said that, I cannot recall anyone losing his 'tot' through spillage!"

Whilst much of the cutters' American gear was replaced with the more familiar British equipment during a series of conversion refits,

FIRST IMPRESSIONS

Pat Patrick, a Leading Telegraphist in *'Walney'* from May 1941 to July 1942, had nothing but praise for the radio equipment:

"The Radio shack was a dream after the antiquated gear in the old *'Resolution'*, where operating was an art form, and lots of receivers ran from batteries, and the directly heated valves were located on the outside of the set. *'Walney's'* Radio office was in a space normally taken up by the main transmitter, but had the most modern equipment and could do all that the total of that in *'Resolution'* could do. It was so easy to operate and once a frequency had been set, one had the confidence that it would work."

Although the cutters' armament at the time of the take-over comprised a 5" gun, three 3", a 'Y' gun, .5 machine guns and depth charges, these were not ideally suited for the task which lay ahead. The .5's were later replaced by the larger calibre and more efficient Oerlikon guns, two mounted above the gun shelter forward, and one each on port and starboard side of the super-structure aft. Single-barrelled 'Pom-Poms' on port and starboard sides of the fo'cstle added extra fire power. The forward 5" gun was later replaced by a 4", and on some cutters the after 3" was replaced by a quick-firing Bofors gun. An innovation towards the end of the war was the installation of rockets on either side of the 4" gun.

In order to up-date the anti-submarine equipment, the American depth-charge gear was removed and British ten-charge pattern equipment installed. In addition, the 'Hedgehog' forward throwing device was fitted on the fo'cstle. Basically a spigot mortar, it fired a pattern of bombs, which were designed to explode on contact. In principal, a hit by any one bomb in the pattern, caused the remainder to detonate. However, the 'Hedgehog' did not enjoy the confidence of all escort commanders during the early stages of its use. It did have a tendency to breakdown, and an incident aboard the destroyer *'Escapade'*, when there was an inboard explosion of 'Hedgehog', causing considerable damage to both ship and personnel, did little to improve attitudes towards it.

A problem endemic in the cutters was the lack of manouvreability to put distance between themselves and exploding depth charges with shallow settings, as Lt. Macleod explains:

"It was on my third night out in *'Landguard'* that we fired out first shallow pattern of depth charges. How much it worried the U-boat we shall never know, but the ship nearly blew herself out of the water. The first charges shook us mightily and a number of contact breakers in the engine-room opened, causing main and auxiliary engines to stop and every light to go out. Inexorably, the pair of depth charges rolled over the stern and fired from throwers, were all set to explode at a depth of thirty feet. This they did, closer and closer as the ship lost way. The last two charges exploded under a near stationary ship — or so it felt.

"We were frantically trying to get the auxiliary generator running again while we still had steam, when an irate Captain requested my presence on the bridge to explain just what was happening. Thereafter, we arranged that the engine-room should be warned when depth-charges were about to be dropped, so that we could hold the vital switches in position until the explosions ceased. To improve communications in these circumstances, a Leading Stoker had his Action Stations on the bridge end of the voice-pipe to the engine room."

The last word on the adoption of the cutters also comes from Lt. Macleod;

"I was amused to see in *'Landguard'* that identically framed pictures in the big day-cabin, were of Horatio Nelson and Franklin D. Roosevelt."

Chapter Three

HMS Culver — The First Casualty

Within days of being officially handed over to the Royal Navy, the cutters were despatched from New York to Halifax, Nova Scotia, where they were quickly pressed into service as escorts for U.K. bound convoys. Notwithstanding their proven endurance in the service of the US Coast Guard, it remained to be seen how they would weather the rigours of all-out war. The first group, comprising *'Culver'*, *'Banff'*, *'Fishguard'* and *'Hartland'*, sailed within twenty-four hours of their arrival, as escort to convoy HX125. Whilst the ships had yet to be tested in battle, the passage crews were no strangers to it. Many of them had already suffered the traumatic experience of having a ship sunk under them, and all had encountered the wrath of the U-boats at one time or another.

The 3,000 miles voyage across the Atlantic, passing through the notorious 'Black Gap', so named because it was an area with poor air cover and subsequently the graveyard for countless merchant ships, lasted fifteen days, ending on the Clyde on 22nd May. For *'Culver'*, it was the first of a dozen or so convoys before her career with the Royal Navy was brought to an abrupt and tragic end less than nine months later. The career of her sister ship *'Hartland'* was also to be short-lived.

On arrival in the United Kingdom, a large number of the passage crews were either assigned to other vessels, or despatched on well deserved and, in some cases, long-overdue leave. For those who left *'Culver'*, their departure was as fortunate for them as it was fateful for so many of the men who replaced them.

Within no time at all, the cutters were assigned to Western Approaches Command, operating out of Londonderry, Northern Ireland. Londonderry was home base for three 'Special Escort Groups',

THE HAND - ME - DOWN SHIPS

whose general function was to shepherd Arctic convoys and Atlantic troop convoys; three groups of destroyers and corvettes to protect North Atlantic convoys, and five groups of sloops and cutters, whose responsibility was the South Atlantic convoys; a total of more than sixty-eight ships. The new additions to this fleet were assigned as follows; *'Culver'*, *'Landguard'* and *'Lulworth'* to the 40th Escort Group; *'Hartland'* and *'Walney'* to the 41st; *'Totland'* and *'Gorleston'* to the 42nd; *'Fishguard'* and *'Banff'* to the 44th; and *'Sennen'* to the 45th. The losses of three of the cutters between 31st January 1942 and 8th November 1942 brought about some diversification in the assignments, as we shall see later.

'Culver' was the first casualty, rent apart by a massive explosion following a U-boat attack, on the quiet, moonlit night of 31st January 1942.

Up till then, and apart from two convoys to Halifax, her activities had been confined to the 'Bathurst run', with straight-through convoys to and from the west African port. There was a break in her operations in September 1941, when she was despatched to the North Woolwich yards of Harland & Wolff, where she was fitted with HF/DF (High Frequency Direction Finding), an innovation in submarine detection which had been developed during the winter of 1940/41. *'Culver'* was the first operational warship to be fitted with the new equipment.

HF/DF was an important contributory factor in bringing about a turning point in the ongoing and costly battle against the U-boats. It caused considerable confusion among German submarine commanders who, unaware of its existence, were puzzled by the ease, accuracy and frequency with which their positions were being targetted by convoy escorts, and later by shadowing aircraft. Their habit of communicating with their headquarters and other U-boats was often the cause of their downfall, since HF/DF proved most successful in obtaining a fix on a submarine's position through the radio transmissions.

Thus equipped, *'Culver'* with Lt.Cdr. R.T. Gordon-Duff RN., in command, sailed on 25th October, to join with the southbound convoy

HMS CULVER – THE FIRST CASUALTY

OS10. In addition to having sister ships *'Gorleston'*, *'Lulworth'* and *'Landguard'* for company, the escort included the ex-American destroyer *'Stanley'*, (torpedoed and sunk two months later), and the Flower Class corvette *'Verbena'*. *'Landguard'* (Lt.Cdr. R.E.S. Hugonin) was senior officer escorts.

At 1947 on the 31st, the hitherto quiet passage was interrupted by the detected presence of enemy submarines. Although it was later assessed that two U-boats had contacted the convoy, it was not known at the time that one of Germany's most successful and experienced submarine commanders, Heinrich Lehmann-Willenbrok, in U96, was one of them. The other was the Italian *'Barbarigo'*. Whilst there is no evidence that the latter attacked the convoy, U96 certainly did. Records show also that other U-boats had been directed to seek out and attack OS10, but none were reported as having been in the vicinity by 1st November.

At 1947, *'Lulworth'*, stationed about 3000 yards off the port bow of the convoy, reported a submarine blowing tanks on bearing 135°. She headed straightway to the bearing and spotted a U-boat breaking the surface. Almost immediately the S.S. *'Bennekom'* was struck by torpedoes and quickly succumbed to the Atlantic, another victim of U96. *'Lulworth'* pressed home her attack, but when within 1600 yards of her prey, Willenbrok took his boat to the depths. The cutter dropped a total of nineteen depth charges in five attacks, but no evidence of a kill was seen, although an additional large explosion was heard. She was then ordered, together with *'Culver'* to assist in picking up survivors from the *'Bennekom'* before rejoining the convoy.

John Loughran, an Able Seaman in *'Lulworth'* at the time, recalls the rescue operation:

"The rescue was a traumatic experience since the survivors were retrieved from a hot, oil sea. These included the Dutch First Mate and two British soldiers who were taking passage to South Africa to join another ship. I was taking a turn at artificial respiration on one of the soldiers, when our doctor came along and asked me to turn the man over. Which I did. After a quick examination, I was informed that I was wasting my time. We buried the Dutch First Mate and the two soldiers at sea. Another survivor, a West African who I only knew as Chris managed to get to a raft. He later spotted a shipmate still aboard the sinking ship, shouting that he was trapped. Chris climbed back on to the burning ship by means of a line and by a feat of sheer physical strength and extreme courage managed to get the man to safety. Another unsung hero of the war at sea."

It was at 2016, during the rescue operation that *'Culver'* came close to being a casualty herself. With the Master and twenty-four crew members of the *'Bennekom'* on board, she picked up hydrophone effect of an approaching torpedo. Her evasive action proved effective and the torpedo was seen to pass harmlessly down her starboard side.

It was not until the following day that U-boat activity was resumed, when U96 was spotted on the surface from *'Landguard'* at a range of approximately 12 miles. *'Gorleston'* and *'Verbena'* were despatched to intercept. Some twenty minutes later, *'Gorleston'* had the U-boat in sight and between 1700 and 1708, fired rounds from her 5" gun at maximum elevation. All these fell short. The cutter's full-speed approach was observed by Willenbrok, who turned away and dived to periscope depth with a possible torpedo attack in mind.

In his report on the persuit of the U-boat, Cdr. Keymer in *'Gorleston'* wrote: "Upon reaching a position 2000 yards beyond the diving position without gaining contact and anticipating a retiring torpedo attack from the most favourable firing position, course was altered up sun's path to 245°".

Shortly after the new course was reached, a submarine echo was reported at a range of 1700 yards and *'Gorleston'* thereafter carried out a number of manouvres to coincide with those of the target. When the range closed to between 100/200 yards a periscope was sighted and the port Pom-Pom's gun crew was ordered to open fire. It was reported in *'Gorleston'* that the periscope was obliterated by a stream of accurate shell bursts. Judging by the wake from the periscope it was estimated that the submarine's speed was about three knots and seen to be moving at right angles to and in the direction of the ship's line of advance. *'Gorleston'* moved in and fired a pattern of five charges. The fact that the second charge produced a column of water some 88 feet high, almost twice that of a normal depth charge could have given the impression that a hit had been scored. Later analysis suggested that one depth charge counter-mining on another could be a more likely explanation.

About one minute after firing, two good echoes were reported right astern of the cutter, then faded out rapidly and were never regained.

At 1754, *'Gorleston'* altered course to investigate further and shortly after counter-attacked a weak and doubtful echo with a pattern of nine charges. In the light of the charges of the first attack having been seen to explode around the area of the swirl from the U-boat's conning tower, together with the rapidly fading echo, it might be considered reasonable that Cdr. Keymer thought a 'kill' had been achieved. Unfortunately for him, no visible evidence of a 'kill' was observed. Since there was seldom, or never, any benefit of the doubt given to escort commanders, submarine 'kills' had to be evidenced by debris or human remains or supported by documentary evidence in order to establish time, place and identity of both attacker and victim. In *'Gorleston's'* case, it was a matter of on the spot speculation against documentary evidence of no submarines having been sunk on the date the action took place.

Disappointing though official findings were, there is some consolation for the men of *'Gorleston'* in that by her actions, the cutter was formally credited with safeguarding the convoy OS10 from further molestation by one of the most successful and experienced U-boat captains of the war, who would have undoubtedly torpedoed more ships had he been able to overhaul the convoy again.

The 40th Escort Group departed the convoy on 14th November and sailed into Bathurst. The routine was all too familiar. A brief run ashore for the off-duty members of the crew, and refuel was little relief before returning to the Atlantic with another UK bound convoy. By 10th December, *'Culver'* was back in her home port and there was speculation among the crew as to the possibility of Christmas at home. They were to be disappointed.

During this brief respite from convoy duties, *'Culver'* was joined by Walter Costick, who had just completed a long commission in the cruiser *'Berwick'*. Coincidentally, another *'Culver'* crew member, Tom Ambrose, had served in the same ship:

"Walter and I served together from 1939 to 1941. I was a signal boy in those days, but was transferred to the W/T Branch due to eyesight problems."

Recalling his joining the cutter, Walter Costick said:

"We sailed almost immediately for Bathurst and ran into bad weather whilst joining up with convoy OS15. This coincided with our having trouble with our Type 271 RDF. I reported this to the Captain, adding that I considered it unreliable. This was passed on to Senior Officer Escorts in the sloop *'Londonderry'*, and it was decided to try and carry out repairs on our arrival in Bathurst. This turned out to be impossible due to the lack of the necessary spares."

Nobody could have forseen at that time, what the dramatic consequence of that situation was to be.

Convoy OS15 was *'Culver's'* last outward-bound voyage, and a comparatively quiet interlude to her sinking two weeks later. On 17th January, she sailed from Bathurst to join up with convoy SL98, comprising 23 merchants ships. With her Captain indisposed, Ld.Cdr. Dalison in the *'Londonderry'* had installed his First Lieutenant, Lt. R.F. Kipling RN., in the ship. The transfer was made at sea, and on the whaler's return trip, Sub.Lt. George Pattinson RNVR., was given passage to replace him as an additional Watch Keeping Officer. George Pattinson had joined *'Culver'* in May 1941 from the destroyer *'Havant'*.

'Lulworth' sailed the same day with the SS *'Langletarne'*, whilst the sloop *'Bideford'* escorted the survey ship *'Challenger'*. The remaining ships in the convoy were temporarily delayed through defects. By 1430 the following day, all ships had met up successfully on the mean course of the convoy advance, and the Group organisation for screening the convoy with smoke against surface attack, was carried out successfully. On the 19th, the Ocean Escort, comprising *'Wild Swan'*, *'Orchis'*, *'Auricula'* and *'Fritillary'* parted company to join up with convoy OS17.

'Culver's' crew were in happy mood and looking forward to leave

on arrival in the U.K. Whilst they were constantly aware of the dangers associated with the 'Bathurst Run', they had no reason to suspect that for most of them, that leave would never materialise.

At 2200 on the 23rd, *'Culver'* was ordered to meet up with the steamship *'Nurterton'* off Funchal, Madiera. Tom Ambrose recalls: "The merchantman was a coal-burner of about four knots. She was belching smoke and her crew waved like mad as we steamed by. I think they were Chinese. On top of the hatches were scores of bird cages and the twittering of the birds could be heard plainly. There was much shouting at the old tub to get more fire under her kettles."

After almost twelve hours steaming, the *'Nurterton'* developed serious boiler trouble and was forced to return to Funchal. *'Culver'* escorted her back, then returned to her station with the convoy, arriving at 1100 on the 27th.

"I saw the old steamer in Liverpool some months later," said Tom Ambrose. "I recall also seeing the survey ship *'Challenger'* in the convoy. Whether it was to conserve fuel or help her keep up with the convoy, I don't know, but she hoisted a sail. It was a memorable sight."

It was during the evening of the 31st, when the convoy was off the coast of Brest, where U-boats were almost continually coming and going, that disaster struck, in the form of U105, under the command of Heinrich Schuch. Schuch had joined his boat earlier in the month and sailed from Lorient on 25th January. His predecessor, George Schewe, who had commissioned the U105 in 1941, had established quite a record of successes for the boat, sinking fifteen ships, totalling over 83,000 tons. It is not unreasonable to assume that Schuch would wish to emulate that success.

There was a full moon on the night of the 31st and in spite of the moonlight being diffused by cloud, visibility was good. The ships in the convoy were being caressed by a gentle swell and routines aboard the escorts were proceeding as normal. Dispersed strategically around the convoy, *'Landguard'* and *'Lulworth'* were stationed on port and starboard sides respectively, with *'Culver'* on the port quarter, and *'Bideford'* on the starboard quarter. Senior Officer *'Londonderry'* was positioned astern.

Up to 2030, *'Culver'* had been on a zig-zag course at a speed of 7½ knots, which might be considered somewhat slow in the light of her zig-zag being 20° either side of her mean course, and the convoy speed being the same. This would perhaps account for her having fallen slightly astern of her station. With the full moon at bearing 120° one might conclude that she was an easy target for any enemy submarine commander bold enough to approach the convoy in the prevailing conditions. To add to her vulnerability, her Type 271 RDF was still out of action. However, it is unlikely that this would have made any difference to the outcome of the ensuing disaster.

Down below, Lt. Jubb, accompanied by the coxswain and bosun's mate, was nearing completion of night rounds.

On the mess-decks, off-duty members of the crew were passing the time with personal chores and good-hearted banter. Those who were writing home were oblivious to the fact that their letters would never be sent. In the wardroom, the officers were either at dinner or preparing for it, totally unaware that the commander of U105 already had *'Culver'* in his sights. On the upper deck, 'First' watchmen had settled down to their four-hour long stint, with an alertness born of much practice in escort duties. The duffle-coated Lt. Kipling was keeping his vigil on the upper bridge, whilst his second officer of the watch, Sub. Lt. Carlow RNVR., was positioned on the lower bridge.

At 2030, when the helmsman was ordered to steer 033° on a course parallel with that of the convoy so that a bearing might be taken, U105 was in a perfect position for her attack. Within four minutes of *'Culver'* assuming her new course, her Asdic operator reported hydrophone effect bearing 332°, off the cutters port beam. His immediate response and report sent Sub.Lt. Carlow dashing to the port wing of the lower bridge to make visual search. Almost immediately he spotted the dark and ominous shape of a submarine, nearly bows on at 2/3000 yards range. What was even more alarming was the swirl of foam from an electric torpedo about to strike the ship. There was no possible way that his reflex order to port 30° and telegraph full speed ahead, could have prevented the ensuing catastrophe. The torpedo struck deep into the boiler room and the ship shuddered violently from the blow. The boiler-room, together with duty personnel was devastated yet, miraculously, ERA Hayman managed to survive. Within seconds, a second torpedo ploughed into the ship's port side, resulting in a massive explosion in the after magazine. At that moment, the coxswain was holding the night rounds book for Lt. Jubb to sign, with the bosun's mate standing beside him. The latter was thrown to the deck by the blast and although he managed to reach the upper deck, neither he nor Lt. Jubb were seen again. The luckiest escape was that of the wardroom steward and pantry hand. Both survived, in spite of their being in such close proximity of the magazine explosion.

The two crippling detonations were quickly followed by those of two primed depth charges which had rolled over the side. The devastating effect of three explosions in such quick succession, caused the ship to cave in amidships. She heeled over to 45° to starboard, disappearing rapidly in a dimishing pyramid of fire, to the groaning of twisted metal and the cries of the men trapped below decks. Within less than a minute, *'Culver'* was engulfed by the black waters of the Atlantic, taking with her 127 members of her crew. The eerie silence which followed was broken only by the calls for help from the small band of thirteen survivors struggling in the water.

'Culver' went down in position 48° 43' N — 20° 14' W — about 700 miles off Brest.

Tom Ambrose recalls those terrifying moments when disaster struck the ship:

"I was off watch when the torpedoes struck, having just finished the dog watches, and being relieved about 1830 for supper. When the First watchmen appeared, I remained in the W/T office chatting instead of going below, which accounts for there being six of us in the office at the time. The next thing I recall in the confusion which followed the explosions, was that I was in the water and my mind was bent on getting as far away from the ship as I could. I was a good swimmer, and being Shotley trained, was no stranger to swimming fully booted and spurred. I remember saying a prayer and looking up at the sky, watching the moon appearing and disappearing behind the clouds. There were shouts from all directions and somehow we got together, clinging to bits of wreckage which kept popping up as they broke loose from the ship. I recollect seeing Sub.Lt. Carlow and the coxswain. Both were injured, though not too seriously as it turned out."

Another survivor, Walter Costick, was also in the W/T office:

"At 2015 I left the office to distribute current news sheets to wardroom and various messes, which was the custom at that time in the evening. Officers and ratings were in happy mood. As I returned to the office I could see the ships in the convoy quite clearly. Reaching the office, I sat adjacent to the confidential book safe, and my staff said there was nothing to report.

"Shortly after, there was an almighty explosion, followed by a more severe one, and then another. The stern of the ship reared up and the angle of the W/T office took on 45°. I shouted to my staff to get out on the starboard side, which they did. As I followed, the water was already up to my neck.

"The ship was disappearing rapidly and I swam on my back as quickly as I could, fearing that I would be sucked under. The ship appeared to have broken in two and was going down in the shape of a 'V'. It was an incredible sight. I had swallowed a lot of sea water and oil and feared that I would perish. Then a piece of wreckage struck me and I caught hold of it. I shouted to others to join me and soon there were several of us hanging on for dear life."

Those who escaped were fortunate indeed, although their survival from the icy cold of the Atlantic was still dependent upon their rescue.

There was little or no hope at all for those below decks, so quickly did *'Culver'* succumb. Taking into account the acute angle at which both halves of the ship were going down, escape by the companionways had to be considered impossible.

The explosions were heard in *'Londonderry'* and snowflake was fired immediately. The cutter was called on radio telephone without response, and it was quickly established that she had been sunk in an attack presumed to have come from outside the convoy screen.

HMS CULVER — THE FIRST CASUALTY

Various Asdic echoes were heard which turned out to be non-submarine, but a later contact was made by *'Londonderry'* some 3000 yards on her port bow. A sweep in that direction by *'Lulworth'* and *'Bideford'* was aborted when the echo faded. It soon became apparent that the lost echo had been the sinking hull of *'Culver'*.

'Londonderry's' arrival on the scene of the sinking was spotted by the survivors, who were desperately trying to maintain contact with one another, but their hopes of rescue turned to despair when the ship moved off again. She had in fact, dropped her boats and joined *'Bideford'* in an anti-submarine sweep towards the north west. That turned out to be a fruitless endeavour. The search was abandoned and *'Bideford'* was ordered to rejoin the convoy, whilst *'Londonderry'* returned to pick up her boats and the survivors.

"I had the dreadful feeling that we had not been spotted", said Tom Ambrose. "Then I realised that *'Londonderry'* had dropped her boats. I heard the whaler's crew calling out and the relief was overwhelming when I was suddenly hoisted out of the water into the boat. I was not really wounded in the incident, but the following morning I found my legs were black and blue."

With the survivors safely aboard, *'Londonderry'* returned to the convoy, resuming her station at 0001 the following morning. Nearly three-and-a-half hours had elapsed since *'Culver'* had been taken by the sea. The convoy had maintained course throughout, whilst on board the rescue ship, the survivors received the best of attention.

"I cannot praise the ship's company of *'Londonderry'* enough," said Tom Ambrose. "After a stiff tot of whisky, I was taken to the bathroom for a good scrub. It was the first and only time in my life that I had my back scrubbed by a burly rating. It felt great!"

Coming face to face with the small band of survivors from his old ship, proved a traumatic experience for George Pattinson:

"It was with the most profound shock that I learned that only one officer and twelve ratings out of my old ship's company were saved. I learned from Lt. Carlow that all he remembered was the bridge being completely wrecked and then coming to in the water. Apparently the ship almost disintegrated with the explosions. All the survivors were suffering from shock and were reluctant to sleep below decks."

Reflecting on the *'Culver'* disaster, it would seem most likely that U-105's encounter with the cutter was pure chance, since there were no reported indications that a submarine had contacted the convoy immediately preceding the attack. However, there is always the possibility that she had been spotted during her return to the convoy after escorting the *'Nurterton'* to Funchal. At 2315 on the 26th an HF/DF bearing on a suspected submarine gave a fix of some fifteen miles, but a thorough investigation by *'Landguard'* and *'Lulworth'* produced no evidence of a submarine's presence.

It is noted in the Admiralty report on the sinking, that whilst *'Culver'* was keeping listening watch, it is probable that no Hydrophone effect was heard until the U-boat fired its torpedoes. The fact that there were no sightings of the enemy by the lookouts, prior to Lt. Carlow's sightings, would suggest that the torpedoes had been fired at periscope depth. Having fired its deadly missiles, the U-boat had then surfaced in order to make a hasty getaway. It is also not unlikely that the U-boat Commander had mistaken the cutter for a small merchant ship, although it was around this time that the German U-boat Command decided to concentrate its efforts on making escorts a primary prey. The cutter's high freeboard and superstructure layout were frequently regarded as having similarities to merchant vessels.

Had Schuch known his ships, it is doubtful whether he would have fired two torpedoes to dispense with a highly vulnerable cutter. In any event he wasted no time in leaving the scene of his only success in a week at sea.

U-105 had, in fact, been recalled by U-Boat Headquarters, together with others, to assist in the search for survivors from the German blockade runner *'Spreewald'* and was participating in the rescue only twenty-four hours after sinking *'Culver'*. Ironically, the steamer had been sunk west of Biscay, the same day, by U-333, whose Commander Peter Cremer, had mistaken her for an enemy ship. The search was broken off on 4th February, with most of the survivors rescued. U-105

HMS CULVER – THE FIRST CASUALTY

arrived Lorient on the 6th.

On *'Londonderry's'* arrival in the U.K., on the 5th *'Culver's* survivors were put ashore and issued with survivors' kit. Walter Costick recalls:

"I was issued with a jumper three sizes too big with trousers to match. When a Leading 'Wren' asked me if I had salvaged anything, I produced ten pounds in notes, a part packet of cigarettes, and a box of matches in a contraceptive — just in case I was ever a survivor!"

Tom Ambrose had a similar experience:

"I received the usual oversize kit which fitted where it touched. When we went alongside in 'Derry' the girlfriends of the unattached men were waiting on the jetty. The 'Derry' girls always seemed to have advance information on the comings and goings of ships. There were floods of tears when they learned that the men they knew were lost. Some were still crying when we left four days later. Some of us went to 'Pompey' Barracks, where I went ashore for a few beers with fellow survivor and old shipmate McGinty Ryan. We gave no thought to obtaining passes. We got out without problems, but on our return and dressed like hoboes, with no I.D. we were promptly escorted to the cells. At least we had a bed, which was more than we could expect in the messes. The barracks were in a chaotic state in those days."

('McGinty' Ryan was Patrick Camillus Ryan of Stephenville, Newfoundland, one of the large number of 'Newfies' who served in the Royal Navy during World War II. A fellow countryman of his, Heber Brown, of Red Bay, Labrador, perished in *'Culver'*.)

George Pattinson recalls the return to home port:

"*Londonderry's* arrival was one of the most moving moments of my life. The morning was perfect. The sun rose with a red glow in a blue sky, bathing the lovely hills and calm waters with a crimson light. On the upper reaches of the Foyle, just before rounding the last bend, the loud speaker on the upper deck filled the gorge with the gentle strains of 'The Londonderry Air'. It was the sign that HMS *'Londonderry'* was about to enter the town bearing her name. The scene presented to me was one of great beauty and a moving climax to a great tragedy and whilst my heart went out in gratitude for my life, it went out also in sorrow for my brother officers and ship's company lying in our ship in the depths of the Atlantic. Then came the captain's voice behind me as his hand rested on my shoulder "Well Pat, I think you have great cause to be grateful this day."

It was of little consolation to the *'Culver'* survivors, that U-105 was later sunk (2nd June 1942) off Dakar, whilst under the command of Jurgen Nissen. It was back to work for them. Tom Ambrose was assigned to the River Class Frigate *'Spey'*, and found himself back on the familiar west coast of Africa run with the 45th Escort Group. On 11th July 1942, *'Spey'*, together with *'Pelican'* and *'Leopard'* shared in the sinking of U-136 (Zimmerman), whilst escorting convoy OS33.

"I remembered *'Culver'* that night," said Tom Ambrose; "and to my shame, I was elated."

Chapter Four

HMS Walney and HMS Hartland Suicide Mission

The invasion of North Africa in November 1942, code name 'Torch', was the first major allied overseas offensive of World War II. Under the overall command of General Dwight D. Eisenhower, with Admiral Sir Andrew Cunningham responsible for naval aspects of the operation, the plan was to land allied forces at three key locations on the North Africa coastline, namely, Algiers, Casablanca and Oran. The three sectors were designated Western (Casablanca), Center (Oran), and Eastern (Algiers) respectively.

This story is concerned only with the assault on Oran and the leading role played by the cutters *'Walney'* and *'Hartland'*. Their task was to ram and penetrate the harbour boom and put ashore specialist troops, for the purpose of preventing the French from disabling shore installations. Boarding parties from the two cutters had the unenviable task of taking the enemy ships tied up alongside the jetties, to prevent any attempts to scuttle.

Since it was vital to the success of the overall 'Torch' operation that the port be taken intact, the assault was not preceded by any softening-up process from land, sea or air. However, a small but formidable naval force, led by the cruiser *'Aurora'* (Captain W.G. Agnew RN.) was on hand to give support should the cutters be attacked during the approach to Oran, and also deal with any enemy ships that might try to escape to seaward.

As early as October 5th, intelligence had ascertained the extent of the harbour's defences and concluded that the enemy naval personnel manning them, were efficient and capable of executing stubborn resistance. The cutters' assignment, code name 'Reservist', was made all the more hazardous by the restrictions within the harbour and the subsequent limitations on manouvreability. It will help, in order to appreciate the gravity of their task, to know something of the geography of the arena in which the ensuing battle was fought. This was to be no battle on the high seas. In fact, it was possibly the only maritime action ever to be fought within four walls.

Oran harbour was seperated from the sea by a stone breakwater of some 3000 yards in length. It varied in width from 800 yards at the eastern end, to 500 yards at the western end. The entrance, located at the eastern end, was 160 yards across, with 12½ fathoms of water at the centre. Prior to the action taking place, all that was known of the boom, was that it comprised an inner and outer obstruction. Just how formidable those obstructions were was a matter of having to wait and see.

Once through, the cutters were faced with 1½ miles of enclosed harbour, which comprised four main basins, each separated by a broad mole, extending from the inshore jetty and accessible by a narrow passage of water between the seaward end of the moles and the sea wall. At the western end of the harbour were two small basins, facing east and separated by the Mole Centrale.

The largest of the four main basins, Avant Port, 670 yards long by 750 yards wide, with a depth of water ranging from 36 to 72ft, more than adequate to accommodate the cutters' 16ft draught, was flanked inshore by a steep cliff. Avant Port was separated from the second basin by the Mole Ravin Blanc. The third basin, Bassin Du Maroc, roughly 450 yards square, was separated from the second basin by the Mole Millerand. The fourth of the large basins, Bassin Aucor, 500 yards long by 420 yards wide, was separated from Bassin Du Maroc by the Mole J. Giraud.

The larger of the two small basins, 330 yards long by 200 yards wide, was reserved mainly for the berthing of naval vessels, since it was adjacent to a small naval barracks. The smaller basin, 280 yards long by 190 yards wide, was partially enclosed by the Mole St. Marie, with an entrance some 76 yards wide and used mainly by small craft.

Such were the confines of the battle area, flanked on the southern side by the guns of the Ravin Blanc Battery, and at the western end by forts Lamoune, St. Gregorio and Santa Cruz. In addition, there were several gun emplacements situated on the moles and jetties. These dimensions give a clear indication of just how exposed the cutters were and how little chance they had for evasive action.

Although the Command in both cutters were doubtless well-briefed in the geography of the harbour and its principal armament, it is unlikely that they were fully aware of the futility of their venture, even though some American sources, particularly Rear Admiral A.C. Bennett USN, had expressed the opinion that the mission was little short of suicidal. However, in the light of the restrictions within the harbour they could have had few doubts as to how vulnerable they would be.

There is a certain irony in the fact that the cutters went in flying the American flag, in addition to the White Ensign. This unconventional step was part of the plan to attempt to minimise resistance to the operation. Since the French were still smarting from the British attack on their Fleet at Mers-el-Kebir on 3rd July 1940, the general concensus of opinion was that if the French could be persuaded that the operation was an American project, there would be less likelihood of all-out retaliation, and perhaps, a more temperate welcome would result.

For political reasons, it was therefore considered expedient for the British to be as inconspicuous as possible, particularly in the early stages of the operation, and their ships to display all the outward appearances of being U.S. men-o-war. However well intended this political ploy was, it could not be assumed that even any pro-ally elements would be sympathetic towards the invasion, nor could the influence of the German Commission and Officers of the German army, who had infiltrated the area in appreciable numbers, be overlooked. Furthermore, it would have been naive to assume that the defences of such a strategically important port would be other than in a high state of alertness. Intelligence had already ascertained just how formidable those defences were. As we shall see, the French were not impressed by the flying of the Stars and Stripes, nor any of the political stratagem.

OPERATION 'RESERVIST'

8th NOVEMBER 1942

The assault on the harbour of ORAN by the cutters HMS 'Walney' and HMS 'Hartland' prior to the Allied landings in North Africa.

WESTERN END

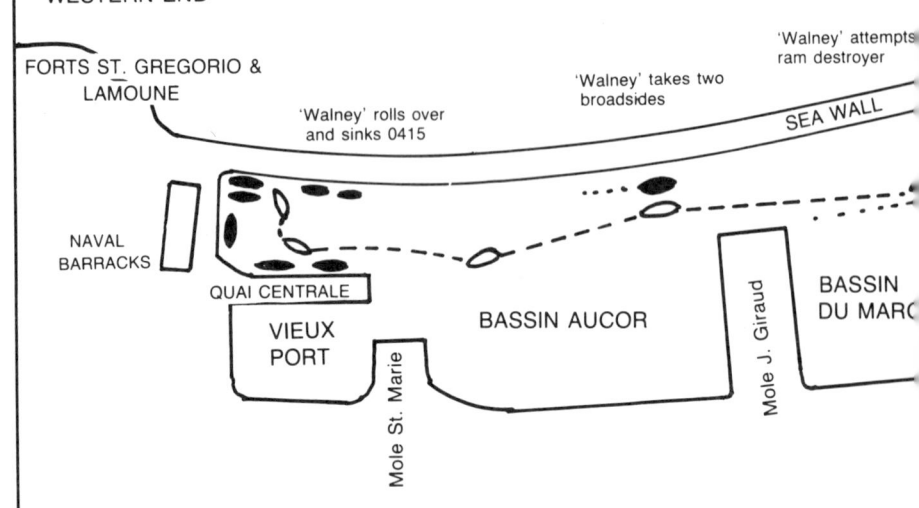

FORTS ST. GREGORIO & LAMOUNE

'Walney' rolls over and sinks 0415

'Walney' takes two broadsides

'Walney' attempts ram destroyer

SEA WALL

NAVAL BARRACKS

QUAI CENTRALE

VIEUX PORT

Mole St. Marie

BASSIN AUCOR

Mole J. Giraud

BASSIN DU MARC

HARBOUR DIMENSIONS (Approx.)

LENGTH: 3000 yds.

WIDTH: (Eastern end) 750 yds.

WIDTH: (Western end) 420 yds.

PLAN NOT TO SCALE

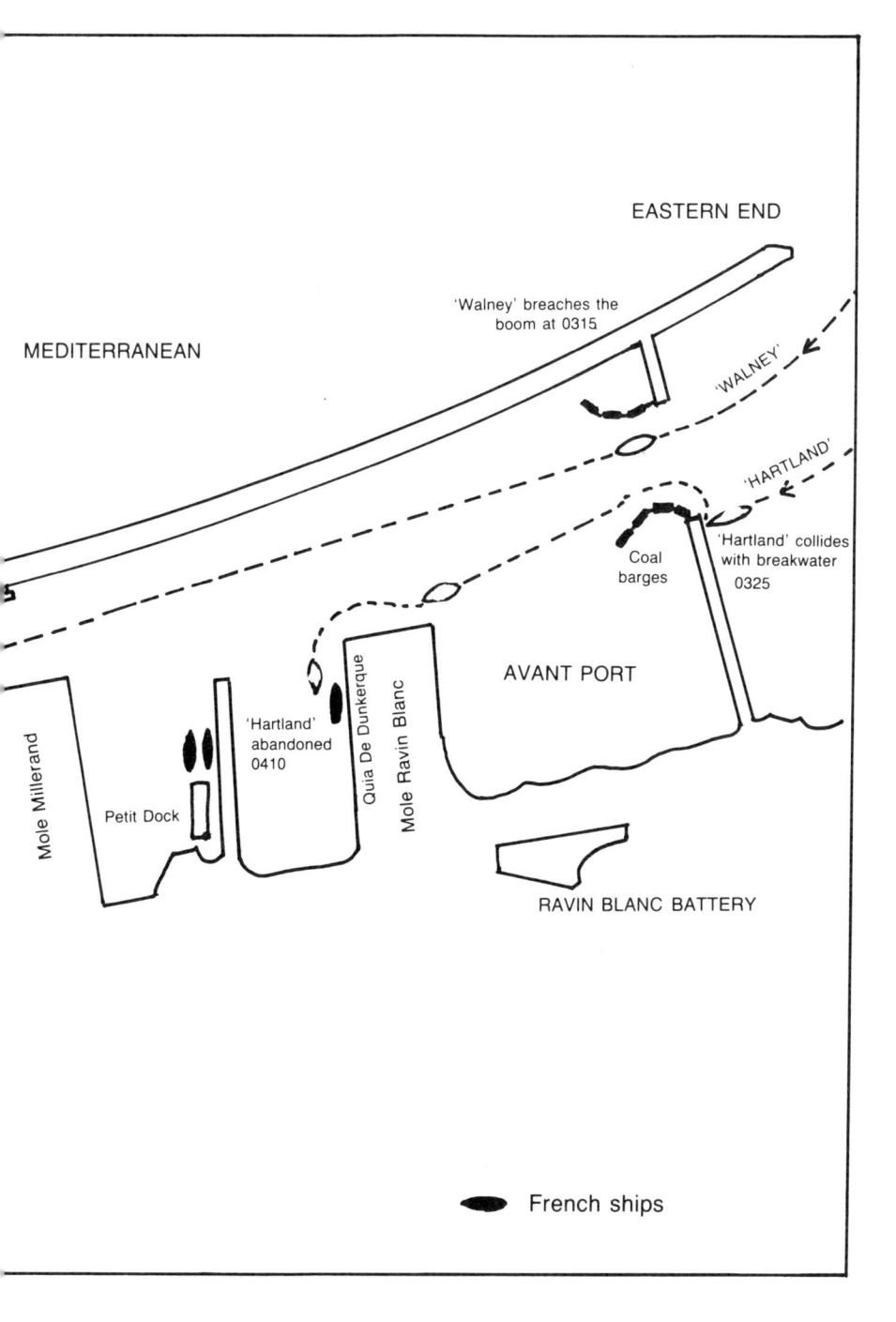

EASTERN END

MEDITERRANEAN

'Walney' breaches the boom at 0315

'WALNEY'

'HARTLAND'

Coal barges

'Hartland' collides with breakwater 0325

AVANT PORT

Mole Millerand

Petit Dock

'Hartland' abandoned 0410

Quia De Dunkerque

Mole Ravin Blanc

RAVIN BLANC BATTERY

● French ships

THE HAND - ME - DOWN SHIPS

The man chosen to head the assault on Oran harbour was A/Captain Frederick Thornton Peters DSO., DSC., RN. Described by his colleagues as the type of man one would expect to see leading some hazardous operation, Captain Peters was installed in the cutter 'Walney'. Born in Charlottetown, Prince Edward Island, Canada, 17th September 1889, he had joined the Royal Navy at the age of 16, and was promoted Lieutenant on 26th March 1912.

He saw service on the China Station, but by the end of 1913, he left the service and returned to Canada. His return to civilian life was brief. The outbreak of the Great War in 1914 saw him back in uniform and within four months he had distinguished himself in the destroyer 'Meteor' at the Battle of Jutland and been awarded a DSO. Peters distinguished himself again in 1918, adding a DSC to his honours. He remained in the Royal Navy until 1920, when, in spite of opportunities for further advancement, he decided to retire. During the ensuing twenty years, his adventurous spirit prompted his participation in a number of ventures, which took him to Canada and the Gold Coast, interspersed with frequent visits to London.

When World War II was declared in 1939, he was back in the Royal Navy within a few weeks, this time commanding an anti-submarine flotilla. Within less than a year of his re-entry to the Service, whilst in the 'Thilmere', he was awarded a bar to his DSC. Later with the rank of Commander, he took the post of Commandant at Brickendonberry Hall, Nr. Hertford, which had been established as a training centre for special agents.

It was inevitable that Peters, with his distinguished naval career would want to return to his small ships. He resigned his position in favour of the 'Torch' operation, thus embarking on the most testing venture of his action-packed life. Ironically, it was to be his last.

In 'Walney' he inherited the services of an already experienced captain and crew, who had seen action in the Atlantic with the 41st Escort Group. The cutter's captain, Lt.Cdr. Peter Meyrick RN., described as a big man with strong physique and inspiring features, had the total admiration and respect of his entire ship's company.

The situation was much the same in 'Hartland', also of the 41st

HMS WALNEY AND HMS HARTLAND — SUICIDE MISSION

Escort Group. Lt.Cdr. Godfrey Billot RNR., and his crew had survived many a 'cat and mouse' encounter with U-boats. The two cutters were almost constant companions for the most part of their eighteen months service with the Royal Navy, mainly to and from Bathurst on the west coast of Africa.

Preparation for 'Reservist', which was later described as one of the most daring exploits of the war, began in October, when both ships were despatched to Belfast, having just returned from escorting convoy SL122 from Freetown. It soon became obvious to the crew that something unusual was afoot.

Ex-Leading Seaman J.H. Finch, in *'Walney'* said:

"On arrival in Belfast, armour plate was fitted internal to the bridge, and various other alterations were carried out, clearly for an ominous purpose, since they were inconsistent with our normal line of work. We were then despatched to a remote part of Scotland, where we spent a great deal of time practising coming alongside and boarding vessels in the dark."

Les Elder, a stoker in *'Hartland'* had joined the ship in June 1941, a month after having the mine-sweeper *'Queenworth'* sunk under him:

"Together with three other stokers, I was detailed to boarding parties. During the dummy run in Scotland, we were sent aboard merchant ships to familiarise ourselves with the engine-room and boiler-room layout. We had no idea why at the time."

The two cutters sailed from the Clyde in late October, in company with a large convoy, scheduled to reach Gibraltar on 6th November. This was one of many carrying men, supplies and equipment to the Mediterranean, in the great build-up to the actual landings, which were planned for the 8th November. It is remarkable that the passage of this armada was almost totally undetected by the enemy.

"We appeared to be wandering about the Atlantic for what seemed an eternity," said J.H. Finch. "However, our course was in the general direction of Gibraltar, but we were still unaware of what our assignment was. We eventually reached 'The Rock' after dark, and to the annoyance of our skipper, ran aground. We were quickly refloated after discharging depth charges. Later we took on American troops with loads of ammunition and gear."

The United States troops comprised 400 members of the 1st Armoured Division, under the Command of Lt.Col. George C. Marshall. This force was distributed below decks in the two cutters. In addition to the troops, *'Hartland'* took on board Lt.Cdr. G.D. Dickey USN., with a 35-strong US Naval contingent which included six marines.

Of the military passengers, J.H. Finch said:

"We already had on board British commandoes who had joined us on the Clyde, under the Command of a very tall, thin officer of the Coldstream Guards. I remember them making bombs with what looked like childs' plasticine. They packed it in tins and jam jars. One commando assured me that it was all quite harmless, and stuck a lighted fag in it just to prove his point. We left Gibraltar in darkness and steered eastwards into the Mediterranean. It was then the 7th. Around noon we rendezvoused with the cruiser *'Aurora'* and passed mail and messages of good luck. When she was out of sight, our captain cleared the lower deck and addressed the entire crew. He revealed to us that our destination was the fortified port of Oran and, jokingly, told us not to worry as the water was warm and there were no sharks!"

Roughly about the same time, Lt.Cdr. Billot was informing his ship's company of the nature of their assignment.

The two cutters made their approach to the North African coast with the main body of ships, designated Group V and headed for the Eastern Sector landing beaches – C. Farrat. They broke off at 2130 on the 7th and headed towards Oran. Just after midnight, both ships went to 'Action Stations'. In the darkness, the crews went quietly and efficiently about the preparations for 'fighting the ship'. These were somewhat different, in many respects, to the routine pre-action preparedness to which they had hitherto been accustomed, with the accent on lightweight weaponry. Not only would the main armament be hindered by the confined conditions in the harbour, but an adequate ammunition supply to the guns would have proved difficult

HMS WALNEY AND HMS HARTLAND — SUICIDE MISSION

in a situation aggravated by the presence of over 200 troops on the mess-decks.

All 5" ammunition was subsequently struck down and the magazines closed off. All close-range ammunition for the .5 machine guns, rifles, automatic weapons, pistols and other small arms, was brought to the upper deck and placed either at the guns, in the fo'csle lockers, or in the gun shelter and laundry.

Careful planning had gone into achieving the most efficient and effective deployment of the ship's company. It is in situations like this that the traditional flexibility of the sailor becomes most apparent. The magazine crews and supply parties were to be used as back-up for the close-range weapons, as well as boarding and landing parties. They were also used for turning out the canoes which were to be used for disembarking the troops. With all this activity, there was little time to contemplate what lay ahead.

Their preparations complete, the two cutters made their approach to the coast at about six knots, making their landfall somewhere near Pointe D'Aiguille, about twelve miles east of Oran. They then steered westward and headed towards the port, maintaining a distance of about half a mile from the shore. In company were two motor launches, ML483, with Lt. I.H. Hunter RNVR in command, and ML480 with Lt. J.H.F. Morgan RNVR on the bridge. Their task was to provide smoke cover for the cutters' assault on the boom.

Arriving about three miles from their objective, the small flotilla faced a two-hour wait in the darkness. For what must have seemed an eternity, the tension grew, with mixed feelings of excitement and apprehension evident on the faces of the crews and the troops below decks. Those on the upper deck stared questioningly shorewards, waiting for the order to go. Whether the delay in sending the cutters in made any difference to the outcome of the savage battle which followed, is a matter for conjecture, but the events of 0200, when a final attempt was made to win over the French, would suggest that surprise and secrecy were not considered essential to the success of the mission. It was at 0200 that the allies' intentions were broadcast to France and French North Africa, via the B.B.C. and American

Radio Stations. In a recorded message, President Roosevelt said:

"We are coming amongst you to repulse the cruel invaders who wish to strip you forever of the right to Govern yourselves, to deprive you of the right to worship God as you wish, and to snatch from you the right to live your lives in peace and security."

This message was followed by a call from Lt.General Eisenhower:

"I have got strict orders that no offensive shall be taken against you on condition that on your side, you observe the same attitude."

However, the French were left in no doubt as to the strength of the invasion force. A statement from the White House said:

"A powerful American force, equipped with adequate weapons of modern warfare and under American Command, is today landing on the Mediterranean and Atlantic coasts of French Colonies in Africa. The landing of this American Army is being assisted by the British Navy and Air Force and will in the immediate future be reinforced by a considerable number of Divisions from the British Army. This combined allied force is designed to prevent any occupation by Axis armies of any part of Northern or Western Africa."

These appeals were supported by leaflets dropped by allied aircraft. The response of Marshal Petain, through Vichy radio broadcast, was short, if not sweet, and ended with; "We shall defend ourselves."

The long-awaited order for the assault on the boom, came just before 0300, and the ships moved off with *'Walney'* in the lead. There was a temporary setback, when she missed the harbour entrance on the first approach. The group then turned to starboard and performed a full clockwise circle for the next run in, with *'Hartland'* approximately 500 yards astern of *'Walney'*. Even at that critical moment, a last-ditch attempt was made to placate the French, when an announcement was made over the loud hailer. It served as little purpose as did all the other political ploys and brought almost instant reaction from the guns ashore.

In unison with the gunfire, the probing beam of a searchlight from Fort Lamoune at the far end of the harbour, stabbed the darkness, picking out the cutters whilst they were less than half a mile from the boom. With the ships now illuminated by searchlight and the gun

HMS WALNEY AND HMS HARTLAND — SUICIDE MISSION

flashes, the heavy armament of Ravin Blanc Battery, together with heavy machine-gun fire from the moles, joined in the devastating barrage at point blank range.

'Hartland' bore the brunt of the opening salvoes, whilst *'Walney'*, screened by the smoke of the two M.L.'s, increased her speed to 15 knots and made her run in.

"Lofty Pearson and I located the centre bearing on the harbour entrance, using our Asdic, then housed the gear," said J.H. Finch.

There was an anxious moment when M.L.483 came into collision with her as she came out of the smoke. In the darkness, nobody could be certain as to what effect the impact on the ship would be, as she hit first the outer boom, and then the inner boom which turned out to be a row of coal barges. Surprisingly, the cutter broke through with hardly a noticeable tremor, due no doubt to her reinforced bows. Engines were then stopped, and when way came off the ship the canoes were slipped with their crews and stores in them. This was achieved in less than a minute. Although all canoes reported themselves clear and under way, one had been damaged by enemy fire before lowering, and sunk shortly afterwards.

As the smoke drifted across the Avant Port, *'Walney'* was exposed to heavy close range fire on both quarters from guns mounted on the jetties and moles. It is remarkable that she suffered so little damage from that initial burst of fire.

The situation changed rapidly as she approached Mole Millerand, when two moored submarines joined in the action. The cutter suffered several direct hits, and all telephonic communications aft were cut. In spite of her decks being swept with fire, the crew managed to complete the launching of the canoes, whilst the ship moved up-harbour at a painstaking four knots. With enemy fire now directed at her from all directions, a new hazard presented itself in the form of an enemy destroyer coming towards her in an attempt to flee the harbour. As it approached, *'Walney'* made a gallant attempt to ram, but steaming at such slow speed, she was unable to complete the manouvre and the enemy passed down her port side.

Although little more than ten minutes had elapsed since she broke

THE HAND - ME - DOWN SHIPS

through the boom, the cutter had already fought her way to within 600 yards of her objective at the furthermost end of the harbour. So far her casualties had been light. Illuminated by gun flashes, and raked by machine-gun fire, the order was given to go to boarding stations. The boarding parties, comprising a British Naval Officer and six ratings, together with seven members of the US Army, clambered into the two port boats, which were then turned out, preparatory to coming alongside the enemy ships. The task of clearing the enemy's decks prior to boarding, was in the hands of sixteen grenade throwers from the American contingent, mustered on the fo'csle. The deck parties were standing by with bow and stern lines ready for use, with power on the winch and capstan.

So far *'Walney'* had been able to keep all her close-range weapons manned, and surprisingly, in spite of being under continuous fire, had suffered minimal damage. However, the worst had yet to come. As she approached the Quaie Centrale to board the *'Epervier'*, another enemy destroyer attempted to break out. With her attention focussed mainly on the *'Epervier'*, which was putting up strong resistance, coupled with salvoes from one of the forts, the cutter was hit by at least two broadsides from the destroyer as it passed down her starboard side. Two shells pierced the ship's side, exploding in the engine-room, devastating the personnel and destroying the lubricating tanks. With the oil supply cut off, the automatic stop value closed and the main engine shuddered to a stop.

Within seconds of this disaster, another shell detonated in the boiler-room, killing most of the men and totally wiping out the two main boilers. Simultaneously, the wardroom flat and steering compartment were ravaged by two direct hits on the starboard quarter. With her steering gear out of action *'Walney'* was now at the mercy of the enemy guns. Yet another direct hit completely demolished the cutter's bridge, killing sixteen of the seventeen officers and ratings gathered there, among them the ship's Captain, Lt.Cdr. Meyrick. The only survivor, Captain Peters, had a miraculous escape, though partially blinded in the explosion. It would have been little consolation to *'Walney's'* crew, that the French destroyer, having inflicted such terrible damage and loss of life before slipping out of the harbour, was later engaged by the British destroyer *'Brilliant'* and sunk.

J.H. Finch, takes up the story from the time *'Walney's'* bridge was shot away:

"Lofty Pearson and I were both concussed and choking on cordite fumes and smoke as we scrambled from the Asdic compartment over the dead bodies of our colleagues. We managed to make our way to the Rec/Gyro room on the starboard side, where kitbags and hammocks were stowed. Other casualties had made their way there. By now, the ship had drifted round so that her starboard side was exposed to the fire. We received a direct hit aft of our position in the storage compartment and the explosion threw me into the pile of hammocks, which collapsed on top of me. I managed to extricate myself and make my way along the row of bunks, between which were the troops. From what I could see, very few had survived.

"I crossed the mess-deck to the port passageway and moved aft towards the wardroom. I was suddenly joined by 'Nutty' Gardner, the wardroom steward, who informed me that some thirty casualties were gathered there. Together we made our way there, to be greeted by the most appalling sight. In the dim light, our surgeon and his sick berth attendant were desperately trying to cope with the wounded, many of which were beyond help. I was facing the pantry, with vertical channelling supporting lead-cased cables behind me. Suddenly there was a massive explosion as a shell struck the starboard quarter and exploded in the wardroom. The cables behind me must have given me protection, because I believe I was the only one to survive.

"Stunned and dazed and my head ringing, I managed to grope my way up the stairs to the port gangway, to collapse on the upper deck. By this time, the ship was well to the far end of the harbour and ablaze."

Surgeon Lt. A.L. Phillips RNVR, together with sick berth attendant S.H. Masterton, perished in the wardroom explosions.

Now without power, *'Walney'* drifted closer to the *'Epervier'*, caught in the French ship's searchlight. This was promptly put out by the cutter's .5 machine-gun fire. By this time, the cutter had suffered so many casualties that she was unable to keep her guns firing. All the grenade throwers on the fo'cstle had been killed, and all but two officers and three ratings from the combined boarding parties. In spite of the heavy losses and the severe damage to the ship, the surviving officers and crew members made a gallant attempt to get the cutter alongside. A headrope was finally got to the jetty, ahead of the *'Epervier'*, whilst Lt. Moseley succeeded in getting a sternline out to a depth-charge carrier, which lodged between the funnels. But with no power on the ship, it was impossible to heave-in and *'Walney'* drifted at right angles to the French ship.

The cutter's guns were finally silenced and she was ablaze forward and amidships. Her crew had been depleted considerably and the carnage among the troops was reported by Lt. Moseley as 'indescribable'.

Amid the deafening din of the battle, and seeing the ship reduced to a floating heap of jagged, twisted metal, the surviving crew members must have despaired of any hope of survival. In the midst of the confusion it was impossible to know when, and from which direction the death-dealing blows were coming.

"I gave the order to un-prime the five-pattern depth-charges still primed," wrote Lt. Moseley; "followed by the order to abandon ship. No attempt was made to get away the Carley rafts or other life-saving equipment, since the whole harbour was full of debris by this time and we were still being engaged by the enemy. Our small arms and mortar ammunition was exploding all over the ship, which decided me to get the survivors into the water and away from the ship as quickly as possible. I swam in the direction of the *'Epervier'* and was hauled aboard. Several of the ship's company were killed in the water by riflemen.

"Their treatment of me caused me much surprise, as when I came on board they were tending their wounded. They had been hit by a 3" shell or splinters in the T.S. and the forward boiler-room and bridgework, director and searchlights were riddled with bullets. As the blazing remains of *'Walney'* drifted down at 0700, the ship's company of *'Epervier'* were too busy to notice me and I was free to have a brief look around."

Lt. Moseley was later imprisoned in the Naval barracks, then moved to a civil prison, and finally lodged in the barracks of the Second Zonave Regiment.

"The supply of food for extra mouths was non-existent and the sanitary arrangements — French," he wrote.

'Walney's desperate fight, in which she was constantly outgunned, ended whilst only a few yards from the western end of the harbour. Like a tired old warhorse, she rolled over and sank.

The devastation of *'Hartland'* began even before she entered the harbour. Whilst her captain could see little of the harbour entrance because of smoke, the sound of the battle from within was clearly audible and the gun flashes and explosions were evidence enough of the reception he could expect.

Les Elder recalls those early moments:

"As part of the plan to hoodwink the French, the members of the boarding parties were given American battle fatigues. But all that was in vain. We were sitting ducks and they hit us with everything they had."

There was a brief delay before *'Hartland'* made her run up to the harbour entrance. In the darkness and smoke, it was virtually impossible to see just how much the boom was breached. Lt.Cdr. Billot, subsequently put into effect the instructions previously received from Captain Peters, to wait five minutes before proceeding.

As *'Hartland'* shaped her course at about 0315, she was picked up by the Fort Lamoune searchlight and immediately subjected to fire from the Ravin Blanc Battery and the French destroyer *'Typhon'*. The opening salvoes were devastating and within minutes, most of her guns' crews had become casualties. So quickly did the French react to the cutter being illuminated, she was able to get only three rounds off before there were too few unwounded seamen to man her guns. *'Hartland'* was a sitting target in the searchlight beam and the fires which were raging fore and aft. The efforts of her supply parties were hampered by continuous fire raking her decks. Their numbers were quickly depleted whilst they were desperately trying to get the fires under control. In addition to the heavy punishment being taken on the upper deck, severe damage was inflicted below. One boiler or main steam pipe was hit, causing a loud escape of steam, which effectively rendered all communications impossible.

Lt.Cdr. Billot was blinded in one eye by shrapnel, resulting in the ship striking the Jettee Du Large, about six feet from it's northern side, before he could recover. Fortunately, the engine-room was responding to telegraphs and after some manouvreing, 'Hartland' entered the Avant Port, and proceeded, still under heavy fire, towards her appointed billet, halfway down the Quai de Dunkerque, on the western side of the Mole Ravin Blanc. The order to launch the canoes was given, but this was not carried out because both craft had been riddled with bullets and rendered useless.

As the ship rounded the Mole, she sailed straight into the heavy armament of the destroyer *'Typhon'*, whose fire was joined by the two submarines which had earlier punished *'Walney'*. At this stage *'Hartland'* was fully committed and headed for the quay, whilst the destroyer's guns continued to pound her at a range of less than a hundred feet. One direct hit put her main motor out of action and all power failed in the ship.

In spite of this setback, she had sufficient way on to reach the jetty, where her First Lieutenant, Lt. V.A. Hickson RN., made a gallant, but unsuccessful attempt to pass a wire ashore. Nothing could be done at the after end of the ship, since the decks were being swept with machine gun fire at point blank range. Anyone who attempted to brave the withering fire was immediately cut down.

With much of her bridge shot away, and out of control, *'Hartland'* started to drift away from the quay. Her captain had not sought another billet for the ship, since a study of reconnaissance photographs had not revealed a better place, bearing in mind the requirements of the military, and at the time, he was unaware of the heavy losses among the combat troops on the mess-decks. In fact, he had called upon them to help capture a pair of tugs lying under the

HMS WALNEY AND HMS HARTLAND — SUICIDE MISSION

cutter's bows, and was dismayed at the poor numbers that arrived. The determined resistance of French seamen on the quay, added to his problems.

As the cutter started to drift, Lt.Cdr. Billot gave the order to drop anchor. He then attempted to make a hurried inspection of the ship to ascertain whether further action could be organised. His activities were considerely restricted when he was hit in both legs and a shoulder. With all her guns out of action and flames funnel high, it was obvious that *Hartland's* end was imminent. With the large amount of explosives on board likely to explode at any time, her captain was faced with no alternative but to abandon the ship. In his report of the action, Lt.Cdr. Billot wrote:

"Soon after this, the French humanely gave up firing, though we did not heave down our colours."

There followed the task of getting the wounded ashore. Whilst this operation was hampered by ammunition going off in all directions, the ship was finally cleared forward by the First Lieutenant, while a small band of officers were getting the wounded away aft in some haste, as the decks and the ship's side were red hot. These officers were eventually ordered ashore by the captain, who followed at about 0500. By this time, the fires had reached the crows nest and more than half the crew were either killed or wounded. About twenty-five minutes later, *'Hartland'* was rent apart by a massive explosion, yet stubbornly stayed afloat. It took a further explosion, a few hours later, to finally seal her fate.

Survivors among the troops installed in the two cutters were alarmingly few. Lt.Cdr. Dickey USN., reported later:

"Upon abandoning ship, officers and men showed the highest kind of leadership and spirit in helping to save the lives of United States soldiers who were unfamiliar with the ship and the use of life jackets. The effort to rescue men from the water continued long after the ship had been abandoned."

Lt. Moseley, in his report to Flag Officer Commanding 'Force H', wrote of *'Walney's'* part:

"I should like to stress that the recommendations I am forwarding are merely representative of the gallantry and heroism shown by officers and men of the ship and the U.S. Army borne. The lack of success in this operation does not detract from the ship's company's feat in fighting their ship for over an hour against overwhelming odds."

Whilst it would perhaps be unfitting to single out any individual acts of bravery in an action where extreme courage was abundant, the actions of the men in 'Hartland', who ensured that the wounded were placed to safety, is representative of the gallantry displayed by all who were engaged in the brief but bloody battle.

Lt. John Evans RNVR., Lt. E.G. Lawrence RNVR.; A/CPO Laurence Hazard; and Gunner Obelkevitch of the US Navy, had, eventually, to be ordered to leave the ship. A/CPO Hazard had remained at 'Hartland's wheel throughout the action.

Telegraphist Arthur Ticehurst, who had joined 'Hartland' on 7th January 1942, from the Aircraft Carrier 'Eagle', was among the survivors:

"Our leading telegraphist was killed, but the rest of us managed to escape. I was dragged along the upper deck by a mate of mine and down into a boat with more of the wounded. We made out way to a merchant ship and were taken aboard. Later, we were landed on the jetty, where we lay until daybreak before being taken prisoner. The wounded were taken to hospital, where the room was infested with bed bugs. I was examined by three doctors and then moved to another hospital for an emergency operation. By the time the Americans arrived, most of the doctors had left and we remained in the care of a handful of Red Cross. I spent the next three months in Oran before returning to the U.K."

Les Elder, another survivor, said:

"Those of us who survived were lucky indeed. When we got ashore, we were quickly rounded up and marched through the streets of Oran. Some of us were even spat upon by some of the people. We were dumped in a filthy prison, but later removed to a French barracks. On my return to the U.K. I got survivors' leave for the second time in eighteen months before being drafted into Combined Operations."

HMS WALNEY AND HMS HARTLAND — SUICIDE MISSION

When dawn broke over Oran harbour, the full extent of the battle was revealed, with debris littering the placid water and the smell of cordite and smoke still hanging in the air. The culmination of this savage conflict by desperate and brave men, was a terrible toll of dead and wounded. Eighty-one of *'Walney's* crew paid the supreme sacrifice, as did thirty-four from her sister ship *'Hartland'*. Few survived among the four-hundred or more troops installed below decks.

During the course of the action, three French ships had fled the harbour, only to run into the guns of the British Naval Force stationed offshore. In a brief engagement, the French *'Tromontane'* was sunk. The remainder headed back into the port, where the *'Tornade'* was beached. The following day, the *'Epervier'* and *'Typhon'* were ordered to sail, but they too ran into trouble with the British cruisers *'Aurora'* and *'Jamaica'*. The French ships were quickly dispensed with, the *'Epervier'* sustaining hits which set her ablaze, causing her to beach herself. The *'Typhon'* returned to the safety of the harbour only to be scuttled across the entrance. Other casualties included the minesweeper *'La Suprise'* and submarines *'Acteaon'*, *'Ariane'*, *'Argonaute'*, *'Ceres'*, *'Diane'* and *'Pallas'*.

By the 10th the eastern half of the port was cluttered with French ships, many of them scuttled, whilst more damaged vessels littered the western end, where *'Walney'* had finally settled. By that time, allied troops were closing in from both sides of Oran, against strong resistance. By 1100 on the 11th, armoured units had penetrated the town and by noon the same day, the French gave up the fight.

Captain Peters, who had been imprisoned by the Vichy garrison, was flown home after his release, but the aircraft carrying him home, Sunderland W6054, crashed on landing at Plymouth at 2100 on the 13th and he was killed. It is ironic that the man who had survived so many sea battles in two world wars, should meet his end as passenger in an aircraft.

A four-inch column in the London Gazette, placed on record a nation's gratitude for the heroism shown by Officers and ratings in the two cutters *'Walney'* and *'Hartland'*, whose numbers were so sadly depleted in the early hours of 8th November 1942. Only those who survived the battle know the full measure of boldness displayed that day, against overwhelming odds.

Heading the list of Honours, is Captain Frederick Thornton Peters DSO., DSC., RN., who was awarded a Victoria Cross. The remaining citations are:

The Distinguished Service Order Lt.Cdr. Godfrey Philip Billot RNR; Lt. Wallace Dempsey Moseley RN; and Lt. Vere Ashworth Hickson RN.

The Distinguished Service Cross — Lt. John Evans RNVR; Lt. Eric Gordon Lawrence RNVR; Lt. John Macleod RNVR; Lt. Robert Denis Sworder RNVR; Lt. (E) John White RN; and Lt. Ronald John Major RANVR.

The Conspicuous Gallantry Medal — Petty Officer Ronald Herbert Frank Hyde C/JX151957.

The Distinguished Service Medal — Acting CPO. Lawrence Thomas Hazard P/JX125131; Ldg. Seaman Samuel Bolton P/JX180491; Engine Room Artificer, Third Class, Robert Sidney Smith C/MX 53378; Chief Engine Room Artificer, George Harry Rolls P/MX49955; Engine Room Artificer, Third Class, George Albert Park P/MX56580; Petty Officer Bert Ballentry Clark P/JX130780; Petty Officer Richard Charles Young P/JX131554; Able Seaman Fred Henry Buck P/JX98914; Able Seaman John Joseph Canavan P/JX264529; and Stoker First Class Frank William Desmond Crosby P/KX123549.

Mention in Despatches — (Posthumous) Lt.Cdr. Peter Capel Meyrick RN; and Lt. Paul Eric Aver Duncan RNVR.

Mention in Despatches — Able Seaman Henry Brown Hamilton P/JX329710; Able Seaman Kenneth Marsden P/JX263443; and Able Seaman Ronald Brockbank C/JX243366.

The Le Petit Lac Cemetery which is situated on the south eastern outskirts of Oran, is a permanent memorial to the men who were lost in the action. Originally a large war cemetery, it was formed in 1943 by the Americans for the burial of soldiers of the allied forces who perished during the North Africa landings. After 1945 all, except United Kingdom and Commonwealth graves, were moved elsewhere, but in 1950 it was re-opened by the Ministere de Anciens Combattants et Victimes de Guerre, as a Free French National Cemetery for men of the French Army, Navy and Air Force. The United Kingdom plot lies undisturbed on its original site, on the western slope of a hill. It is the final resting place for two hundred and twenty men from all three services and the Merchant Navy, who died during the landings. Included are thirteen men from the cutters *'Walney'* and *'Hartland'*.

They are, from *'Walney'*: — Able Seaman A.C. Beck; Telegraphist K.W. Lawrence; Able Seaman A. MacDonald; Stoker 1st Class J.S. McPherson; Leading Seaman L.W. Merrick; Telegraphist L. Lavill; Leading Stoker S.W.O. Spratley; and Leading Signalman K. Brighton. From *'Hartland'*: — Engine Room Artificer V.O. Lillie; Able Seaman A.E. Moore; Able Seaman D. Sayle; Ordinary Seaman H. Shipley; and Gunner (T) A. Thompson.

Lt. Moseley concluded his report on the action with the following comment:

"It is my opinion that the naval side of the operation might have been successful if carried out by two modern Fleet destroyers and that even the cutters could have accomplished it if they had entered the harbour two hours earlier."

A 'suicide mission' had been predicted, and that is what it turned out to be.

Familes mourned loved ones who did not return from Oran. For Kathleen Cunningham, it was a tragic end to a marriage which was all too brief. Her young husband, Sub.Lt. Peter Ward RNVR, was killed during *'Hartland's* assault on the harbour boom. He had been drafted to the cutter after surviving the hazards of the notorious Russian convoys.

Chapter Five

HMS Landguard (1)

At least two more cutters, *'Landguard'* and *'Fishguard'*, underwent strengthening of hull and bow, which had strong similarities to those carried out in *'Walney'* and *'Hartland'*. Whilst it is uncertain which of them had been first choice for operation 'Reservist', there is no mention of the former in the US Operational Plan of 5th October 1942, whilst *'Walney'* and *'Hartland'* are clearly indicated as the chosen vessels for the mission.

Lt. K.M. Macleod, in the *'Languard'* at the time, recalls:

"Following a visit by senior British and American officers, when *'Landguard'* underwent close inspection, especially her messdeck, we were taken to a US repair ship moored in the Foyle, and steel plates were welded to her bows at and below the waterline. All this was unexplained, but very sinister. Then came a sudden panic! A merchant ship with engine failure and an important cargo was adrift in worsening weather in the vicinity of Rockall and off we went with instructions to tow and escort her to safety."

The dramatic build-up of events which led to the rescue attempt, had its beginnings on 1st September 1942, when the British steamer *'Empire Tarpon'* sailed from Mobile for New Orleans, en route for Great Britain, via New York, with her holds packed with general cargo, much of which was vital to the war effort. What followed is a classic example of courage and good seamanship in the most adverse weather conditions. Ahead of her lay the long haul round the coast of Florida to New York, before making the hazardous passage across the Atlantic, a distance of over 5,000 miles. Hardly had she left Mobile, when the steering broke down and she was forced to anchor in the South West Pass while temporary repairs were carried out by the engineering personnel, using the limited facilities at their

THE WHITE HOUSE
WASHINGTON

April 5, 1941

My dear Mr. Secretary:

    Consultation having been had with the Chief of Naval Operations of the Navy and with the Commandant of the Coast Guard, I find that:

    (1) The defense of the United Kingdom is vital to the defense of the United States;

    (2) Sections 4 and 7 of the Act of March 11, 1941 have been complied with by the necessary agreement on the part of His Majesty's Government in the United Kingdom;

    (3) It would be in the interests of our national defense to transfer the defense articles set forth in the annexed schedule.

    I therefore authorize you immediately to make the transfer to His Majesty's Government in the United Kingdom of the defense articles set forth in the annexed schedule.

    I would appreciate it if you would arrange with the Chairman of the British Supply Council in North America for the time, method, and other details of the disposition.

    Very sincerely yours,

    Franklin D. Roosevelt

The Honorable
    The Secretary of the Treasury.

The US President's letter of authorization for the transfer of the cutters to the Royal Navy.

'Culver' alongside the jetty at Bathurst, in August 1941, prior to sailing to the United Kingdom with convoy SL84. (G. Pattinson)

The thirteen survivors from 'Culver' grouped on board their rescue ship 'Londonderry'. The only surviving officer was Sub. Lt. Carlow (second from left, front row.) Regrettably it was not possible to identify all the survivors individually. (G. Pattinson)

▲

 his fo'cstle view of 'Culver'
 ows the early armament
 the cutters before
 nversion. The taking of
 e picture coincided with
 ashday. (G. Pattinson)

▶

 e officers of 'Culver' prior
 her sinking. (Back row l
 r): Lt. Cdr. (E) G.S. Thorp
 N., Lt. G.F. Watson
 VR., Sub.Lt. G.
 ttinson RNVR., Sub.Lt.
 rlow RNVR., Lt.Cdr. R.T.
 rdon-Duff RN., (captain),
 Sub. Lt. R.G.R. Bensley
 VR., and Sub.Lt. W.
 otrowski (Polish Navy).
 ront row): Gunner A.G.
 nnett DSM.,RN., T/Lt.
 H. Jubb RNR., and
 Surgeon Lt. R. Troup
 VR.

The final moments in the destruction of the cutter 'Hartland' in Oran harbour on 8th November 1942. (Imperial War Museum. A140...

The cutter 'Walney' lies on her side in the harbour, sunk after her gallant action at Oran. (Imperial War Museum. A13693).

'Banff' rides at anchor at Kilindini, August 1944, flying the Admiral's Flag at her masthead. (James Nesbitt).

Lt.Cdr. James D'Arcy Nesbitt RNR (standing right) paying a visit to his ship HMS 'Banff' during her stay in Massawa in the Red Sea. (J. Nesbitt)

'Banff' crew members pose with a Zulu rickshaw operator on the beach at Durban, S.Africa. (Back row l. to r.) 'Brum' Hemmings and 'Lofty' Elkins. (Centre l. to r.) Reg Stanley, Moss, 'Jagger' Cross and Doug Blake. (Front row l. to r.) Ted Worral, Griggs, Kettle, and Steve Hieway. (Reg Stanley)

The cutter 'Landguard' whose wartime career was ended by an inboard explosion in 1945. ▲
(K.M. Macleod)

Officers in 'Landguard' 1942. (Back row l. to r.) Sub.Lt. Robertson RNR., Sub.Lt. Watson RNVR., Sub.Lt. Lewis RNVR., Sub.Lt. Challis RNVR., Sub.Lt. Bird RNVR., Sub.Lt. Waclieski (Polish Navy), Gunner, T., and Medical Officer. (Seated l. to r.) Lt. Gladstone (First Lieutenant), Lt.Cdr. R.E.S. Hugonin RN., (Captain), and Lt.(E) K.M. Macleod (Engineer Officer). (K.M. Macleod) ▼

Always with the working parties was a Sinhalese boy, who was adopted by the crew and named John Landguard. He is pictured here with the ship's mascot. (J.O.C. Willson)

The working part of Tamils and Sinhalese aboard 'Landguard' (Seated from l. to r.) Petty Officer Jackson (Coxswain), Sinhales (Captain), Able seaman Brown; The Chief ERA., and the Sinha

▲ *The 'Landguard' football team in Colombo with the Slave Island Mohamodans. Gordon Cooke, who supplied the photograph is seated third from the left in the middle row.*

*r days as static depot ship in Colombo towards the end of the war.
lerk, Petty Officer Gordon Cooke (Bosuns Mate), Lt. R.N. Kinder RN.,
d clerk. (Gordon Cooke)*

By the KING'S Order the name of
Able Seaman Ronald John Robert Coulson,
H.M.S. Lulworth,
was published in the London Gazette on
13 October, 1942,
as mentioned in a Despatch for distinguished service.
I am charged to record
His Majesty's high appreciation.

First Lord of the Admiralty

▲ Ron Coulson's 'Mention in Despatches' for his alertness in spotting the Italian submarine 'Pietro Calvi' at 12 miles range at night.

'Lulworth' proceeds alongside an oil tanker at Port Swettenham in September 1945. (Bob Game) ▶

'Lulworth' anchored off Aden in January 1945. (David Thomas)

Members of 'Lulworth' football team pose for the camera in Colombo. (David Thomas)

'Lulworth's motor boat alongside the quay at Alguada lighthouse. Shortly after the boat was wrecked on the rocks in bad weather. (David Thomas)

The deck party aboard 'Lulworth' take in the slack after passing a tow rope to a merchant ship. (David Thomas)

▲ 'Lulworth' crew members take a break among the palms of the Cocos Islands in October 1945. (Bob Game)

'Lulworth's liberty boat heads for shore in the Cocos Islands with the football team in tow. (Bob Game) ▶

'Lulworth' carves a path ▶ through masses of water hyacinths in the Bassein river, whilst making her way upstream to liberate the town of Bassein. (David Thomas)

(Dream of Florence)

"Firenze sogno" Ballata

I

Firenze fiorellin bella
un dì ti ho sognata nel cielo
che in cielo apparivano fiumi
come fiammelle
belli orrendi mirabili
le bocce fiammanti
in fiore. Oh amore
il tuon di ciò tutto fulgea
per le città mie
ospiti il mio cuore
Napoli

Sull'Arno d'argento
si specchia il firmamento
contro la tua collina e un canto
si perde lontano
nella spiaggia della luna

II

— Tutti tre nel mio balcone
mia ch'io nel mio balcone
ogni sera una madonna baciai
Bellon coloriti di porpora
e gigli in fior.
Venti schiudetevi ancora
che posa l'amor,
gemo piano di nuovo ti
Madonna coroliti
nell'ozio vola
ai miei toini ella già
la gioia regina.
Tutto fiorisce
Sull'Arno d'argento.

▲ Italian ballad written out for John Loughran by Emilio Trucco, a survivor from the Italian submarine, 'Pietro Calvi'. Emilio had a fine tenor voice and had broadcast on Radio Nazionalt Italiano.

London 14-1-42.

Dear Tima,

The first news is to wish you a happy X-mas and a happy New Year. Boy & Boy I never will forget you. I never knew you before, but you was very good to me and Chriss. I hope to see you very soon. I wish every body at home a happy new year. I am very sorry I could find in any case, no room in the position Truhos, Trust will to forget rusedime, I always will remember you Jan Form.

I hope you will answer me soon.
your friend Ali.

From. Johan Mohamed. Ali.
C/o Osbourne Hotel. (Room 6).
Endsleigh Place W.C.2.
London. England.

Copy of the letter received by John Loughran from Johan Mohamed Ali, a survivor of the torpedoed SS Bennekom. The signatures of the thirty-two survivors from the sunken Italian submarine 'Pietro Calvi' (on the right) also supplid by John Loughran.

'Lulworth' fires a salvo during night action off Burma in March 1945. (David Thomas).

disposal. Although the old ship managed to resume her passage, there could have been little room for optimism concerning her general condition. A recurrence of the steering problem rendered her uncontrollable and she struck the river bank. No time was lost in refloating her and she rode at anchor whilst her engineers made a further attempt to put matters right. As in the first instance, the repairs were of a temporary nature. Nonetheless, she eventually made New Orleans without further incident.

When the *'Empire Tarpon'* set off on the 2,000 miles passage to New York, the Master must have had doubts as to whether the old ship would survive the voyage without further mishap. Such doubts were confirmed when there was not only further trouble with the steering, but the discovery of leaking boiler tubes must have caused even deeper concern. In spite of the setbacks the steamer made New York and straightaway underwent repairs of a more permanent nature.

Three weeks after leaving Mobile, the ship was considered ready to continue her passage to the United Kingdom. She sailed from New York on 24th September and headed out into the Atlantic. Within a week, there were further problems with the boiler tubes, coupled with the discovery of a serious leak in No. 1 hold. It called for superb seamanship to maintain way on the ship with her condition worsening daily. By the 6th October, *'Empire Tarpon'* had fought her way to a position off Rockall, beset by one problem after another. So serious had her position become, that she was no longer able to continue steaming. Now at the mercy of mounting seas, her Master called for assistance. That distress call was answered by three ships of the 40th Escort Group, *'Londonderry'*, *'Bideford'* and the cutter *'Landguard'*.

"The passage through the Minches was fiendish," said Lt. Macleod. *'Bideford'* suffered such wave damage that she was compelled to return to base. *'Londonderry'* and *'Landguard'* struggled on and in due course found Rockall and the distressed ship."

By this time, the tug *'Dexterous'* had been despatched to assist in the rescue. To attempt a towing operation in such appalling sea conditions, was hazardous enough for both the damaged steamer and the rescue vessels, but the importance of the vital cargo, made it necessary for risks to be taken. It was not until the following day, with everyone praying for an abatement in the weather, and the hapless merchant ship wallowing helplessly at the mercy of the sea, that an attempt was made to pass a tow across. The task fell to *'Landguard'*, but whilst trying to get alongside the steamer from astern, she misjudged the manoeuvre and her bows came up under the violently pitching merchantman's stern, incurring damage to the cutter's forward section. In spite of this near disaster, and with both ships being tossed around like corks, the evolution was finally accomplished.

However, the major role in this drama was being played out by the sea itself. With a ferocity, not unfamiliar to the supporting cast, she suddenly flung the two ships apart with such fierceness that the tow parted. A second tow shared the same fate. The lack of success in maintaining the tow, coupled with the deterioration in the steamer's condition, prompted the rescuers to remove the crew. This was accomplished without loss. The arrival of the tug raised hopes of salvage. Furthermore, in spite of her condition, the old steamer resisted all attempts by the sea to claim her. Later, on the 10th, after a further assessment of the situation, the merchant ship's crew were returned together with a boarding party from *'Landguard'*.

'Empire Tarpon' was again taken in tow, but with 23ft of water in her No. 1 hold she proved extremely unmanageable, and hopes of beaching her in Vatersay Bay, in the outer Hebrides, seemed remote. The violent seas persisted and a sudden furious squall caused yet another tow to part. A second tug was called for with the old ship 150 miles west of Barra. By this time *'Landguard's* condition was also causing concern. Her badly damaged bows tended to hamper her, and it was decided she should return to base. Meanwhile the tugs persisted in their attempts to salvage. By the evening of the following day, their efforts were finally rewarded and they had the ship in tow, moving at an agonizing 3½ knots towards Loch Boisdale. However, the continual battering by mountainous seas had worsened the situation in the merchantman's No. 1 hold. The cargo of cotton swelled to such

an extent that it buckled deck plates and burst the hatches. As the sea continued to pour in, such was the strain on the tow, that it parted, with the battered hulk within sight of a landfall. In spite of having brought her so close to home, it became obvious that her end was imminent.

'Empire Tarpon' was finally abandoned at 1900 and, within three hours succumbed to her inevitable fate. She sank 20 miles south west of South Uist with every member of her crew taken to safety.

Captain George Boyle had served in 'Empire Tarpon' as an able seaman from early January to April 1941. How the ship came to such a dramatic end came as no surprise to him:

"'Empire Tarpon' was originally the American vessel 'Harpoon'. At that time she was a wreck. We attempted to sail from the Tyne in January 1941, but broke down whilst still in the river and dropped anchor. This fouled a submarine cable putting a large part of Northumberland's telephone communications out of order. About a week later, we made another attempt to put to sea, but the engine broke down again. The Master was reluctant to drop anchor and left it rather late, with the result that we collided with the training ship 'Satellite', which was moored to the bank. On our third attempt, we got underway and joined up with a convoy bound for America, via Oban. Once again the engines failed, this time at Loch Ewe, where we had a three-weeks stay undergoing repairs. Most of that time we were without heating. We eventually made Oban and spent several weeks waiting confirmation that the ship was fit to make the Atlantic crossing. A few days after sailing we broke down again and were towed into the Clyde by an Admiralty tug. There we paid off and to the best of my knowledge the ship was declared unseaworthy and would probably end up as a blockship."

Some five months previous to the 'Empire Tarpon' disaster, 'Landguard' had been engaged on the Freetown run. The convoys were often slow and frequently comprised tankers, which were prime targets for U-boats. The experience gained during these convoys had resulted in many new techniques in anti-submarine warfare, and in spite of sometimes constant harassment, the enemy were deterred

THE HAND - ME - DOWN SHIPS

from making attacks. Keeping the U-boats at bay was as important as trying to deplete their numbers. After all, the main object was to get the merchant ships to their destinations with their valuable cargoes.

A good example of how escorts employed these tactics successfully, and how the cutters quickly adapted to their new role against the enemy's 'shadow and attack' strategy, is shown in the assault on Convoy SL109, which comprised thirty-one ships, and sailed from Freetown, bound for Gibraltar, on 4th May 1942.

During seventy-two hours of continuous U-boat activity, the ships of the 40th Escort Group, *'Bideford'*, *'Hastings'* and the cutters *'Landguard'* and *'Lulworth'*, held the enemy at bay, with the loss of only one merchantman. Their success was made all the more noteworthy in the light of the number of set-backs experienced during the three-day period.

As was usually the case, the first few days of the voyage were comparatively quiet, but at 1510 on the 11th, the first submarine was sighted from *'Lulworth'*, at a range of twelve miles. The cutter set off to intercept at a speed of 14½ knots, with *'Landguard'* and *'Hastings'* in company. The target was identified as probably Italian. With the range closing visibly, *'Lulworth'* closed up her guns' crews ready to engage the U-boat on the surface, but by the time she reached a firing position, the submarine crash-dived. The game of hide-and-seek began. *'Lulworth'* and *'Hastings'* were immediately ordered to close within 4,000 yards on either beam of *'Landguard'*, with the intention of carrying out a sweep over an area of approximately eight square miles. Since *'Hastings'* was unable to match the speed of the cutters, and was left about three miles astern of them, *'Landguard'* and *'Lulworth'* pressed home the attack with depth-charges set at medium settings. The subsequent explosions from *'Landguard's* charges caused her A/S training gear to fail, and it was necessary to send a man to the Directing Gear position to train by hand, maintaining communications by telephone. The defect was traced to a burned out balance resistor which took three hours to trace and repair.

HMS LANDGUARD (1)

In the meantime the search and chase was continued by her companions. When the contact was lost, 'Hastings' and 'Landguard' returned to their stations with the convoy, leaving 'Lulworth' in the vicinity to continue the search. About an hour later, she resumed contact with the target, and launched a further depth-charge attack. It was now her turn to have her intentions foiled by mechanical breakdown and almost an hour elapsed before she could resume her search. In spite of the interuption, she quickly regained contact and pressed home another depth-charge attack. Although there was a noticeably strong smell of oil, there was no visible evidence of a 'kill'. 'Lulworth' returned to the convoy at about 0100.

The early hours of the 12th saw both 'Landguard' and 'Hastings' in trouble, with more mechanical faults, which were attributed to the depth-charge attacks of the previous day. 'Hastings' was forced to shut down one engine, but managed to stay underway. 'Landguard', being a single-screw ship, was not so fortunate. She had serious condenser problems and had to shut down completely, rendering her most vulnerable in the light of the U-boat activity. This situation could have had serious consequences for both the cutter and the convoy, since it was not possible at the time, to estimate just how long repairs would take. An additional complication was a breakdown in her Type 271 RDF.

Rather than leave 'Landguard' to her own devices, it was decided to take her in tow, so that she might remain with the convoy. A tow was passed to the merchantman 'Royal Star', and to the credit of it's Master, and Lt.Cdr. R.E.S. Hugonin RN., in the cutter, the two ships maintained station in the convoy for the three-and-half hours it took to put matters right. It was a most commendable display of good seamanship on the part of all concerned.

Meanwhile, the engineering staff in 'Landguard' worked feverishly to remedy the faults. It was to their credit that the condenser problem was resolved by 1615, when the 'Royal Star' slipped the tow.

However, there remained the problem of the Type 271 RDF. Although arrangements were made for spares to be supplied by sister-ship 'Lulworth' this proved impossible in the light of subsequent events. It was fortunate that a temporary repair proved satisfactory, making 'Landguard' more or less, fully operational.

During 'Landguard's incapacitation, the other escorts in the group were kept busy defending the convoy. 'Hastings', with her repairs completed, had been proceeding to her station on the port beam of the convoy when, at 1539, she sighted the conning town of a submarine at 10 miles range, but because of her lack of speed and a possible recurrence of engine failure, 'Lulworth' was despatched to assist. Although 'Hastings' opened fire at the target, it soon became obvious that the U-boat's superior surface speed was taking it well out of range of the escort's guns. She therefore gave up the chase and set course for the convoy. Apparently this action did not go unobserved aboard the U-boat, since it was spotted from 'Lulworth' following 'Hastings' back to the convoy, which at that time was out of sight. The cutter opened fire with her heavy armament and although her shots fell short, the action produced the required result. The submarine appeared to lose any further interest.

About the same time, 'Landguard' was making her way to the port bow of the convoy when, at 1733, her masthead look-out reported a submarine at 12 miles range. Although she gave chase, with 'Bideford' in company, she too suffered the frustration of having a U-boat match her speed. Nonetheless, her attempts to deter the submarine with fire from her 5" gun, had the required result of putting the U-boat commander off his intentions.

The persistent daytime shadowing by enemy submarines suggested that they were trying to take up stations for a night assault. Unfortunately, although there were several sightings by the escorts, it was impossible to determine with any certainty, just how many of them were in contact with the convoy. The possibility of there being more than one sighting of the same submarine could not be ruled out. By 2142, the escorts were dispersed in anticipation of a hectic night.

This assessment of the situation proved to be correct. The darkness was suddenly pierced by the eerie glow from a rocket, which appeared to have been fired from the starboard side of the convoy. Minutes later, more rockets, together with 'Snowflake' illuminated the sky and sea.

HMS LANDGUARD (1)

Shortly after came the report that the steamer *'Denpark'* had been sunk. Devastated by two torpedoes, the merchantmen went down in under four minutes.

Escorts *'Landguard'* and *'Bideford'* were immediately despatched to the scene of the sinking, where the SS *'Nordlys'* had begun to pick up the survivors. *'Bideford'* assisted in the rescue, screening the rescue ship at the same time. Although there were no indications of a submarine in the area, the RDF operator in *'Landguard'* later reported an object, quite small, but growing in size, which suggested a submarine surfacing. Course was at once altered towards the bearing and the cutter was rewarded with the sighting of the blurred shape of a surfaced U-boat, a mere two thousands yards distant. With the target in such close proximity, she straightaway increased speed with the intention of ramming. When the range had been reduced to less than a thousand yards, 'Snowflake' was fired, with the two-fold purpose of ascertaining the submarine's inclination, and deterring it from an attack on the convoy. At such close range and the submarine well within electric-torpedo range of the convoy, it was considered more important to spoil a possible attack, even at the risk of missing the chance to ram. By then, the enemy was clearly visible, painted grey, but with no number on the conning tower.

Strange as it might seem, the submarine was apparently unaware of *'Landguard's* approach, because the cutter was able to score several hits with Pom-Pom and .5 machine-gun fire before the enemy sought shelter in the deep. But so close was *'Landguard'* by that time, that when she dropped her pattern of depth-charges at shallow setting, the swirl from the U-boat's dive was visible little more than fifty yards off the port side. With the target moving slowly left, the cutter prepared for another depth-charge attack, but as she closed, the contact suddenly disappeared. Nonetheless, she pressed home her attack with a ten-charge pattern on the submarine's estimated position, 10° off her starboard bow. The first explosion shook the ship, putting her Asdic out of operation. Twelve minutes elapsed before the fault could be rectified, by which time *'Bideford'* had joined in the action.

THE HAND - ME - DOWN SHIPS

'Landguard' rejoined the search with her Asdic repaired, but even after a careful all-round sweep, first for hydrophone effect, then using transmissions, she failed to regain contact with the enemy. Whilst it is not unreasonable to assume that the U-boat had either been sunk or badly damaged, a thorough search in the darkness, failed to reveal any wreckage or other evidence of the attack being successful.

U-boat activity continued into the following morning and included many false alarms. At 0140, 'Landguard's attention was drawn to a small indication at about nine miles range. Course was altered immediately. The range closed rapidly at first, but later slowed down. It was considered unlikely that this contact was the submarine attacked earlier, but another U-boat looking for a target. By the time the range had closed to above five miles, the RDF operator had assessed that the target was too large to be a submarine, and by 0230, a ship could be clearly seen. This turned out to be the 'Nordlys' which, after picking up survivors from the 'Denpark', was steaming on course 330° in an attempt to rejoin the convoy. It would appear that the Master of the merchantman had mistaken 'Landguard', coming up astern of him, for a submarine, and proceeded to zig-zag so effectively, that the cutter had difficulty in closing him. This was not only an excellent feat of seamanship, but a classic example of the tenacity displayed by Masters of merchant ships in their efforts to get their valuable cargoes delivered safely. Furthermore, the Master of 'Nordlys' showed considerable courage in stopping to pick up survivors, at a time when the sea was brightly lit and with U-boats still extremely active in the vicinity. However, it was fortunate for him that 'Landguard' turned up to guide him to safety. Had he continued on his course he would, more than likely, have been sighted by a shadowing submarine.

During the early hours of the 13th, with both 'Landguard' and 'Lulworth' at the head of the convoy, it was decided to take advantage of a lull in U-boat activities, so that the Group's RDF officer, installed in 'Lulworth', should be transferred to carry out more permanent repairs to 'Landguard's ailing RDF. This did not materialise, because at 0728, with the transfer imminent, a surface object was sighted at a distance of ten miles. This was confirmed as a submarine and the convoy took the necessary evasive action. *'Hastings'* was despatched to ensure that the enemy 'kept his head down'.

There was a further sighting at 1418, but there were doubts as to whether the enemy had spotted the convoy. However, it was considered that the U-boat was shadowing the convoy by keeping station on *'Landguard'*. With this in mind, the cutter remained on her original course to give the impression that she was unaware of the enemy's presence. This ploy failed to deceive the U-boat commander, and it became necessary for *'Landguard'* to accelerate with the object of heading the submarine off. This action had the desired effect and at dusk, the cutter returned to the convoy on an evasive course to resume her night station. In the light of the numerous daytime sightings, another eventful night was anticipated.

At 2035, 'Snowflake' was fired from the *SS 'Ingria'* in the leading column of the convoy. She had sighted a submarine dead ahead at 1500 yards. It was at this point that the Commodore Ship, the *SS 'Thomas Holt'* showed the enemy that merchant ships had a sting in their tail. With the area illuminated, she rendered great assistance by firing tracer from her Oerlikon guns, claiming several hits on the target, followed by an unsuccessful attempt to ram. Still on the surface, the damaged U-boat tried to escape towards the port side of the convoy, but was forced to dive when *'Landguard'* and *'Lulworth'* covered him with 'Starshell'. Whilst he was barely clear of the port wing of the column of ships, *'Lulworth'* and *'Bideford'* attacked with depth-charges, but intensive as it was, it failed to produce any evidence of a 'kill'. Nonetheless, it served the purpose of putting yet another U-boat off carrying out a damaging attack on the convoy.

Little over an hour later, *'Landguard'* narrowly missed becoming a casualty herself, when her A/S operator reported hydrophone effect of torpedoes at 120°. The subsequent evasive action brought sighs of relief from those on deck, when the torpedoes were seen to pass harmlessly down the cutter's starboard side. A search for the enemy brought negative results.

By this time, the activity of the past seventy-two hours had taken its toll on the escorts' fuel and depth-charges. With little more than five per cent of their depth-charges left and the need to refuel imminent, there was still need for concern. As it turned out, the frustrated U-boat commanders must have realised the futility of their efforts to get at the convoy. There were no further sightings and no further attacks. The convoy was handed over to the 37th Escort Group, minus only one ship.

In his report, Lt.Cdr. Hugonin, in *'Landguard'* praised the actions of the escorts and the ships in the convoy, adding:

"It is considered that extremely good work was done by the engine-room departments of *'Landguard', 'Lulworth'* and *'Hastings'* in executing major repairs very rapidly at a time when lengthy breakdowns would have proved fatal."

Chapter Six

HMS Landguard (2)

In August 1943, the Germans introduced a new and deadly weapon into the war at sea; the Hs293 radio-controlled glider bomb, designed to be used in stand-off attacks. The weapon was, principally, a glider version of the SC500 high-explosive bomb powered by a Walter rocket motor. The first flight tests were carried out on 16th December 1940. These proved unsuccessful, but a few days later, with the faults rectified, a successful launch was made and a high percentage of direct hits registered. Designed to be used mainly in Luftwaffe anti-shipping attacks and launched from Dornier Do217 bombers, the Hs293 was capable of rapid acceleration, attaining speeds in excess of 600 km per hour in less than 15 seconds. The bomb had a launching weight of 2870 lbs; a wing span of 10 ft; were 11 ft in length; and carried 727 lbs of high-exoplosive in a warhead located in the forward section. The weapons were carried under the wings of a bomber, launched and guided by radio-control and had a range of approximately ten miles. The Dornier Do217 was capable of carrying two Hs293's outboard of the engine nacelles, whilst the M-5 version carried one bomb slung beneath the fuselage.

Trials were completed in March 1943 and German missile-carrying aircraft Groupes were re-organised to make the best use of the new weapon.

The first operational use was on 25th August of that year, when Dornier Do217's of the Luftwaffe's 11/KH100 Groupe, based at Cognac in the South of France, launched an attack on the 40th Escort Group in the Bay of Biscay. The first British ship to suffer damage from an Hs293 bomb was the cutter *'Landguard'*, then under the Command of Cdr. T.S. Fox-Pitt RN. The 40th E.G.'s presence in the Bay of Biscay at that time is explained by Sid Simkin, then serving in the ship as

THE HAND - ME - DOWN SHIPS

a coder:

"Our apparent object was to prevent homeward bound U-boats reaching their bases at Lorient and Bordeaux. We had sailed from Belfast on 29th July, and within three days, during the early hours of 1st August, we were fending off the attentions of three JU88 and one Focke-Wulffe aircraft which were shadowing the group. They appeared to have no taste for battle and left us in peace to continue our patrol. We were later despatched to within twenty miles of the French coast to search for American airmen whose plane had ditched in the area.

"The search took place in darkness, which sometimes meant steaming with lights on and firing the occasional luminating rocket. In spite of an extensive search we could find no signs of the unfortunate airmen and the search had to be finally abandoned. Any hopes we might have had about a quiet patrol were soon dispelled when it was reported that three enemy destroyers were headed in our direction. These ships, believed to have been of what the Germans referred to as the 'Narvik Flotilla', whose main armament comprised four 5" guns, six 37mm and eight 21" torpedo tubes, would have been more than a match for the lesser armed ships of the 40th Escort Group. It came as good news that we were to join up with the 2nd Escort Group and the destroyers *'Grenville'* and *'Atherbaskan'*. Further encouragement came from a signal from C in C Plymouth, that the cruiser *'Charybdis'* was proceeding with all haste from Gibraltar to join us. We felt a great deal more confident when the reinforcements arrived. However, the enemy must have been alerted of the extent of our assembled force. They altered course, and without firing a shot, used their superior speed to put distance between us. Attempts by supporting aircraft to slow down the enemy's retreat had to be abandoned due to shortage of fuel."

'Landguard' later returned to base, where she spent four days before returning to resume her duties in the Bay of Biscay. This particular operation was code-named 'Operation Musketry'. *'Landguard'* was but a few days off becoming the first operational target for the enemy's latest anti-shipping weapon. In the meantime,

HMS LANDGUARD (2)

she, still with the 40th Escort Group, was engaged in investigating reports that German U-boats were taking advantage of Spanish territorial waters, and that the Spanish might be indulging in unneutral activities. There was constant alertness for enemy shipping which might be making use of Spanish ports. This entailed a number of investigations of merchant ships and fishing vessels. Sid Simkin takes up the story:

"We were established between Cap Ortegal and Cap Villanto, waiting for our relief by the 1st Escort Group. In the meantime we sighted and picked up what appeared to be a paravane, (an instrument fitted and designed to cut loose secured mines). In the light of our suspicions of activities in and around Spanish ports, we used the paravane as an excuse to enter their waters, and anchored off the small village of Ria de Camarinas. The countryside around was pretty barren, except for clumps of trees here and there. Soon we were plagued by Spanish craft whose crews were intent on bartering mementoes in exchange for tinned gear and white bread. This activity promptly ceased when a police launch arrived on the scene and the ill-kept and hungry Spaniards were made to return all our victuals.

"A Spanish launch followed suit, came alongside with due ceremony and their officers were piped aboard. There was little trace of friendliness from these representatives of the Spanish Navy, but it was noted that the best-dressed (obviously a senior officer), was somewhat unsteady on his legs when he departed the ship. By the time we sailed, we had more or less achieved what we went in for. Nonetheless, our seaward passage was hastened by the appearance of a cruiser and two destroyers of the Spanish fleet. The last day of our patrol loomed up with the usual shadowing by Ju88 enemy aircraft. We had got used to this activity by now, but when the Dorniers appeared, we were certainly not prepared for what followed."

The ensuing attack was observed by General Sir Charles Elles, who was at that time, on *'Landguard's'* bridge. In his report he wrote:

"Hostile aircraft were observed astern of us — they passed astern on the starboard beam, with the object, as appeared later, of attacking down wind. *'Bideford'* was to the right of our line, about two miles to starboard of *'Landguard'*. The remainder of the group were in line abreast to our port side. These were not attacked. The aircraft returned downwind to the course of the ships. Bombs were released at a uniform height of some 1000/1500 ft. in the direction of flight, and a second or two after release, rocket smoke was observed. It appeared that each bomb made two or three emissions of rocket smoke. This cut out after about five seconds, after which I could not see the bomb again until it was four to five hundred yards from *'Landguard'*. I observed eight bombs in all. Four were grotesquely inaccurate, having been released from 6,000/10,000 yards. One bomb, discharged against *'Bideford'* fell level with her bridge on the port side, almost on the side of the ship. Three bombs were discharged against *'Landguard'*. One fell within forty yards of the ship on the port side, the second amidships on the starboard side, and the third twenty yards from the ship on the port side, level with the bridge. The third bomb approached on a very definite curve with its wings banked.

"The bombs consisted of two cylinders, one above the other, each of about 12 inches diameter and the top cylinder about eight feet long. Two wings were attached horizontally — total lateral span ten feet. The whole appearance of the glider bomb was exactly that of a miniature dive-bomber aircraft. They struck the water at say 120 miles per hour and exploded with slight delay, force of explosions less than a depth charge. The aircraft carried only one bomb. The shooting of the four successfully discharged bombs was astonishingly accurate against these small targets. A very interesting experience, as the bombs could be seen clearly at distance and short ranges. Observers previously warned would no doubt be able to follow the flight from end to end."

This unfamiliar weapon certainly caused consternation among members of *'Landguard's'* crew. John Pye, a Signalman in the cutter said:

"The German aircraft had released missiles which appeared to be chasing us."

Aubrey Brooks added: "The Dorniers were reported by a bridge look-out whilst they were still out of range of our anti-aircraft fire. I was halfway through the standard enemy aircraft warning signal in morse, when an almighty explosion shook the ship. I continued the transmission; then another explosion, and a third. I completed the transmission. The ship altered course and the Dorniers broke off the action."

The news of the attack and this unexpected appearance of such a deadly new weapon was quickly signalled to Admiralty. That signal reads:

'New weapon used today by Do217. Projectile appears like paravane and same shape. Release takes place at about 1000 ft. when aircraft approximately abeam on reciprocal course to ship about 3/5 miles range. Rocket propulsion carries it ahead of aircraft then projectile peels off in general direction of ship, i.e. rocket begins flight pointed away from ship, alters course to approach again at end of flight. Control appears to be optical based on evidence Radio Valve and supposed amplifier base with lens slots recovered. One carried by each aircraft. Explosive normal.

251607A (August 1943)

Later the same day, the 40th Escort Group was relieved by the 1st Escort Group, comprising *'Egret'* (Senior Officer); and the destroyers *'Athabaskan'* and *'Grenville'*.

'Landguard' and her companions in the 40th E.G., were indeed fortunate to have survived the glider bomb attack. Three days later, *'Athabaskan'* was severely damaged in another glider-bomb assault, whilst *'Egret'* received a direct hit, culminating in a massive explosion and sank. She was the first warship to be destroyed by the new glider bomb.

Towards the end of 1943, *'Landguard'* was assigned to the Eastern Fleet. She sailed from Milford Haven on 13th September, escorting a coastal force group to Gibraltar. By the 20th October, she had passed through the Mediterranean, bound for the East Coast of Africa to join the Kilindini Escort Force. Apart from a break of almost a month spent in Durban undergoing refit, she was engaged in a variety of operations, all of which were vastly different from those experienced in the Atlantic. This miscellany of 'odd jobs' proved to be monotonous by comparison. On the 6th March, whilst off Aden, she sank the derelict LCT492, which was drifting and a danger to shipping. A week later, she sailed from Aden as escort to the dry dock AFD53, which was being towed by the tugs *'Cheerly'* and *'Bold'*, bound for Colombo.

In January 1944, she had a change in command, when Lt.Cdr. Bernard M. Skinner RN., relieved Cdr. Fox-Pitt as Captain. He was the only Naval officer to have held command in two cutters: *'Landguard'* from January 1944 to January 1945, and *'Sennen'* from May 1945 to 16th February 1946. It is ironic that Lt.Cdr. Skinner survived an action-packed career in World War II, only to lose his life, four years later, whilst in the Frigate *'Amethyst'*. The Frigate's exploits, in what became knownas the 'Yang-tse River Incident', made newspaper headlines at the time, when in 1949, she was seriously damaged by Chinese Communist fire. Upon Lt. Cdr. Skinners re-asignment from *'Languard'* in January 1945, Lt. R.N. Kinder was installed as Captain. He remained with the ship until April 1946.

It was during this period that *'Landguard'* suffered a somewhat undignified end to her career when, as a result of a catastrophe in her engine-room in March 1945, she was rendered unseaworthy and forced to spend the remainder of the war as a static depot ship.

Sister ship *'Banff'* was in company with *'Landguard'* at the time of the incident. Her Captain, Lt.Cdr. James D'arcy Nesbitt RNR., said of it:

"Both ships were under orders to exercise 'Hedgehog' together and then *'Banff'* was to exercise towing *'Landguard'*. We had done the exercises quite happily, then *'Landguard'* started hers whilst we lay off about a mile away. Suddenly *'Landguard'* was blowing off steam and was obviously in trouble. I sent the motor skimmer away with a doctor and deck officer to find out what was wrong. A signal from *'Landguard'* informed me that there had been an explosion of high-pressure steam in the engine-room and that two E.R.A.'s had been seriously injured and that she was unable to move. One of her 'Hedgehog's had apparently countermined on another on its was to the bottom."

Ex-ERA Charlie Anderson, was on duty in *'Landguard's* engine-room at the time:

"What happened I cannot imagine, but the subsequent explosions appeared to be directly under the ship. So violent were they that I was thrown to the plates. However, everything appeared to be normal in the engine-room. I sent Stoker Roberts to inspect the lower engine-room and Leading Stoker Grieg to check exciters. Roberts reported smoke coming from the lubricating oil switch-box. I gave the order to start the standby lub. oil pump, which orders Roberts carried out, leaving both pumps running to allow the auxiliary pump to take the pressure. Roberts then reported that the switchbox of the stand-by pump was getting hot and there was smoke. I immediately sent for Chief ERA Fowler and ERA Locke, who came down at once to attend to the switch boxes. As I was crossing the plates to inform the bridge, the main turbine started racing. First I brought the Rev. control lever into secure position, but it had no effect. I noticed that the lub. oil sight glass and also the gauge to main turbine bearings was showing normal working pressure. I sent Stoker Ayres to take gags out of auto-stop-valve and was standing by to shut it immediately the gags were removed, when there came a series of explosions from the turbine. I was thrown to the plates and blinded by oil and smoke."

Ex-Stoker Roberts takes up the story:

"Our next move after ERA Locke appeared on the scene was to shut off the main steam valve over the boiler-room. We ran up the ladder, but could not see even across the engine-room, the steam was so dense. So we went back down the ladder, through the shaft alley and up through the hatch to the mess-deck level, then through the boiler-room and shut off the main steam valve. Unfortunately there were some casualties. When I later saw the extent of the damage, I suppose we were lucky that there were not more injured."

With *'Landguard'* incapacitated, *'Banff'* went alongside and passed over a tow. The disabled cutter was towed into Colombo, where a tug took over. So serious and extensive was the damage that all hopes of returning her to sea duty were abandoned.

THE HAND - ME - DOWN SHIPS

ERA Gordon Cooke was drafted to *'Landguard'* from *'Largs'* on 5th October 1945:

"On my arrival, the story of how the ship came to be in her predicament was explained to me. She had only a 'care and maintenance' party on board and was being used as accommodation ship for Post Office personnel. In my charge were some sixty Tamils and Sinhalese labourers who were employed on general cleaning duties."

Jim 'Tug' Wilson, also in *'Landguard'* at the time, has one particular memory of those working parties:

"The Tamils were accompanied by a young boy who lived on the streets and was both deaf and dumb. He was quickly 'adopted' by the crew and we gave him the name John Landguard."

Gordon Cooke resumes the story of *'Landguard's* last days:

"The Regulating Coxswain was a Seaman Petty Officer. He frequently told me that when he left the Navy, he intended to produce a hair-cream, for which he had a secret formula. Whether he ever did I don't know. During our stay in Colombo, we moved twice. The biggest move came when we were towed round the coast to Trincomalee and moored up there. Boring as life was in general, there were some moments of light relief. One day the Shipwright informed me that he had been called to open the Captain's safe, since the keys could not be found. He set about the task, having first to dismantle the desk in which the safe was located, and eventually completed the job successfully. He had discovered inside the safe a beautiful ship's clock, with an Indian's head imprinted on the face. It was in fact, a replica of the ship's crest, when she was *'Shoshone'*. Our 'chippy' was so impressed with his find, that he suggested it might 'get lost' inadvertently, when he left the ship. In order to keep it out of sight until his departure, he hid it behind the safe and re-assembled the desk round it. He was still on board when I left the ship on 21st October 1946, so I shall never know whether he realised his intentions."

Lt.Cdr. Nesbitt, took advantage of the availability of one of *'Landguard's* officers, to solve a problem of his own in *'Banff'*:

HMS LANDGUARD (2)

'My 'number one', John Bryant, an Australian, was sadly overdue for leave, so I got him a trip in a Carrier bound for Fremantle. I replaced him with *'Landguard's* First Lieutenant, Lt. Arthur Masterson Smith RNR. He stayed with us for a long time. In fact, during a visit to Durban, we finished the Christening of his baby son in my cabin, with all Chiefs and P.O.'s present."

Chapter Seven

HMS Lulworth — U-Boat 'kill'

The sharp eyesight and alertness of a masthead look-out, sixty feet up in the crow's nest aboard the cutter *'Lulworth'*, in spotting an enemy U-boat at 12 miles range, resulted in a dramatic encounter with the Italian submarine *'Pietro Calvi'*, and earned the man on watch, Able Seaman Ron 'Tubby' Coulson, a mention in despatches.

The action occurred during the passage of convoy SL115, comprising 29 ships, which sailed from Freetown at 1100 on 5th July 1942, bound for the United Kingdom. The escorts of the 40th EG., comprised (Senior Officer) *'Londonderry'*, *'Hastings'*, *'Bideford'* and *'Lulworth'*. In company were the *'Salisbury'* and *'Wolverine'*.

Up to the 14th, in spite of some U-boat activity, the convoy had proceeded unmolested, but when *'Lulworth'*, with Cdr. Clive Gwinner in Command, was despatched to investigate a strong HF/DF bearing, there began one of those rare actions in which a single ship was in combat with two enemy submarines at the same time. It was during the evening when the look-out reported an object at 12 miles range, but the sighting was brief and the target quickly vanished from sight. Within minutes, 'Tubby' Coulson made a second sighting, which prompted the despatch of Sub.Lt. W.R. Chalk RNVR., aloft to give verification. The look-out moved up into the upper crow's nest, an innovation in the cutter which gave at least two miles extra visibility. 'Tubby's assessment that the object was a submarine moving at speed, was confirmed by Sub.Lt. Chalk, whereupon *'Lulworth'* proceeded to close the range, apparently unobserved from the target.

It is surprising that the submarine's commander, Primo Longobardo, should have allowed himself to be caught off guard, since the 40 years old submariner had more than twelve years experience in U-boats and was recognised by the Italian Navy as one of the most

HMS LULWORTH — U-BOAT 'KILL'

experienced of their submarine commanders. He had also, the distinction of having done a cruise in U-99 with Germany's most successful U-boat ace, Otto Krestchmer, an experience which should have added to his already wide knowledge of submarine warfare. Adolf Hitler apparently shared the appreciation of Longobardo's experience, since he honoured him with an Iron Cross.

However, it is not unreasonable to assume that Longobardo was a little rusty when he took command of the *'Pietro Calvi'*. After all, he had been shore-based for some time, first in Command of the U-boat School at Pola from April 1941, and later on the Staff of Admiral Submarines in Rome. There can be no doubt that in the light of his considerable experience, he was unhappy with the prospect of fighting the remainder of the war from behind a desk, hence his expressed desire to return to sea duty. He rejected the offer of Command of the Italian Cruiser *'Engenio Di Savoia'* and was eventually returned to the more familiar surroundings of submarines, joining the *'Pietro Calvi'* in Bordeaux. There is a certain irony in that Longobardo chose to give up the safety of a position on the Admiral's Staff to return to sea, because it was barely three weeks after taking up his new command, that he found himself in conflict with *'Lulworth'*, in an action which was to cost him his life. His adversary, Cdr. Gwinner, was no less experienced and had already gained a reputation for his skill and tenacity in the war against the U-boats.

Once aware of the approach of the cutter, Longobardo plunged his boat to 250 ft, in a crash dive of such haste, that his guns were still on their mountings. It took Cdr. Gwinner about forty-five minutes of patient search to pinpoint the submarine's position. At 2030, his A/S operator reported and classified a submarine echo on the starboard side at 1600 yards. There followed a series of tactical manoeuvres in which the U-boat attempted to elude the cutter, but these were successfully anticipated in *'Lulworth'*. At 2041, the first pattern of depth charges was dropped, set at 140 feet. Although these exploded right above the target, they proved to be set too shallow to do any damage. Nonetheless, they had the effect of forcing Longobardo to seek safety in more depth. This action was also anticipated by his pursuer, and in the second attack the charges were set at 300 ft. This pattern straddled the U-boat and the subsequent explosions caused it's motors to stop temporarily, fractured a number of seams in the pressure hull, and blew in several rivets. Whilst the U-boat's personnel worked feverishly to make good repairs, the depth-charge crews in *'Lulworth'* reloaded the throwers and rails in preparation for another attack.

In the light of the damage to his boat, Longobardo decided to come up and take his chances on the surface. He was well-armed with two 4.7 guns, four 13.2 mm, and eight 21" torpedo tubes, which would put him on at least equal terms with the cutter. When the order to surface was given, the submarine suddenly went out of control and plunged to 400 feet. This sudden change in events was detected in *'Lulworth'* and Cdr. Gwinner pressed home another attack with his charges set at 350 and 550 feet. The accuracy of this assault put any hopes of the *'Pietro Calvi's'* survival beyond all reach. With her main ballast tanks wrecked, increased leaks in the pressure hull and the starboard diesel out of action, she suddenly surged to the surface at an acute angle with a heavy list to port. *'Lulworth'* had run on and momentarily lost contact. When the upper bridge look-out reported the submarine on the surface, Cdr. Gwinner immediately altered course to starboard and fired 'Snowflake' to illuminate the target. In his report of the action, he wrote:

"By its extreme limit of illumination, just saw the stern of the U-boat and its bow wave and wake. Considering that I was inviting a torpedo with this type of illumination, being alone and unsupported at the time, I turned towards the enemy and fired five rounds of starshell at it. By this illumination the 3" and .5 guns crews were able to pick up the target which they never again lost. The forward 20" searchlight was trained on the enemy and its beam exposed."

Aboard the *'Pietro Calvi'*, guns crews were scrambling to their stations, obviously prepared to fight to the bitter end, but trapped as they were in the cutter's searchlight, they were a sitting target for *'Lulworth's'* gunners. Cdr. Gwinner pressed home his attack. He wrote:

HMS LULWORTH — U-BOAT 'KILL'

"I could now see that the enemy had both his 4.7 guns trained on us, but the ratings manning our .5's did magnificent work, and I am convinced that with the aid of their mates manning the port and starboard 3" guns, who scored at least two hits with high explosive, were the sole reason why only two rounds were fired at us by a vessel as well, if not better armed than ourselves. One direct hit from the port 3" burst in the conning tower and killed the captain and all the personnel whom he was trying to get to operate their 13.2mm Bredas. Another direct hit aft on the pressure hull, and the hail of machine-gun fire killed the entire personnel of the Italian's after gun."

Although the outcome of the battle was inevitable, the surviving crew members of the submarine showed no signs of surrender. Two rounds from their 4.7's passed harmlessly over the cutter, but two torpedoes loosed from the stern tubes, caused *'Lulworth'* to take evasive action. One was seen to pass within ten feet of the ship's side.

With his ship and crew still at risk, Cdr. Gwinner decided to go in for the kill:

"I was now determined to ram the enemy if he did not surrender. I ordered the A/S dome to be raised and keeping on a steady bearing and bows on to the U-boat, closed the range at full speed. At the last minute, he went hard to starboard, and although I followed, I just shaved past his stern. Keeping the wheel hard over, I tried to catch him on his port side, but again, reversing his wheel, he slipped across my bows. Reversing the wheel, I managed to give him a pretty hard knock on his starboard quarter, just ahead of his after hydro-planes. The effect of this collision was to push him well over to port and cause a number of men to be washed into the sea."

Despite the damage to the submarine, the crew displayed great courage in their desperate fight for survival, and considerable skill in their efforts to out-manouvre the cutter. But with no place to go, Cdr. Gwinner called for the survivors of the action to surrender.

John 'Paddy' Loughran, was a loader on one of the cutter's .5 machine-guns:

"I heard a voice over the loud haler, call to the Italians to lower their ensign. The three-badge Able Seaman operating my gun, suggested that they did not understand the order and that there was nobody in *'Lulworth'* who could speak Italian. When I told him that I had some knowledge of the language, albeit a bit rusty, he straightaway headed for the voice-pipe. I was hastily summoned to the bridge. I could not remember the Italian for 'lower', so I called several times — 'Giu la bandiera' (down with the ensign). It took several minutes before the penny dropped. I was next asked to tell the survivors to swim to the ship. We had already picked up some of them, and, as I recall, were little more than a hundred yards from the submarine at the time."

No doubt realising that further resistance was pointless, the Italians finally gave up the fight. *'Lulworth'* approached the U-boat on its port side, and when within some fifty yards of it, sent away a boarding party.

A member of that boarding party, in the charge of Lt. P.R. Law RNVR., was Les Kennett, who had joined the cutter in 1941, after two-and-a-half years in the Tribal Class destroyer *'Ashanti'*:

"I was on the boat's falls in the port waist, when the First Lieutenant asked why I wasn't in the boat. I told him that I was not armed. The next thing I knew, was being handed a belt and revolver and was clambering into the boat. Although the whaler was safely slipped, it was quickly noticed that we were taking in water, of all places through the bunghole. Whoever had removed the bung had forgotten to replace it. Engineer Officer Lt. North came to the rescue and stopped up the hole with a handkerchief. We managed to get alongside the submarine, which was rolling heavily. There were some very hairy moments, when we almost came to grief.

"I was appalled by the horror of the sight that greeted us. The dead, including the Captain, packed the bridge area and the deck was strewn with dead and wounded. Some of the survivors were grouped on the deck, whilst others had jumped into the sea. Within a short time, the submarine gave a lurch and started to settle by the stern.

"Whilst we were still aboard the U-boat, I heard a shout from *'Lulworth',* warning us that a second submarine was approaching on the surface, and on *'Pietro Calvi's* blind side. Someone shouted —

'we'll be back'. I recall thinking, I bloodywell hope so!"

This new and unexpected threat to the ship, his crew, and possibly the convoy, left Cdr. Gwinner with no alternative but to turn his attentions to it. Reluctant as he was to abandon his boarding party and the survivors, he was confident that Lt. Law had things under control.

With his searchlights still concentrated on the damaged U-boat, and the second submarine beyond the hull of the first, Gwinner decided to play possum, with a view to leading the commander into thinking he was undetected. Gwinner hoped, by this means, to lure the new target into a perfect position for a counter attack. This strategy proved successful. As the approaching submarine came into full view and clear of the Italian's conning tower, the cutter's searchlight was switched on to him. Temporarily blinded by the searchlight's glare, the U-boat ran into a hail of machine-gun fire at 1000 yards range and hits were seen to be scored on the conning tower. Having gained the advantage, *'Lulworth'* headed straight for the target at maximum speed, but by the time the range had closed to less than 800 yards, the enemy crash-dived from sight.

During the ensuing chase, the drama around and aboard the *'Pietro Calvi'* continued. The boarding party, comprising Lt. Law, Engineer Officer Lt. North, a Norwegian Midshipman, a Stoker and ERA, were hurriedly assessing the condition of the submarine and trying to salvage what documents they could. With great presence of mind and personal courage, the boarding officer entered the U-boat, having first to shift the decapitated body of the captain, which he discovered jammed in the conning tower. He made his way to the captain's cabin where, after a quick and intelligent search, found a sealed copy of the inter-U-boat recognition letters for July; the chart upon which the *'Pietro Calvi's* last course from Bordeaux to the position where she was attacked was plotted; a personal letter to the captain containing some interesting sidelights of enemy U-boat operations off the U.S. seaboard, and a diary of the submarine's movements. It was apparent that all confidential books had been destroyed. He observed sediment in the bottom of the wash-basin, indicating that papers had been burned in it.

Time was now running out for the Italian submarine, with her angle increasing by the minute and well down by the stern. The whaler's crew felt increasing concern for the boarding party, added to which they were having great difficulty in fending the boat off the sinking vessel.

"As she settled further in the water, we shouted warnings to Lt. Law that the boat was going down fast," said Les Kennett. "In spite of our efforts to control the whaler, our gunwhale became wedged under the submarine's guard-rail and she was pulling us down with her. Our Norwegian Midshipman, with some assistance from the boat's crew, managed to push us free. Subsequent events happened so fast that he was left aboard with other members of the boarding party."

The fate of the boarding party now hung in the balance. The stricken submarine, still rolling heavily, gradually settled further by the stern, and within minutes slid stern first from sight. In the blackness of the night, the boarding party, with the exception of Lt. North, managed to swim clear and make the safety of the whaler. Lt. North, who was washed overboard when the submarine succumbed to the sea, was never seen again.

"It was very dark," said Les Kennett. "We could hear shouts from all directions, mingled with the sounds of *Lulworth's* depth charges as she attacked the second submarine."

By this time, the struggling survivors in the water were despairing of their rescue, whilst the cutter, now some distance from the scene, was making her approach for a second depth-charge attack on her quarry. So accurate was this onslaught that there was confidence in *Lulworth'* that the target had, at least, been seriously damaged, although there was no visible evidence to support it. *Lulworth'* broke off the action when *'Hastings'* was ordered to take over the chase.

When the cutter returned to the spot where the Italian submarine had sunk, she found the survivors floating around in an area of about 300 square yards. Her first task was to recover her boat, together with the members of the boarding party. She then began picking up the thirty-six survivors from the *'Pietro Calvi'*. An extensive search for Engineer Officer North proved fruitless.

John Loughran, who had learned his Italian whilst at the Irish College in Rome 1932/36, was charged with the role of interpreter during the interrogation of the Italian prisoners, and the translation of documents salvaged from the U-boat.

"The diary comprised a succession of reports on weather, sea, flotsam, etc.," he said. "The submarine's previous mission was also detailed. This was off the American east coast, when five ships were sunk, totalling 50,000 tons, most of them unescorted merchant men."

In his capacity as interpreter, John Loughran came into daily contact with many of the survivors:

"I recall one saying, when we brought him on board — 'do you shoot me now? I assured him that we would not. My hardest task was interpreting for the doctor in the sick bay, where there were two survivors with serious injuries. Fortunately they made it to Gourock, where they were taken ashore on stretchers. One of the survivors, 33 years old CPO. Agastino Isola, died on board from his wounds and was buried at sea with due ceremony the following day.

"Another survivor, 22 years old Electrician, Emelio Trucco, had a fine tenor voice. He told me that he had broadcast on Italian Radio, and was kind enough to write out for me, the lyrics of two well-known Italian ballads."

Convoy SL115 arrived 26th July having suffered no shipping losses. John Loughran recalls one light-hearted moment when they docked:

"All the prisoners had been blindfolded and led ashore. Many of them shook hands with me as they disembarked, one of them confiding in me — 'I can see through this thing!"

The closing comments in the story of the sinking of the *'Pietro Calvi'*, come from the narrative of 'Monthly Anti-submarine Report' for August 1942:

'There was a good deal of confusion in the U-boat but no panic, even among that half of the crew which consisted of young ratings, expected to gain experience and confidence as best they could during a patrol. The older men, who were well-trained seamen, kept their heads and one at least, was imperturbable. Fifty and bespectacled, Ernesto Maccotta, the Supernumerary Engineer Officer, leant composedly against a bulkhead and made a note in his diary of the number of depth-charges as they burst around the vessel. The Engineer Officer was not among the rescued. He was last seen on the bridge, adjusting his spectacles so as to get a better view of the affair, and it seems that he made no effort to be saved.'

An interesting footnote to the *'Pietro Calvi'* story, and fitting tribute to the courage of the captain and crew, is that after the war, an Italian submarine was named *'Primo Longobardo'*.

Chapter Eight
HMS Lulworth — Foreign Commission

Whilst the action against the *'Pietro Calvi'* was, without doubt, the most noteworthy during *'Lulworth's* two years of escort duty in the Atlantic, Cdr. Gwinner and his crew had frequent brushes with the U-boats. In all of them Cdr. Gwinner was a constant source of encouragement, and much revered by his entire ship's company.

On leaving the ship in February 1943, he took command of a Group under the legendary Captain F.J. Walker RN., whose tally of U-boat 'kills' was unequalled. Of *'Lulworth'* and her crew he said:

"I was most fortunate in having most excellent officers and ship's company, who I shall always remember, not perhaps by name or face always, but by their unfailing loyalty and support, without which I could have achieved nothing."

Lulworth's previous and subsequent activities are related through the men who served in her.

Maurice Bevan joined her shortly after she was assigned to the 40th Escort Group:

"I went aboard as an Ordinary Seaman with a 'White Paper', with three others and one Paymaster C.W. rating from Chatham. For all of us, it was our first ship. We all worked 'part of ship' with the 'Buffer', a dour little Yorkshireman who, as an active service Petty Officer, had little love for H.O.'s and probably C.W.'s in particular. The ship's company was mainly ex *'Resolution'* and many of them heartily disliked serving in a ship of two thousand tons, and an American one at that, after an HM ship of nearly 30,000 tons. Apart from our Captain, First Lieutenant and Gunner (T), the remaining officers were RNR, RNCVR, or RNVR.

"Our first disaster was a split fresh-water tank during a depth-charge trial before sailing, and disaster it was when we reached the tropics, short of water and subsequent rationing. We had a rough time in the Atlantic, of which I still have vivid memories. Although the cutters were comparatively dry ships below decks, thanks to their high freeboard, we did have one outstanding incident when the main mess-deck food store burst open, covering the decks with cocoa, split peas and sea water, making it practically impossible to stand up anywhere."

Referring to convoy OS4 to Bathurst, with sister-ship *'Gorleston'* in company, Maurice said:

"The escorts anchored in the river Gambia, with a 6 knot current and some sharks in attendance. We were there for five or six days, refuelling and victualling and for many of the newcomers on board, there was the first experience of going ashore in the tropics and seeing bananas and limes growing on trees. Bathurst, in those days, consisted of little more than a waterfront, a bazaar, a church, the Governor's residence, and an RAF flying boat mooring. It was in a temperature of over 100°F that we were subjected to a violent tropical storm. Returning to the quay after a church parade, we found the river in full flood, a merchant ship ashore, a crane overturned, and the river coloured a bright yellow, looking more like an ocean than a river. Within no time at all it was flat calm and liberty boats left at 1400.

'The return voyage was, in some ways, a nightmare. Somewhere in the Atlantic we ran into a U-boat pack, which attacked the convoy at night, on the surface. There was a similar attack the following night and a merchant ship was lost. I was an ammunition number, between decks, hoisting up shells for the 5" gun. I found it all very primitive and hair-raising at the time. We were fortunate when the U-boats broke off the action to turn their attention to richer pickings, a south-bound convoy. For the latter part of that voyage we were out of bread, vegetables, cigarettes and chocolate. Our diet comprised mainly biscuits and dried beans, with very little water. The latter tasted of paraffin, resulting from the paint store having sprung a leak into the forward fresh-water tank.

"The C.W.'s were put into a Watch-keeper's mess and made bosun's

HMS LULWORTH — FOREIGN COMMISSION

mates for the round trip. We sat our Captain's Board at Bathurst. It comprised the Captain, First Lieutenant and the Senior Watchkeeping Officer, a Lieutenant RNVR. As I recall, the Paymasters and three of our four seamen passed.

Quite the most exciting incident in my time in *'Lulworth'*, was being on watch in bright moonlight, with the Navigating Officer. He turned to me and said, quietly — "can you see what I can see"? I replied yes; and there sitting on the surface on the starboard side, was an Italian submarine. 'action stations' was sounded and an attempt to ram followed, but we were just too late."

Maurice Bevan was commissioned Sub.Lt. RNVR in May 1942. Much of the credit for the short time it took him to qualify, he attributes to Lt.Cdr. Gwinner, whom he described as 'a typical escort commander, full of dash and eagerness', and the First Lieutenant.

Arnold Sayers CBE., joined *'Lulworth'* as a Midshipman in December 1942:

"I joined the cutter in Gourock and some time after, the captain told me, that when he asked 'King Alfred' for a Midshipman to join the ship, he said — 'we have only left a lazy one and a stupid one — which would you like?. I cannot remember into which category I fell! We sailed as escort to a convoy for Gibraltar. The weather was awful — mountainous seas, so that for a time, zig-zagging was almost impossible. I was desperately sick and staggered down from my watch feeling like death. The only comfort was that my captain was sick too. However, the trip enabled me to find my sea-legs and I was never sick again. It was whilst in Gibraltar that Lt. Southcombe, the First Lieutenant, sent for the Midshipman to chuck him in the 'oggin', but somehow I managed to escape. I remember little of the homeward voyage to Londonderry."

C.J.S. Lancaster does recall that passage:

"I was an officer in the Canadian corvette *'Moose Jaw'*. We were part of the U.K. bound convoy in which we were in company with *'Lulworth'*. Both she and *'Moose Jaw'* were detached from the escort to try and intercept a blockade runner, heading for Brest. I vividly remember when we received a signal from Gwinner, saying — 'on sighting the enemy, I will close while you circle.' We had only a 4" gun for our main armament. Luckily for us, the runner, the *'Rakotis'*, was intercepted by a Dido Class cruiser. We returned to our stations with the convoy, much relieved."

Arnold Sayers happier memories included a visit to St. John's, Newfoundland:

"We had some happy times there, although there was little enough time to see the countryside. What I especially remember was deep snow and a visit to a Mrs. Job, the sister-in-law of an aunt of mine, as the Job family had interests in the Newfoundland Fisheries for a great many years. They offered to fill our freezer with salmon, which we gratefully accepted. Believe me, salmon can become the most boring and unappetising fish, and the cook ran out of ideas to make it taste different."

A later voyage to Iceland, prompted another fishy story from Arnold Sayers:

"On the way we got an enormous 'blip' on the Asdic. The ship went to 'action stations', but the only reward from our depth-charging which followed, was to find the ship surrounded by herring."

George Jackman, in *'Lulworth'* from 1941 to 1946, recalls the incident:

"We had on board the Commander of the Escort Group, whom I believe was a keen angler. He dashed off for a rod and line, whilst a boat was sent away to harvest the catch. During this bit of light relief he was called to the bridge and laid his rod on the deck with a fish still struggling on the hook. When he returned, he found his fish between two slices of bread, put there by some wag from the lower deck!"

In September 1943, with Lt.Cdr. R.S.C. Woolley RNR, in command, *'Lulworth'* put the rigors of the Atlantic behind her and embarked on a foreign commission that was to last until November 1945, embracing some 64,000 miles. On the 16th, she sailed the picturesque reaches of the Foyle for the last time and joined up with a convoy bound for Gibraltar. She arrived on the 29th.

"We were issued with tropical clothing," said Arnold Sayers:

HMS LULWORTH — FOREIGN COMMISSION

"including topees, so we guessed that our destination was further than the Mediterranean."

John Loughran said of Gibraltar:

"One of the big attractions was window shopping and amazement at some of the fantastic prices asked for goods. Having a quiet drink at the 'Universal Bar', with its all-girl orchestra, was a popular pursuit. During the evening performances, one might be lucky to see a matelot or GI come hurtling through a window into the street."

'Lulworth' sailed from Gibraltar on 3rd October and headed into the Mediterranean. Shortly after sunset, the following day, the convoy came under attack from enemy aircraft.

John Loughran takes up the story:

"Out of the gathering darkness came twelve enemy bombers. What a diapason greeted them! The thunder of anti-aircraft fire disrupted the heavens and still they came in, with everything in their favour, the failing light, the vast array of closely packed ships and the grey hills of Africa for camouflage. The torpedo bombers flew so low in their daring attack that it was almost impossible to engage them for fear of hitting convoy or escort. The action was brief, with one aircraft confirmed as destroyed and four ships damaged.

"On the 8th we came in sight of the cliffs of Malta and collected the Malta portion of the eastbound convoy. On arrival at Port Said on the 16th, we re-fuelled and stored ship. The following day we entered the Suez Canal, and around noon anchored in the Great Bitter Lake to allow the passage of a north-bound troopship. The waiting time was passed with 'hands to bathe over the side'. Four hours later we proceeded on our way, emerging from the canal at Port Taufiq."

The passage through the Suez Canal provides many interesting sights for those for whom it was a first-time experience, as Arnold Sayers recalls:

"I remember seeing Egyptians squatting with their backsides towards us, doing their morning WC duties. There appeared to be a row of them."

By the 21st, 'Lulworth' had travelled through the Red Sea and was in sight of Aden, where she made a brief call before proceeding to

THE HAND - ME - DOWN SHIPS

Kilindini.

"The heat in Aden was intense," said Arnold Sayers; "but we were able to return to the cool of the ship in the evening. The town is a crater with all the hubbub of an eastern community. There were countless market stalls selling fruits and vegetables, and whilst the water melons were juicy, they were likely to cause a variety of tummy upsets. However, there were all sorts of other delights, including camel hump, which helped vary the diet. It was really quite good and tasted like veal. An officers' shirt cost 1 Rupee (or 1/6d old money) and would be ready in 24 hours. There were plenty of opportunities for swimming inside the shark net, and many of us patronised the local open-air cinema. Watching a film, however poor, always seemed more enjoyable with the stars looking down on a perfect night."

Lt.Cdr. Peter Dixon, who served in *'Lulworth'* until joining the cutter *'Gorleston'* on the staff of Captain Joe Baker-Cresswell RN., recalls:

"The time spent in *'Lulworth'* in the Indian Ocean was quiet, compared with what I experienced in the destroyer *'Mohawk'*, and then as Watchkeeping officer in the *'Valiant'*. The Maelstrom of the Mediterranean was how this was called.

"Our wardroom rations were sometimes supplemented with turtle steaks and turtle eggs. These, even when scrambled were most inedible. Wild bananas meant a variation of vegetable."

'Lulworth' made frequent trips between Aden and her Kilindini base, the monotony being broken from time to time by the ship's first XI football team's activities. Often played on pitches totally devoid of grass, they scored many successes over teams from the big ships, including *'Ramillies'*, and the cruisers *'Newcastle,' 'Danae'* and *'Phoebe'*. The depot ship's team also fell victim to the *'Lulworth'* side, though crew members of *'Woolwich'* and *'Chitral'* would be loathe to admit it.

"Most of the alarms experienced during our Aden/Kilindini activities, were caused by dhows," said John Loughran. "These seaworthy craft were frequently spotted far out to sea, some making the crossing between Africa and India. At night we would get a Radar contact. Then it was full speed ahead to the bearing, a flash from the 4" gun and a bright man-made star parachuting to the water, and like some spectre ship, appeared the inevitable dhow. On one occasion we spotted one flying a distress signal. As we approached, four powerfully built members of the crew pulled away in a primitive boat and hailed us, reporting that they had no water. They gratefully received sufficient precious water from 'Lulworth' for their needs and continued on their way."

On New Years Day 1944, the cutter was despatched on another rescue mission, to escort and assist in the salvage of the crippled Liberty ship, the American freighter 'Robert F. Hoke', which was being towed by the 'Empire Bombadier', and well down by the stern. She had taken a torpedo in the after hold, but had managed to keep afloat. When the tug 'Masterful' arrived on the scene, a party from 'Lulworth' was dispatched to assist with the transfer of the tow. The following day, the damaged freighter was beached at Sharma Bay, on the northern side of the Gulf of Aden, waiting the arrival of the salvage tug 'Ocean Salvor'. The wait was brief. When the vessel arrived, it tied up alongside the 'Robert F. Hoke' and the complex diving and sealing operations began. It fell to the lot of a working party from 'Lulworth' to make the damaged ship as shipshape as possible.

"The least envied task was that of clearing the huge refrigerator, which had ceased to function fourteen days earlier," said John Loughran. "Clad like men from Mars, complete with masks, our party ditched thousands of pounds of once prime meat. The sharks had a great time! After work the lads were taken by motor boat to Sharma's lovely beach, where the clinging odour of rotten beef was washed away."

After pumping and sealing, the damaged freighter was finally towed away and moored in Aden harbour.

On their return to Kilindini, 'Lulworth's crew got a welcome leave, which provided them with an opportunity to spend ten days inland at either Nairobi or Nakuru, in the bracing altitude of 6/9,000 feet. Ex-naval men who have experienced this welcome break from the heat of Kilindini, will remember the nearly 200 mile journey in an old-fashioned train with the traditional wooden, and uncomfortable seats.

"Nothing seemed too much trouble for the Naval Welfare Officials at Nairobi," said John Loughran. "The administrator, Lt. Bulteel RNVR, was something of a legend among the thousands of naval personnel who enjoyed his kindness and efficiency. It was during this leave that two of *Lulworth's* Able Seamen, J. Page and P. Wynne, received an award for bravery. They both received the Bronze Medal of the Society for Protection of Life from Fire, for outstanding courage shown in rescuing a woman from a blazing house in Nakuru."

The brief holiday over, *Lulworth* returned to escort duties, and though these activities were mainly uneventful, they, together with two years arduous duty in the Atlantic, were beginning to take their toll on the ship. By September 1944, she was despatched south to Durban for an extensive overhaul, which lasted for nearly three months. The cutters' crew took full advantage of the opportunity to savour the overwhelming hospitality of the people and the grandeur of Natal.

"Norman Winram, our Engineer Officer, and I went by train to Johannesburg," said Arnold Sayers. "We visited the longest bar in the world at the Rand Club, went 7,000 feet down into a gold mine, and then made a day trip to Pretoria, where the Government building looked splendid, flanked as it was by masses of Jacuranda trees in full bloom, with red Cannas in the Park Gardens. I sent some bulbs home, but I don't believe they ever grew. Thence we went by train, in great comfort, via Bulawayo to the Victoria Falls Hotel, where we had three happy days. The hotel was excellent, the weather good, although the Zambesi was at a low ebb. Nevertheless the magic of the falls was wonderful and as it was a full moon we were able to see the lunar rainbow."

Both ship and crew benefitted from the prolonged stay in the most favourite of South Africa's ports. However, even with the war drawing to a close, there was still much for *Lulworth* to do. After a brief stay in Colombo, she was despatched to the Bay of Bengal and Akyab, from whence John Loughran brought away a most disturbing impression:

HMS LULWORTH — FOREIGN COMMISSION

"Akyab was a dead city, though it had previously housed forty-thousand people. The surviving inhabitants had fled, leaving behind them a sad heap of rubble and ankle-deep clinging dust everywhere. It was during our visit that the harbour was subjected to an attack from the air. Every ship in the port opened up, together with fire from the shore batteries. It seems unbelievable that so many aircraft could survive such a concentrated hail of fire. After repeated attacks, during which the enemy planes baulked at the barrage, the only bombs dropped landed on the shore. The casualties were light and we secured 'action stations' in the early hours of the morning."

By 22nd April, *'Lulworth'* was at Kyaukpyu, about eighty miles further down the coast of Burma, where she assisted in the assembly of landing craft from various ports in The Bay of Bengal. She was present, when on 1st May, Gurkha troops were dropped in the paddyfields on the west side of the Rangoon river, where they accomplished the task of destroying gun emplacements that could impede the progress of shipping. Throughout that day, the convoys came in to anchor in the approaches to the river. At 0200, the following day, the landing craft went in against negligible resistance from the enemy.

'Lulworth's' next assignment took her down to the mouth of the Irrawaddy, about 150 miles west of Rangoon, where she was charged with the task of restoring the light to Alguada lighthouse, which had remained extinguished throughout the Japanese occupation. John Loughran takes up the story:

"On the morning of the 20th, a party went ashore in the motor boat, taking with them oxygen cylinders, tackles and all the necessary tools. A strenuous day was spent on repairs to the lighthouse, before returning to the ship. In the late evening of the same day, they returned with more equipment, but by this time the sea had risen, making their approach to the tiny pier, between jagged rocks, extremely hazardous. The one accident that could possibly happen did. The boat was lifted by a wave and thrown crashing on to the rocks. It was a total loss. Fortunately the boat's crew survived without injuries. In wet clothing, and without food, they were forced to spend an uncomfortable night ashore before their rescue the following morning. The memorial to their miserable night out is an entry in *Lulworth's* Log, which reads: — 'Bearing Alguada Light — 100°."

Lulworth's run of 'out of the ordinary' duties, continued with a 'show the flag' call at the newly liberated town of Bassein, little more than seventy miles north of where she had restored the light to the Alguada lighthouse. The passage entailed steaming up river through acres of water hyacinth, a most unlikely place for a two thousand ton ship.

In his diary of *Lulworth's* eastern fleet activities, John Loughran wrote:

"Bassein had just recovered from the effects of the occupation. Among those who had endured most were the Catholic nuns, who conducted an orphanage and school housing some 500 souls. The sisters were invited to a meal on the ship, when they told of their experiences under Japanese subjugation. The captain had a table laid with the best food on board, including sugar, milk, butter, biscuits and chocolate. The look of astonishment on the visitors' faces was worth witnessing. They had almost forgotten what such delicacies looked like.

"The party included French, English, Irish and Burmese. All save the latter were suffering from malnutrition. Before they left the ship, the captain presented them with two large sacks of foodstuffs, whilst the librarian offered a wide range of books to help restart the educational programme. The fruits of their teaching were clearly seen, when a dance was held on the quarter-deck. Almost all the guests were ex-pupils of the convent. They proved to be women of culture and charm and their conversation was a delight. Many were graduates from Rangoon University. Other honoured guests were the Mayor and his wife, and a guerilla leader, together with his wife. The guerilla leader, named Rene d'Attaides, was of Portuguese descent. He came on board like a walking arsenal.

"Belts of bullets festooned his person and he carried two murderous-looking pistols in hip holsters. With his swarthy complexion, drooping moustache, wide-brimmed hat and his condifent swagger, he looked the personification of the bad men of the old American West. One could see that he was a hero among the inhabitants, having been a thorn in the side of the Japanese throughout the occupation."

Whilst *'Lulworth'* was pursuing her duties in and around the Bay of Bengal, the good news came that the war in Europe was over. V.E. Day, 8th May 1945, was cause for celebration. There was much cheering from the crew and toasting of the Allied Forces, mixed with relief that reunion with families and friends was not far off.

However, the jubilance turned to sadness, when in the early hours of the next morning, came the distressing news that two of the cutter's officers, Lt. Peter Chalk and Sub.Lt. Maurice Garnish were lost, when the sampan carrying them from shore to ship capsized. The tragedy cast a shadow over the entire ship's company.

During the following three months, with the end of the war imminent, age and service groups, due for demobilisation, began to leave the ship. It was the parting of the ways for shipmates, many of whom had served in *'Lulworth'* since she was first commissioned in May 1941. The long-awaited news that the forces of oppression had finally been brought to their knees, reached *'Lulworth'* on the 1st August 1945, but the celebrations which followed, did not mark the end of her service in foreign waters. Prior to joining the mighty force that was mustered to carry out the final mopping-up operation of World War II, there was much scurrying to and fro with small convoys.

'Lulworth' returned to Colombo on 20th October. After four-and-a-half years service with the Royal Navy, her role in the war had been fulfilled.

Chapter Nine
HMS Totland — From civvy to sailor

By 1943, the number of HO's serving in the cutters had increased. These, mostly young men who had enlisted for the period of 'Hostilities Only' (hence the term HO's) came from all walks of life and a wide range of trades and professions, and most were in their late teens when they first went to sea. The transition from civilian to sailor had, by necessity, to be achieved in the shortest possible time, which meant that many training programmes, some of which might have taken several months in peacetime, had to be condensed into a few weeks. Whilst the purpose of such famous training establishments, like *HMS 'Ganges'* was to provide basic training in such subjects as seamanship, gunnery and communications, it was mental and physical fitness for the task ahead, that appeared to be the prime objective. The real work therefore, began at sea.

The relationship between the 'regulars' and the HO's, though somewhat strained at first, improved with the passage of time. The 'regulars' on their part were generous in passing on their wider experience to the newcomers who, in turn, generally responded with a willingness and application which did them credit.

An H.O., himself, the author's early experiences, epitomizes those of almost every fledging sailor who, on completion of his basic, and perhaps later 'specialist' training, was thrown into the war, via the privation of life at sea.

"By the time I was eligible to enlist, the cutters had been plying the Atlantic convoy routes for about eighteen months. Three of them, *'Culver', 'Walney'* and *'Hartland',* had been lost whilst I was resident in the comparative safety of training establishments, *'Ganges',* and later at *'Pembroke'* and *'Queen Charlotte'.* For me, that period comprised a progression of leaps from the frying pan into the fire.

The discipline of *'Ganges'* had little comparison with the harshness of *'Pembroke'*, whilst my specialist gunnery training at *'Queen Charlotte'* on the bleak coastline of Ainsdale, in mid-winter, was sheer purgatory. I must confess that I emerged much the wiser and fitter for the experience. Whilst on a business trip, long after the war, I took a detour to re-visit Ainsdale. A foolish whim, because I had long since learned that sentimental journeys invariably end in disappointment. I was not surprised therefore, to find that the old barracks had been demolished and in its place, much to my amusement, stood a holiday camp. All I recognised from all those years ago, was a pathetic patch of concrete at the head of the beach, where the old dining hall had once stood.

"My training completed, I was returned to *'Pembroke'*, where I spent several weeks in seemingly pointless activity, young, full of enthusiasm and impatience. Each day, as was the custom, I visited the drill shed to cast an eye over the 'doomsday board', on which was displayed the names of those chosen for draft. When my name came up, I reported to the drafting office, where I learned I was to join a ship in Belfast.

My excitement at the thought of finally going to sea, turned to apprehension, when I discovered through *'Pembroke'* intelligence, that I was destined for an ex-American destroyer of the four-stacker variety, which, my informant confided — 'pitched like bucking broncs and you can stand on the quarter-deck and put your hand in the 'oggin'. All this was not very reassuring to a young Ordinary Seaman about to make his first encounter with sea duty.

The following day, a party, comprising myself and three other Ordinary Seamen, in the charge of a one-badge Able Seaman, embarked by lorry, headed for the railway station, each of us encumbered with kit-bag, hammock, and suitcase containing the sum total of our personal belongings.

"The train journey was as unforgettable as it was uncomfortable. The carriage was bulging at the seams with personnel from all three services, greatly outnumbering the civilians. There was standing room only. Sailors snored away in the luggage racks and even the toilet seats were commandeered. In the packed corridors, tired-looking men stood shoulder to shoulder, jealously guarding their personal effects. I choked on the tobacco smoke and the soot gusting in through a half-opened window, whilst my slim form was wedged between a large Royal Marine and the voluminus bust of a corporal of the Womens' Auxiliary Air Force, who did not appear to share my embarrassment. I survived the journey, as I did the stormy crossing from Stranraer, and finally arrived in Belfast, completely spent and anxious to remedy the gnawing hunger in the pit of my stomach.

"My first sight of my new billet sent my heart plunging to my boots, although her outward shabby appearance was probably due to the savagery of the elements in which she had been working, rather than the fact that she was a relic of the First World War. My companions and I were no sooner on board than we were informed that our services were not required, since the ship was about to undergo an extensive refit after prolonged operations in Icelandic waters. The news was as welcome as the excellent and satisfying meal that followed.

"The following morning, our party was despatched much refreshed, on the long journey south to Chatham. Within a week of arrival, after what must surely be one of the shortest commissions on record, I was on the move again, to join *HMS 'Totland'*. This time, *'Pembroke'* intelligence was totally confounded, although I received many speculative suggestions, from as many 'reliable' sources, which ranged from water-boat to cruiser. By this time I had already logged several hours of sea-time, albeit on the ferry between Stranraer and the emerald Isle. Rough as the passage was, it was hardly indicative of the sort of seas I was to experience during the next three years.

"When I arrived at the quayside in Londonderry, I was overawed by the activity. I had never before seen such a diversity of ships gathered together at one time. The air echoed the sound of welders and riveters at work and there was a general urgency about everything which left me breathless. I revelled in the excitement of it all as my gaze flitted from ship to ship.

I had no idea what *'Totland'* looked like, but I was doubtless looking for a ship that matched all the expectations and hope I had built into a mind's-eye picture during my days in training. After tripping my way over endless cables, wires and other dockyard bric-a-brac, a burly docker pointed the ship out to me. I confess that at first sight, she was a bit of a disappointment, though she did display a certain elegance. As I made my way up the gangway, I had that gut feeling that this was 'my ship'. Boarding her was the fulfilment of a boyhood dream, when I had run away to sea at the age of fifteen, only to be intercepted by an anxious father halfway between Wisbech and King's Lynn dock.

"My arrival on board was logged by a seemingly disinterested seaman, whose pencil appeared to be minus a point. My arrival coincided with that of a tall officer, with bushy eyebrows and a slight stoop. He approached from the quarter-deck with hurried gait, leaning forward slightly as though hoping the momentum would prevent him falling forward onto his face. He introduced himself as Lieutenant Stark, then thrust out a hand and welcomed me aboard. It was a reassuring and happy start to what was to be a three-year relationship with ship and crew.

"Welcomes over, an equally tall Leading Seaman, whom I later learned was named Merton, and effectionately known by the ship's company as 'Bombhead', took over and conducted me along the port waist and down to the mess-deck. I was greeted by the enquiring, but not unfriendly glances of the assembled mess-members. It was stand easy and there was much laughter and great swilling of tea. Since the ship had just returned from the Caribbean, there was an abundance of tropical fruits visible around the mess.

In spite of the friendliness, I felt exactly what I was, an ordinary seaman HO, fresh out of training. My lack of surefootedness as I stumbled down the companionway with my gear, must have been a sure give-away, and they must have noticed that the pale blue of my collar was attributed to peroxide rather than length of service. The air of informality, which I later learned was typical of most small ships, was not only encouraging, but surprising, after the regimentation of the training establishments. The tea was better too — hot, strong and sweet. I enjoyed my first constitutional since leaving

THE HAND - ME - DOWN SHIPS

Stranraer.

"I was surprised to find that the Leading Hand of the mess, 'Shorty' Burrows, who, like the others was clad in a faded boiler suit, with blue badges fraying at the edges from constant washing, had greying hair. To a slip of a lad like me, he looked old enough to be my father.

I was soon in conversation with members of the mess and it was apparent that most counties in the British Isles were represented. A welcome bonus, was the news that there was another 'Fenman' on board, a Coder named Don Miller, who hailed from March, only a few miles from my home town of Wisbech, in Cambridgeshire. However, since it was customary for members of particular branches to isolate themselves somewhat from those of other branches, I saw little of him during my time in the ship.

"My first meal on board was a feast, compared with those I had hitherto endured in barracks. The ship was on "canteen messing", which meant that the mess caterers had a choice of menu, unlike the 'take it or leave it' general messing in shore establishments and big ships. However, preferable as 'canteen messing' was, it required that each member of the mess take his turn at preparing food, preparatory to it being cooked by the qualified galley staff. My turn at that particular duty had yet to come.

The following day, I was allocated my 'action station' (the port Pom-Pom), my abandon ship station (one of the Carley Rafts), which I felt was a bit premature, and my 'part of ship' job. I had already been assigned to the Port Watch. Since I was a Gunnery Rating, as yet untried, I soon made the acquaintance of the Gunner's Mate, a dour Yorkshireman, who had joined the ship from the *'Resolution'* on the day she was commissioned. During the ensuing days, I was able to take stock of the rest of the ship's company. There were as friendly and cosmopolitan a bunch as you could hope to meet. So broad were some of the accents, that at times, communication was a little difficult, especially with a broad-speaking Glaswegian and a two-badge Geordie.

A tower of strength to everyone, particularly the younger ratings, was the 'Buffer', John Dexter, another veteran from the *'Resolution'*.

A man of seemingly unlimited patience, he appeared to be continually absorbed in the day-to-day overseeing of working parties and general shipboard activities. Of similar ilk was Leading Seaman Gainty, a short, wiry man, balding on top, with a tanned leathery face, framed in a perfect black 'set'. His carefully groomed moustache was painstakingly twirled at the extremeties into needle sharp points, which gave the impression of his having modelled for the familiar seafarer on packets of Players' cigarettes. Like most sailors, Gainty rolled his own, and whilst in the mess, appeared to have the stub of a hand-rolled smoke attached permanently to his lower lip.

"The overseas contingent comprised two from South Africa, one from New Zealand, and several 'Newfies' (men from Newfoundland), that I readily recall.

"The Captain, Lt.Cdr. F.A. Ramsey RN., with a DSO and a DSC to his credit, looked every inch the part. He always appeared to have the flicker of a smile at the corners of his mouth, as though enjoying a private joke. More to his credit was the way in which he generated confidence among the ship's company. To have served in the company of such men, not forgetting Coxswain Lewis, proved to be as good a start as any young sailor could hope to get. I was quick to appreciate that in spite of the time spent in training, preparing for this moment, my real education into the ways of ships and the sea was only just beginning. I was yet to learn the individual and collective responsibilities which being a crew member entailed. Furthermore, I was to experience the premature coming of age, which is synonymous among all teenagers who venture their lives at sea.

'*Totland*' sailed on 16th April 1943, in company with sister ship '*Gorleston*', '*Weston*' (Senior Officer), '*Wellington*', and River Class Frigates '*Ness*' and '*Exe*', bound for the Mediterranean. The passage out of the Foyle, provided a spectacular and memorable view, with the railway, backed by tall trees, running along one bank, and the occasional red fox, scampering along the water's edge on the other. It was an all too brief, though pleasant diversion from the purpose of our being there.

"There was little time for day-dreaming during the following days.

Apart from being kept busy with watch-keeping and 'part of ship' duties, I had to learn to cope with the everyday complexities of being afloat. Even the most trivial things were affected by the movement of the ship. On the third day out, the wind freshened and the up and down movements became more violent. Moving fore and aft was like clawing up a hill one minute, then careering down a hill like a runaway train the next.

"My first watch-keeping duty was mast-head look-out. I cannot recall ever having been prepared for this eventuality during my training, unless that was the purpose of having to scale the heights of the magnificent mast at *'Ganges'*. Petty Officer of the Port Watch was Geoff George, another 'regular' from *'Resolution'*. Typical of the unflappable professionals, his enviable calm and quiet Suffolk brogue, was a source of assurance to us all. I confess I was somewhat apprehensive when he despatched me aloft. Furthermore, I was getting comfortably used to the warm, though smokey atmosphere of the gun-shelter, where the off-duty watch-keepers were gathered.

"I pulled on my duffle coat and braced myself for what lay ahead. As I stepped out of the gun-shelter onto the deck, I was met by a stiff wind, which momentarily, took my breath away. Steadying myself against the roll of the ship, sometimes staggering as the sea gave her a nudge, I made my way aft and then up onto the superstructure, where I stood for a moment gazing up at the crow's nest, just a blurred shape in the darkness, some sixty feet above my head. I clutched grimly to the steel ladder and began the ascent. The higher I went, the more accentuated was the roll of the ship, whilst the freshening wind prompted me to tighten my grip as I groped my way cautiously upward.

"As I neared the top, a head appeared over the lip of the crow's nest, and the look-out clambered out onto the ladder on the opposite side of the mast. He clung there, expertly, as I lowered myself into the tub, then handed me the binoculars. He said something, but his words were whisked away on the wind. Then he disappeared down the ladder, leaving me with a sudden awareness of the responsibility with which I was encumbered. Away on the port beam I could make out the dark shapes of the ships in the convoy in the distance, seemingly stationary on the black water. Not a light in sight and the only sounds the throb of engines, the occasional boom as the ship plunged her bows into the oncoming sea, and the sound of water rushing wildly from the bow sternwards. An occasional glance downwards assured me that the ship was still there! One moment the deck was directly below me. A moment later I was hovering over the waves. I could make out the occupants of the bridge, huddled in their warm duffle coats, whilst from behind, I could smell the acrid fumes from the smokestack. Ribboning away astern, the ship's wake looked like the tail of a giant kite.

"As I continued to brace myself against the constant buffeting, it was little consolation that out there in the blackness, there were others sharing a similar experience. Between scanning the sea and sky with binoculars, and trying to differentiate between what was real and what was a trick of the dark, my thoughts turned to the vastness of the ocean and the first realisation of how far we were from land.

I was engulfed by a feeling of insignificance. If nothing else, I acquired a keen sense of responsibility, not to mention an ideal, though not very comfortable, retreat for reflection. As the trick wore on, I began to think that I had been forgotten. I was finally shaken from my thoughts by a banging, which vibrated up the ladder to the masthead. I was unaware at the time that it was customary to hammer on the ladder with a fist, to alert the look-out that his relief was imminent. Peering over the top, I could make out the dark shape of my relief climbing towards me.

Extracting oneself from the crow's nest proved more difficult that getting in, but after groping around with a foot for a rung on the ladder, I completed the manouvre successfully and handed over the tenancy. The coming down process was a little disconcerting. When the ship rolled away from me, I was pressed tight against the ladder. When it rolled towards me, I clung on for dear life for fear of being plucked off by the wind.

"It was a relief to find the deck under my feet again. Hanging on to the safety rail, I clawed my way forward along the port waist, head down against the wind and spray. By the time I reached the gun-shelter, I had received a thorough drenching from an all-consuming sea, resulting from the ship dropping her bows into a trough. I scrambled into the gun-shelter, with the taste of salt water still on my lips. The atmosphere inside was as thick as pea soup and there was the usual chit-chat about nothing in particular, plus the all too familiar griping from one member of the Watch. The cocoa, that pillar of support which is I believe, peculiar to the Navy, and almost as traditional as the daily 'tot', had just come up. I poured myself a mug full, squatted in a corner and lit a cigarette. I had adequate time to recover from my first mast-head experience, before returning to that exalted position twixt the deck and the sky.

"The convoy's passage, arriving Algiers on the 22nd, had been uneventful. I was a little disappointed, not that I was overkeen to see action, but I might be forgiven for having wanted to put to the test, at least some of what I had been taught in the gunnery school. My only taste of combat to date, was at the rear of the Drill Shed at *'Ganges'* when I attempted to settle a difference of opinion with a giant of a 'Geordie'. In spite of the fact that he mercifully spared me punishment by extinguishing the lights with a peach of a left hook, I was fearful of having to go through life permanently disfigured. When the real thing came along, I found myself nothing more than a bystander.

'Totland' had sailed from Algiers on the 24th with convoy MKF13, comprising eight ships. The escort consisted of *'Weston'* (Senior Officer), with *'Ness'*, *'Wellington'*, *'Exe'* and sister ship *'Gorleston'*. The escort was later joined by the cruiser *'Bermuda'* and the powerful 'M' Class destroyer *'Orkan'* (ex *Myrmidon*) which was torpedoed and sunk in the Atlantic some four months later.

During the afternoon of the 29th, two enemy Focke Wulf Kurier aircraft were sighted, with their attention obviously directed at the convoy. The alarm was sounded and guns' crews rushed to their stations. I waited with mixed feelings of excitement and some apprehension, for the fireworks to begin. When the enemy came within my vision, they appeared like black specks in the sky, and it was obvious, even to an unblooded beginner like me, that they were way beyond the range of our anti-aircraft weaponry. In fact, the enemy made two uninterupted passes over the convoy at about 10,000 feet, dropping their bombs harmlessly into the sea. From my position on the port Pom-Pom, I could only stand and watch. As they disappeared into the distance, their departure as silent as their arrival, I felt disappointment at having not fired a single shot, although I was grateful that the enemy's aim had been so poor.

"Although there were HF/DF indications of some U-boat activity during the night, no attacks resulted and we arrived on the Clyde safely on 2nd May. I had taken my first steps towards acquiring my sea legs. I had learned also that in spite of what comedians would have us believe, there is absolutely nothing funny about sea-sickness. Most important, as far as I was concerned, was the fact that I was one step nearer to earning my place among the brotherhood of cuttermen."

Chapter Ten
HMS Totland — First Caribbean Convoy

Following *'Totland's* handing over to the Royal Navy, she sailed for Halifax, Nova Scotia, together with cutters *'Sennen'* and *'Walney'* and a crew drawn mainly from the battleship *'Resolution'*. A week later, she and her sister ships, together with the armed merchant liner *'California'*, were despatched as ocean escort to convoy HX128/SC32. The combined convoys, due to split later, comprised 72 ships, among them the ill-fated *'Laconia'*, sunk on 21st December 1942 by U156 (Hartenstein). Commodore of the convoy was Vice-Admiral Somerville in the *'Cape Clear'*. Departure time was 1100 on 20th May 1941.

Coincidentally, on the evening of that day, intelligence learned that two capital ships of the German Navy had been seen proceeding from the Baltic. These turned out to be the battleship *'Bismarck'* and the heavy cruiser *'Prinz Eugen'* which, within a few days, were to cause Convoy HX 128 to take diversionary action. At 1922 on the 23rd, the two enemy ships were sighted, moving southward through the Denmark Strait. Their detection by Radar, in the British cruiser *'Suffolk'*, accompanied at the time by the cruiser *'Norfolk'*, marked the beginning of what turned out to be one of the most startling and shocking events of the war at sea. The task of intercepting the German raiders, was assigned to the battleships *'Hood'* and *'Prince of Wales'* accompanied by six fleet destroyers. Meanwhile, another Naval Force, composed of battleships *'King George V'* and *'Repulse'*, together with the aircraft carrier *'Victorious'* and the 2nd Cruiser Squadron, was heading westward in support.

The long-range battle began in the early hours of the 24th, culminating at 0600, when the *'Hood'* was straddled by a salvo of 15" shells from the guns of the *'Bismarck'*, which caused her to erupt in a massive explosion and quickly succumb to the sea. Her companion, the *'Prince of Wales'* suffered damage and casualties during the action. Although it was suspected that at least one hit had been scored on the *'Bismarck'* from a salvo from the *'Hood'*, the two enemy ships continued their passage south.

On the night of 24th/25th May, the second Naval Force launched torpedo attacks against the German battleship, which resulted in the destruction of her steering gear. Now at a distinct disadvantage, the *'Bismarck'* changed course towards her home base. By this time the net was closing in. The battleship *'Rodney'* was already sailing westward to intercept the German's course, whilst warships from Force 'H', the battlecruiser *'Renown'*, the aircraft carrier *'Ark Royal'* and the cruiser *'Sheffield'* were on their way from Gibraltar.

The chase was now crossing the path of Convoy HX128. In the light of this development, the battleship *'Revenge'* was despatched from Halifax to give the convoy support. An added safety precaution was to order the convoy to reverse course for twelve hours. The continued pursuit of the *'Bismarck'* was possibly the reason for the postponement of the despatch from Iceland of the escorts of the 3rd and 12th Escort Groups. It might also be reasonable to assume, that apart from securing the convoy's safety, these decisions were aimed at preventing the seventy-two ships, together with their escort from impeding the action against the two German Capital ships.

As the chase continued, any threat from the *'Bismarck'* and *'Prinz Eugen'* was removed and the battleship *'Revenge'* returned to Halifax.

At 1036 on the 27th, the *'Bismarck'*, battered to near destruction by ships and aircraft of the British Fleet, sank within 500 miles of Brest.

The *'Prinz Eugen'* managed to elude her pursuers and reach the safety of Brest on 1st June.

The loss of the *'Hood'* was as much a blow to the British, as was the sinking of the *'Bismarck'* to the Germans. The respective 'pride' of the two Navies, had been sent to the depths of the Atlantic within three days of one another. Even more devastating was the combined losses of 4,319 men. One hundred-and-eighteen survived the *'Bismarck'* whilst only three lived through the destruction of the

THE HAND - ME - DOWN SHIPS

'Hood'.

The passage of convoy HX128 lasted sixteen days, arriving the U.K. on 6th June. In spite of several attacks by U-boats, only one ship, the *'Empire Storm'* of 7,290 tons was lost.

Within a few weeks, following a conversion refit on the Clyde, *'Totland'*, together with *'Walney'* and *'Sennen'* was despatched to St. John's, Newfoundland, as escort to convoy OB34. This was all too familiar territory for the cutters, where negotiating the awe-inspiring icebergs was a common experience.

Within two days of arrival, and still in company with her sister ships, she joined up with homeward-bound convoy HX139, and by this time, the 'big ship' men who had been retained among her crew, were settling down, albeit not willingly, to life in small ships. Upon her arrival in her home base of Londonderry on 29th July, she was ordered to the Thames for further refit, changes in her armament and ammunitioning. Bob Bate recalls the visit:

"When the 5″ gun was removed, the shell room was converted for the storage of depth-charges. Whilst ammunitioning at Woolwich, the quarter-deck was chock-a-block, and the Petty Officer in charge was pressing the lads to get them struck down as quickly as possible. One of our Newfoundland ratings, Henry Langdon who, because of his immense strength was familiarly known as 'Horse', started to manhandle them, much to everyone's amazement. After he had, single-handed, moved two or three of them, his only comment was — Jesus! them things is heavy! He seemed surprised and relieved when we drew his attention to the lifting tackle."

On her return to Londonderry on 22nd August, *'Totland'* was assigned to the 42nd Escort Group, and with it her introduction to the 'Freetown Run'. At this time, there was considerable U-boat activity off the west coast of Africa, and many merchant ships and tankers fell victim to them off Sierra Leone. On the 31st August *'Totland'* and *'Sennen'*, with the 42nd Escort Group, were assigned to shepherd the combined convoys OS4 and WS11 southward. When the convoys split off Freetown, the two cutters did an about turn to escort the tankers *'Vanjar'* and *'Sandar'* to Gibraltar. This mission

HMS TOTLAND — FIRST CARIBBEAN CONVOY

safely accomplished, they were then despatched to join the escort for convoy SL89, where they came into conflict with enemy submarines about 400 miles west of Ireland. In spite of the vigilance of the escorts, one ship, the merchant ship *'Aurania'* was lost.

Her next encounter with the enemy was during the passage of convoy OS12, when, on the night of 28th/29th November, *'Totland'* sighted a U-boat shadowing the convoy. Her persistance in pursuing the marauder and subsequent depth-charge attacks, were rewarded by the sound of an underwater explosion and the appearance of a large oil patch, but this was not considered evidence enough to credit her with a 'kill'.

Her activities on the 'Freetown Run' continued until early July 1942, when she was sent to Middlesbrough for further refit. With her refit completed, she resumed the now all too familiar passages to and from the west coast of Africa, until 14th November, when she was assigned (still with the 42nd Escort Group) to escorting troop and supply ships to the Mediterranean to sustain British Forces landed in North Africa.

It was during one of her visits to Gibraltar, that Bob Bate had an unscheduled encounter with the C in C 'H' Force, none other than Admiral Sir James Somerville:

"Tom Dodds and I were having a quick dash round the armament, doing the routines, and had got as far as the after .5's, when suddenly, we spotted the Admiral coming aboard. Tom and I grabbed tools and other bits and pieces and nipped forward to the gun shelter, so as to be out of the way of any verbal explosion which might follow, because there was nobody on the gangway to pipe the Admiral aboard. When we got to the gun-shelter, the coffee percolator was gurgling away on the bulkhead, ready for our stand-easy cuppa. Within a few minutes, in walked the Admiral, who asked if the percolator was working all right. We explained that it was and offered him a cup of coffee. When he saw the thick basins we were drinking from, he declined."

'Totland' was by now only weeks away from the most taxing convoy of her career, the first to the Caribbean, Convoy UC1, largely

comprised of oil tankers. If there was anything that would draw U-boats to a convoy, it was tankers. With this piece of intelligence in mind, a specially strong escort force was mustered to protect the thirty-two ships of the convoy. With Captain B.W.L. Nicholson DSO, RNR officiating as Commodore in the *'Athel Regent'*, the escort comprised the sloop *'Weston'* (Senior Officer — Commander L. Durnford-Slater RN); *'Exe'*, *'Ness'*, *'Folkestone'* and the cutters *'Totland'* and *'Gorleston'*. Because of the importance of the tankers, four destroyers from the U.S. Navy's 14th Destroyer Division, *'Madison'*, *'Lansdale'*, *'H.P. Jones'* and *'C.P. Hughes'* were added to the escort strength.

Within a week of the convoy departing for Curacao on 16th February 1943, and when beyond aircraft protection, the first U-boat attacks began, and it was soon evident that this was a well-organised assault by several, working in pairs. Among them was U522, with Herbert Schneider in command. This comparatively new submarine, commissioned in June 1942, had wrought havoc on a convoy in November 1942, claiming the merchant ships *'Hartingdon'*, *'Maritima'*, *'Mount Felton'* and *'Pathenon'*, totalling over 21,000 tons.

The experienced Schneider was quick to get into action against convoy UC1 and on the night of the 23rd, south west of Mogador, spotted the straggling *'Athel Princess'*. Although he scored torpedo hits on the 8,882 ton tanker, which resulted in her being abandoned, the ship managed to stay afloat.

The action continued through the night and in spite of the vigilance of the escorts, the enemy claimed the *'Empire Norseman'* and *Baton Rouge'*. Another ship, the *'British Fortitude'* sustained damage, but managed to stay with the convoy. None of these casualties were attributed to Schneider, in fact, he had sunk his last ship, and his short career in U522 was about to come to a dramatic close.

'Totland' was credited with seven out of twenty-seven attacks on the marauding U-boats, despite her actions being inhibited by a series of mechanical breakdowns. On one occasion, having contacted a U-boat by RDF, and then Asdic, she forced the enemy to dive and straightaway launched an attack with charges set at minimum depth.

HMS TOTLAND — FIRST CARIBBEAN CONVOY

The old cutter bogey struck again. The subsequent depth-charge explosions caused her engines to stop and by the time she had got under way again, the target had eluded her. With the contact lost she was despatched to give assistance to the survivors of the *'Baton Rouge'*. Hardly had she begun picking up the oil-soaked remnants of the tanker's crew, when she discovered that she could not go astern. More valuable time was lost whilst the engine-room personnel worked frantically to put matters right.

At 2100, with her faults rectified, she detected another submarine at 3,000 yards and raced in to intercept. Whether she had been sighted first no longer matters, but the torpedo which passed dangerously close to her port side is evidence of how close she came to being a casualty. When she fired 'Starshell', the enemy quickly dived from sight. Ten minutes elapsed before *'Totland'* regained contact and sped to the bearing to launch an attack with 'Hedgehog'. Again a U-boat got off the hook, when the forward-throwing device mis-fired. In the ensuing confusion, the submarine made it's escape, and the cutter was diverted to another search for survivors, this time from the *'Empire Norseman'*.

Newfoundlander Bert Dunn said:

"After the close shave with the torpedo, the 'Newfies' were talking about it among themselves. One of them described it as a 'direct miss'. I recall also, a Merchant Navy Officer among the survivors we picked up. As he stepped onto the quarter-deck, he said — 'that is the best time I have been torpedoed'. When I asked him if he had been torpedoed before, he said — 'yes — this is the seventh."

The trauma of saving survivors from the sea is, to some extent, born of — 'there, but for the Grace of God, go I.' It is always the more heart-rending in the case of tanker casualties, where the injuries, mostly extensive burns, are so horrific. *'Totland'* took on board a number of such cases. Whilst the less-badly injured were transferred to a rescue ship, the serious cases were retained on board and given the best possible attention. On arrival at Antigua, with no further losses to the convoy, the burial took place of the casualties who had died at sea.

THE HAND - ME - DOWN SHIPS

The Commodore, in his report, praised the co-operation and communications between the British and American ships, stressing the value of the faster U.S. Escorts in forcing U-boats in touch with the convoy to keep their heads down.

On 25th May 1943, *'Totland'* received an accolade from the Vice-Chief of Naval Staff, informing her that one of her attacks on a U-boat on 23rd February, had been assessed as 'probably successful'. His congratulations anticipated confirmation from post-war research, that *'Totland'* did destroy U522. The brief career of Herbert Schneider had lasted little more than eight months, during which he was credited with having sunk a total of nine ships, totalling 59,000 tons.

On 7th July 1943, Lt.Cdr. H.E. Tourtel RNR, took over Command in *'Totland'*, at which time she had been assigned to West Africa Command, and based at Freetown. Her duties were of a localised nature, operating between her new base and at Takoradi and Lagos.

This activity was to last for the coming seven months.

All sailors who have visited the West African ports have memories of what were then, somewhat primitive places. Runs ashore were only as interesting as one was prepared to make them and at first sight, presented a once in a lifetime opportunity to observe the geography of the area and the life style of the population. For others, they offered just another opportunity to indulge themselves in a rationed intake of alcohol. Residents of foreign ports, like those in the United Kingdom, were reasonably sympathetic towards the imbibing habits of visiting members of the sea-going fraternity. They were well aware of the sailors' need to let off steam after long spells at sea, particularly during the war when both physical and mental endurance was often stretched to the limit.

The numbers who over-indulged themselves were in a minority group, who had to be sadistically-minded to put up with the suffering which was often the consequence of a boozy run ashore. The situation was worsened for some of them by the availability of such quick-acting brews as 'Red Biddy' and 'Palm Wine', which only the foolhardy ventured to sample. Both of them were capable of nullifying reason and immobilising limbs.

HMS TOTLAND — FIRST CARIBBEAN CONVOY

The most sensible visitors to Freetown, did their limited drinking at the 'King Tom', where beer was served up in thick glasses fashioned from empty bottles, from which the tops had been expertly removed. Beer intake was controlled to some extent, by the issue of 'beer tickets', barely adequate in quantity to achieve a state of intoxication. However, you could be sure that those who did, were guilty of a little wheeling and dealing with their more temperate shipmates. Whilst the deportment of most sailors did them and the Service credit, the occasional drink-induced incident was inevitable. The most memorable of these, as far as 'Totland' was concerned, involved one of her L.T.O.'s.

A three-badgeman of portly dimensions and generally good nature, his tendency to lose count of his intake of 'Elephant Ale', was common knowledge among his shipmates. It was obvious to them, if not to him, that his excesses would one day land him in trouble. Nobody anticipated than when that moment arrived, he would work off his high spirits on officers of the Italian Navy.

'Totland' was anchored off Freetown, together with other naval vessels, including an Italian warship. The Italians had only recently surrendered. On the day the incident occurred, the LTO's run ashore coincided with that of three officers from the Italian vessel. As was his custom, he outdrank his companions at the 'King Tom' and returned to the jetty to await the liberty boat. Also gathered there, were other members of 'Totland's crew and the Italian officers, resplendent in their tropical whites. Whether or not the LTO had a personal dislike for Italians, is neither here nor there, but he suddenly broke loose from the supporting arms of his colleagues and flung his weight at the unsuspecting officers, pushing them unceremoniously into the harbour. Not surprisingly, there were cheers from many of the assembled sailors.

Although the unfortunate victims suffered no more than a soaking and some damage to their dignity, their assailant was to pay dearly for his indiscretion. The dispensation of punishment by a very cross and embarassed captain, was as harsh as it was swift. Stripped of his rating and hard-earned good conduct badges, the unrepentant LTO

THE HAND - ME - DOWN SHIPS

was furthermore doomed to a period of incarceration aboard the base ship *'Edinburgh Castle'*.

His departure from the ship was watched from the fo'csle with some sadness. Whilst nobody doubted the seriousness of the offence, there was much sympathy for him. As he was escorted to the ship's side, it was obvious from his hesitant gait, that his compatriots and attempted to make his humiliation easier to bear, by plying him with contributions from their rum allowance. As the prisoner made his way down the Mediterranean ladder to the skimmer that was to carry him off, the captain stood impassive on the quarter-deck. There were half-hearted cheers from shipmates gathered on the fo'cstle. As the boat pulled away, the last seen of the unfortunate LTO was his portly figure, arms waving, standing unsteadily in the bouncing skimmer, and his stream of expletives fading into the distance.

Apart from the excellent facilities at the 'King Tom', there were many sources of entertainment for the crew during *'Totland's* frequent visits to Freetown. 'Stand easy', that welcome break from shipboard activities, saw many of the crew lined along the guardrail, enjoying a front seat view of the aquatic skills of the Freetown children.

Most popular of these was throwing pennies into the clear shimmering water for the youngsters to retrieve. So expert were they that they could recover a sinking coin long before it reached the clearly visible sandy bottom. Swimming naked, they stored their trophies in the mouth, and it was not uncommon to see a smiling youngster with cheeks puffed out like a balloon. For an encore they would wim around on their backs, puffing away at a lighted cigarette.

At one time, the surest way of teaching an ordinary seaman how to distinguish the 'lee' from the 'windward' side of the ship was to send him on deck to dispose of the contents of the gash bucket. However, like most warships, the cutters had a gash chute for the disposal of garbage. This was playfully used for the bombardment of local vendors of tropical fruit when they came alongside in their boats to peddle their wares. Only the most inexperienced of them fell for that time-worn piece of tomfoolery.

On 22nd March 1944, *'Totland'* arrived in Gibraltar, making a

HMS TOTLAND — FIRST CARIBBEAN CONVOY

dramatic and embarassing entrance by colliding with the jetty, an incident not unwelcomed by the ship's company, because it resulted in a stay in 'Gib' whilst repairs were carried out to her damaged bows.

Stoker Lou Costello recalls:

"It was a most embarassing incident for us all, the captain in particular. We were making our approach to the quay, at a fair rate of knots, when the 'full astern' signal was rung down on the telegraph. Too late, we ploughed into the wall. Had it not been for the cutter's strengthened bows, it could have been a disaster."

Stan 'Charlie' Coombes was on deck at the time:

"I was a member of the cable party. As we continued on our collision course, I remember seeing a matelot sweeping the jetty. He looked up, and realising that we were not going to stop, held up his hand like a policeman on point duty, and shouted — whoa, whoa — then dropped his broom and made off. Those of us on the upper deck were thrown off our feet by the impact."

It was during the stay in Gibraltar, that the ship was assigned to the East Indies Fleet, and with repairs completed, was ordered through the Mediterranean with convoy KMS50, bound for Port Said.

It was during this passage, with the constant threat of attack from the air, that *Totland's* progress was brought to an abrupt halt. John Dexter recalls the incident:

"We were on convoy escort duty, when one of the escorts reported sighting E boats, and we were ordered to make smoke. Unfortunately very little smoke emerged from the funnel, but a hell of a lot issued from the boiler room. This was followed by an evacuation of the boiler room, where we discovered on investigation a fire was burning.

"The ship came to a stop and attempts were made to put out the fire with steam extinguishers. In the meantime, crew members were stuffing all manner of stuff into air vents to eliminate draught".

Lou Costello was on duty in the engine-room at the time:

"We got a message from the boiler-room saying that there was a fire and, as I recall, our chief stoker played a significant part in putting it out, not without great risk and discomfort from the dense smoke. At the time it had all the appearances of being more serious than it actually was and some of the crew were anticipating an 'abandon ship' situation. There was a corvette standing off for such an eventuality. Fellow stoker 'Happy' Day, was in a bit of a sweat because he could not find his savings book, indicating that he did not intend leaving the ship without it. When I asked him how much he had in it, he said — 'eighteen shillings'. What I said to him is unprintable!"

The fire was finally brought under control, leaving a great deal of clearing up to do and sighs of relief from the crew.

'Totland' then proceeded through the Suez Canal bound for Aden. Whilst passages through the Canal were usually uneventful, exept for the occasional hold-ups resulting from heavy traffic, there were occasional mishaps.

John Dexter, in 'Totland' recalls:

"During our passage through the Canal, we were required to give way to a troopship, passing in the opposite direction. Unfortunately our manouvre went slightly wrong and culminated in our running aground. In order to get ourselves back into deeper water, we took a rope across to the opposite bank, secured to a bollard and pulled ourselves off on the capstan. During our continued passage to Aden, the captain expressed his concern with the ship's erratic course. Since nobody could doubt the efficiency of the helmsman, it was concluded that the problem must be mechanical. On arrival in Aden a careful examination of the ship was carried out and it was discovered that during our grounding in the Canal, we had lost a large section of the rudder. We subsequently went into dry dock for repairs."

The author has memories of that stay.

"The spell in dry dock, provided many of us with the first opportunity of seeing the ship high and dry. It was most impressive looking up the thirty-two feet from her keel to her gunwale. One was also able to appreciate her proportions. Although only 250 feet in length, her draught was only inches less than a 'D' Class cruiser, and her beam of 42ft 2ins. only four inches less. Her seaworthiness and performance was explained in that brief view of her chocked up in the dry dock."

HMS TOTLAND — FIRST CARIBBEAN CONVOY

With her repairs completed, *'Totland'* sailed for Kilindini. It was during this passage that she 'crossed the line', and preparations were put in hand for the traditional ceremony, for the benefit of those crew members who had not, as yet, been initiated. The author, unpaid sailmaker in the ship, had learned and inherited the job from 'Bunny' Austin, a two-badge Able Seaman who had left the ship on compassionate grounds.

"I was given instructions to construct a suitably large canvas bath especially for the occasion. Up to then my sail-making activities had been limited to making gun covers and a miscellany of other small tasks, which included a number of canvas bags. The latter was the idea of the captain, with the intention of filling them with fresh drinking water, and placing them around the upper deck. It was remarkable how cool the water kept in those canvas bottles.

"I regarded the bath as a challenge, coupled with the suspicion that the security of my 'quiet number', depended on what sort of job I made of it. We carried a modest stock of canvas, much of it scrounged from larger ships as and when the opportunity arose. The ability to scrounge successfully was a necessary requisite in a sail-maker's duties. Since the ship was well-equipped with a large sewing machine, inherited from the Americans when the ship was taken over, I was able to make short work of running up the canvas. The most testing aspect of the task, in view of the volume of water the bath was expected to hold, was the fashioning of rope 'cringles' with metal thimbles (eyes) inserted, by which the bath would be suspended.

When the day for the ceremony arrived, 25th June 1944, whilst in Longtitude 46° 30' East, some 300 miles north of Mombasa, the bath was hauled to the fo'csle and lashed securely between two ammunition lockers and the 4" gun shield. For me, this was the moment of truth! I watched with bated breath whilst the bath was filled with sea-water. It bulged and bellied like a mad thing as the water level rose, to the accompanying leisurely roll of the ship. The occasion, with all its boisterous sky-larking went without a hitch. The bath remained intact throughout, and my position as ship's sailmaker was assured."

'Charlie' Coombes recalls one incident:

"When it came to the turn of 'Doc' Burgess to be shaved and ducked, somebody's timing went adrift. When the moment came for the 'Doc' to be tipped into the bath, the ship took a good roll to starboard, and the contents of the bath followed suit. Much to poor 'Doc's discomfort he landed in only a few inches of water onto the hard deck."

In August, *'Totland'* was despatched from Kilindini for exercises with the submarine *'Truculent'* a wartime activity which nowadays is referred to as 'war games'. However this was a war-game with a difference, the difference being that we were still at war, and the intervention of an enemy submarine was not beyond possibility.

Ex-Stoker Lou Costello remembers that exercise:

"Together with 'Happy' Day, I was sitting on the fo'csle, when 'Happy' said he saw a torpedo pass under the ship. I didn't see it, but 'Happy' swore that he did."

The author can confirm that 'Happy' Day was not suffering from delusions:

"I was look-out on the superstructure aft. It was a glorious day and we were all aware that we were engaged in an exercise. I was scanning the sea and sky on a 90° arc from astern, when my attention was attracted by the track of a torpedo on the starboard beam, heading directly for the ship. Since the enemy was still active in these waters, the question as to whether it was a dummy or the real thing, flashed quickly through my mind. Although I was prompt in reporting the sighting, I had been anticipated and the ship was already turning in a tight turn to starboard. By this time the torpedo was almost upon us and I knew that my doubts would be answered within a few seconds. There was neither bump nor explosion. Instead, I was relieved to see the torpedo speeding on its way on the port quarter. I was never to know whether it was friend or foe."

Between small convoys and divers other chores, *'Totland'* made two visits to the one-time Italian Naval Base at Massawa, in the Red Sea. It was an unpleasant place as far as climate was concerned, and the shore-based accommodation comprised wooden huts. Its only good points as far as visiting sailors point of view, was the supply of ice-

HMS TOTLAND — FIRST CARIBBEAN CONVOY

cold fresh drinking water and the outdoor cinema.

On the 14th October 1944, *'Totland'* was despatched to Durban as escort to convoy MC13, much to the delight of the ship's company. She remained there for some months, undergoing a major refit. It was during the stay that the author celebrated his 21st birthday.

"I was treated to a birthday party, put on by some friends I had made during a spot of leave at a place called Nottingham Road, Nr. Pietermaritzburg. They owned a small hotel there. This 'home-from-home' diversion from sea duty came as a pleasant surprise. In fact, it was fortunate that these celebrations took place three days after my official coming of age, because at midday on the 21st Anniversary of my being introduced into the world, my shipmates made sure that it was an occasion to remember. As was the custom I was plied with a liberal helping from each of their rum rations. Whilst I have never doubted the medicinal value of the daily 'tot', I was totally unprepared for the consequences of a drop too many. I was violently ill. Afterwards I decided to become the sheer quintessence of sobriety. Well almost!!"

It was just prior to Christmas in Durban, that *'Totland'* was despatched to investigate a report of enemy submarine activity. After an intensive, but fruitless search she returned to harbour. It was some months later, whilst in Colombo, that the crew learned that it had been rumoured that *'Totland'* had been sunk whilst based at Durban. They were delighted to report (in the words of Mark Twain), that the news of their demise was 'a gross exaggeration'.

During the stay in Colombo, Seychelles was among the many ports of call. Whilst the crew enjoyed runs ashore in this idyllic spot, three members, 'Ginger' Rich, the author, and another, were ferried to another ship to provide music for a ships' dance. The three of them had formed a trio some time earlier, and already put their expertise to good use whilst in Durban, playing with local bands.

'Ginger' Rich was an accomplished pianist, whilst the author contributed the percussion. The third member of the group was a trumpet player who had purchased his instrument from a crew member of sister ship *'Gorleston'*.

"I only bought it because the chap who owned it was driving me up the wall with his playing," he said.

When the shipwright instigated the formation of a ships concert party, he could not have envisaged that its career would be brief. The author explains:

'As far as I can recall, the concert party gave only one performance, although it did have one or two accomplished performers, especially Frank 'Whacker' Payne, whose ukelele playing was to be commended, and of course, 'Ginger' Rich. The one performance was presented on board the ship, where a temporary stage was erected illuminated suitably with coloured lights. Apart from the struggle to get the piano on deck almost all the behind-the-scenes activity went very well.

"I think it was the opening of the show which could have been responsible for our short run. With the captain and fellow officers seated on the quarter-deck with visitors from other ships and ashore, one of the officers who, I think was the First Lieutenant, made the announcement that there was to be a surprise guest, in no less than the Admiral. Visits by Admirals invariably produced a surge of activity, verging on panic. Worse still were unheralded visits when all and sundry were caught on the wrong foot.

"Since our little surprise had been a well-kept secret, we should have anticipated what the possible outcome would be. It was immediately obvious from the pained expression on the captain's face, that being caught with his immaculate tropical shorts at the dip, caused him displeasure. He rose from his seat as though projected from an ejector seat in unison with his fellow officers, who doubtless shared his alarm. There was much shuffling of feet, whilst heads turned enquiringly towards the gangway.

"The 'admiral' (yours truly clad in Pirate of Penzance fashion) made his entrance, displaying a number of ficticious 'gongs' suspended from a two-foot long boom, slung from his tricorn hat and secured to his chest, port side. He was followed by a flunky in command of a small wheelbarrow which supported the end of a very large sword, which had been fashioned by the shipwright.

"The initial shock was followed by much laughter, though the captain looked more relieved than amused."

'Sennen' (Bill Dawes)

'Sennen' Officers on the quarterdeck. (l. to r.) Warrant Engineer Office E.C. Webb, Lt. T. Knox RNVR., Warrant Gunner S.C. Hatcher, Sub.Lt. J.O.C. Willson RNR., Sub.Lt. G.L. Greenlees RNVR., and Lt. E.M. Ferris RNVR.
(J.O.C. Willson)

▲ 'Sennen' (ex-Champlain) in her peace-time role on International Ice Patrol with the US Coast Guard framed between two icebergs. (Right) Dressed overall for a Royal visit in Halifax, Nova Scotia, in 1939. (Pete Wev).

A group of 'Sennen' crew members in tropical rig. Picture by Les Suffolk, standing on the right of the group.

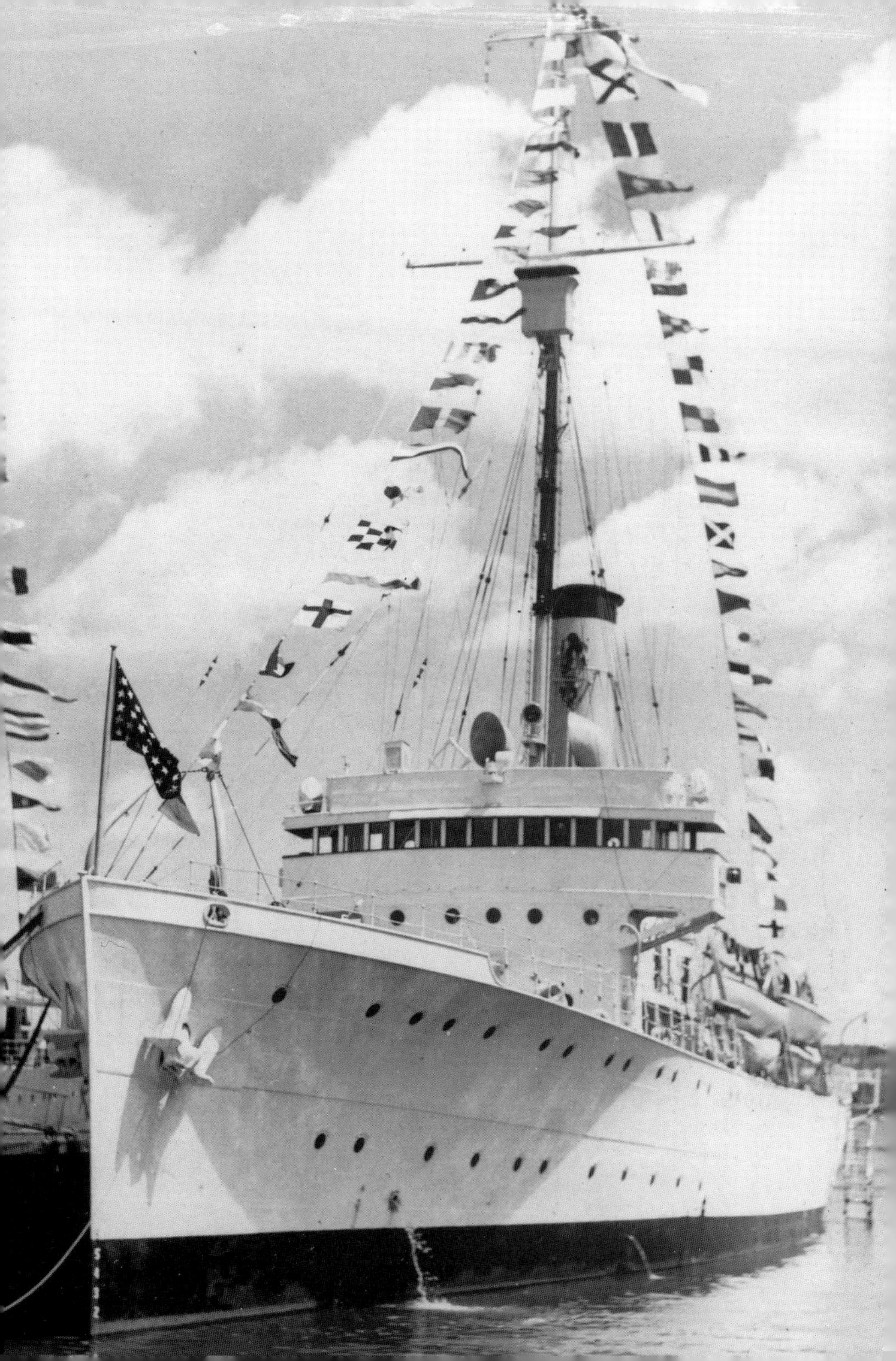

'Gorleston' in her tropical livery during her foreign commission. (Russell Linsell).

Lt.Cdr. Ronald Keymer RN,, pictured on the bridge. He was Captain of 'Gorleston' for two and a half years following her transfer to the Royal Navy in 1941.

German Luftwaffe radio operator and navigator Gerhard Schwenk, rescued from the Mediterranean by 'Gorleston'.

Gerhard Schwenk leaves 'Gorleston' at Gibraltar bound for prisoner of war camp.

▲
A line of ships is under attack from a Heinkel III bomber similar to that shown below. Gerhard Schwenk is standing on the right.
(Gerhard Schwenk) ▼

▲ The 'Gorleston' concert party staging their non-stop revue 'Round the Bend' in Durban.

▲ Stoker Dalby is provided with a guard of honour when leaving 'Gorleston' at Colombo for early demobilisation. (Tom Hebden)

Crew members of 'Gorleston' revelling in the traditional 'crossing the line' ceremony. ▼ (T. Hebden)

Under the Auspices of the
SOUTH AFRICAN LEGION OF THE B.E.S.L.

NON-STOP REVUE
ROUND THE BEND

Presented by
OFFICERS and RATINGS of
H.M.S. NON-SUCH
(BY KIND PERMISSION OF THE COMMANDING OFFICER)

AT THE

CITY HALL
DURBAN

Friday, 6th April, 1945
at 7.45 p.m.

Producers:
TOMMY FIELDS . SID. VICCARS . JOHN WETTERN

PROCEEDS IN AID OF
LONDON'S BOMBED-OUT VICTIMS

"NOT FOR OURSELVES . . BUT FOR OTHERS"

W.F. 17   J.R. DN 9219—1500—3-45

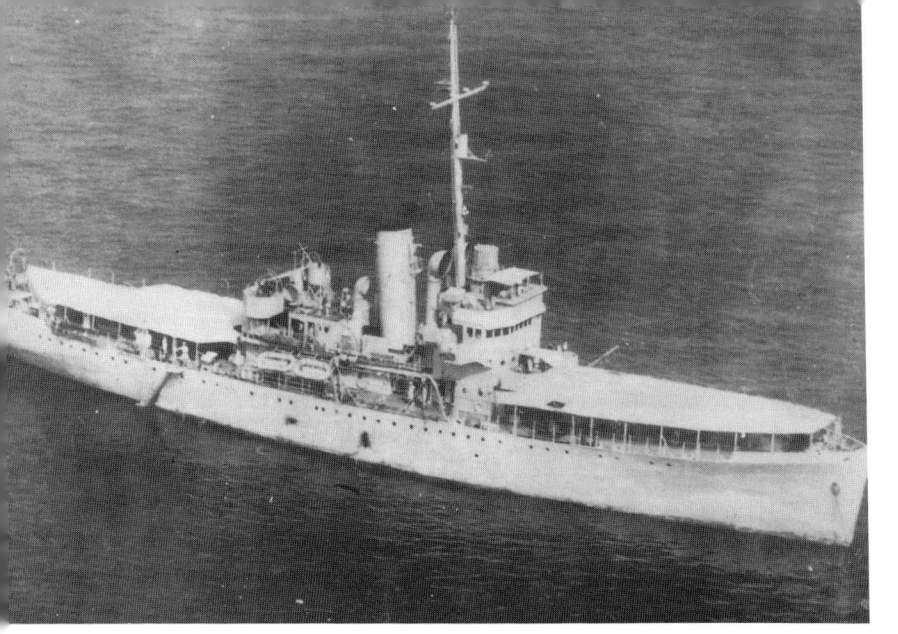

'Totland' with awnings up at Freetown.

Among the many Newfoundland ratings who served in the cutter 'Totland' are (left to right) Bill Gosse, Henry 'Horse' Langdon, and Bert Dunn. (Bert Dunn)

Crew members of HMS 'Totland' take a break from duty with a game of 'deck ukkers'. (Bob Bate)

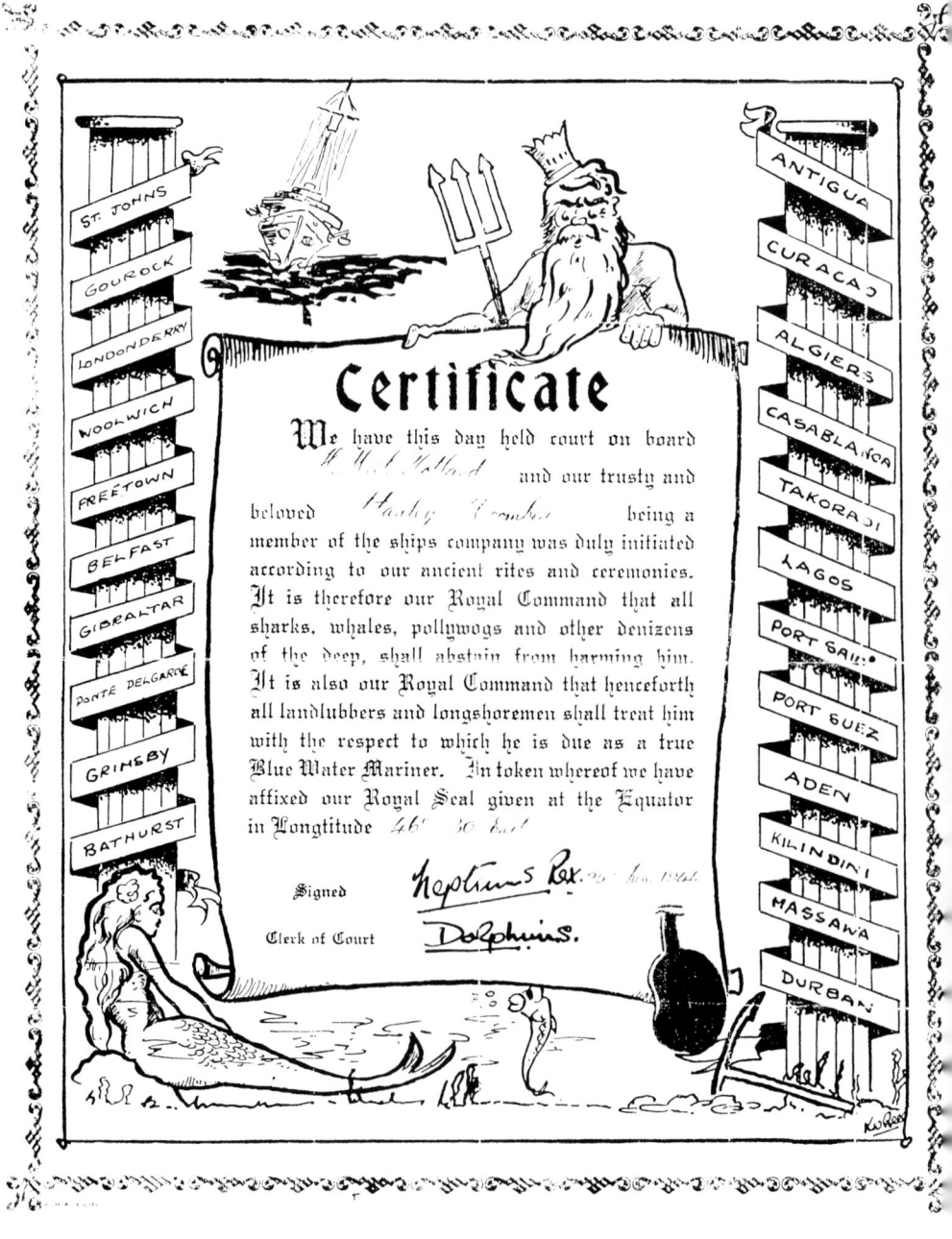

'Totland' 'crossing the line' certificate supplied by Charlie Coombes. The document was designed by the author in 1944.

Stephen Hannaford  George Lee  Bert Dunn

James Kelly

James Cheeseman  Cyril Clemens

Oliver Chappel

Harold Langdon  Jack Prince

Bert Humphries  Bill Gosse

No fewer than eleven Newfoundlanders served in the cutter 'Totland'. They represent only a small proportion of 'Newfies' who served not only in the cutters but in other ships of the Royal Navy. Their good humour, excellent seamanship and hardiness was typical of these men from across the Atlantic. They earned a place in the annals of the War at Sea. (Bert Dunn)

▲ Ex-'Fishguard' crew member J. Byrne, supplied this picture of the cutter.

Masters of improvisation, cuttermen cool off from an improvised shower. (Les Suffolk). ▶

THE COMMANDANT OF THE UNITED STATES COAST GUARD
WASHINGTON, D.C. 20593-0001
1 April 1991

To the Members of the Cutters Association:

Greetings and congratulations from the United States Coast Guard! Fifty years ago, the first "White Ensign" Cutters were transferred from the United States Coast Guard to join His Majesty's Royal Navy in the fight for freedom. The origins of your proud organization flow from that historic transfer under the now famous Lend-Lease effort. Indeed, it also marks one of the memorable occasions in the history of the U.S. Coast Guard.

Thank you for your service in a noble cause during a dark hour in the world's history. It was your valor and determination that helped achieve victory in those troubled times. Today you have great reason to look with pride on the professionalism of the young sailors, in both the Royal Navy, and the U.S. Coast Guard, who are serving shoulder to shoulder in the Persian Gulf in the cause of freedom. You helped to establish the traditions and standards that have become our guide. For this, and your continued interest in our Service, I thank you, one and all.

The 38,000 men and women of the U.S. Coast Guard join me in saluting you and wishing you a very, very

HAPPY ANNIVERSARY!

Sincerely,

J. W. KIME
Admiral, U. S. Coast Guard

Copy of USCG Admiral Kime's letter to the Cutters Association on the 50th Anniversary of the transfer of the ships.

Cutters Association secretary Sid Simkin (left) finds time to talk business with treasurer Jack Waterman at the 1992 reunion. (David Thomas)

Commander Craig P. Coy USCG (left) presents Admiral Kime's congratulatory letter to Lt.Cdr. Peter Dixon, Chairman of the Cutters Association. (David Thomas)

Nearly fifty years on ex-cuttermen listen attentively to the Chairman's speech at the 1992 reunion. (David Thomas)

'Totland' was represented at the first reunion of cuttermen since 1946, by (l. to r.) Vic Harland, Charlie Coombes, Lou Costello, John Dexter, Bob Bate, Geoff George and Ken Reed. (John Dexter)

Ex-crew members of 'Lulworth' meet up again after nearly half-a-century. (l. to r.) Les Kennet, John Loughran, James White, Ron Coulson and Peter Dixon. (David Thomas)

Among the 'Gorleston' veterans (l. to r.) Russell Linsell, P.J. Keeling (both Engineer Officers in the cutter) and crew member Jack Waterman. (David Thomas)

Recounting their days in the cutters (l. to r.) Eric Swann and David Thomas of 'Lulworth' and Pat Patrick 'Walney'.

NEWS

Editor: Ken Reed.
The Laurels, Fleet Hargate.
Spalding, Lincs. PE12 6LH.

Secretary: Sid Simkin,
67 Orchard Way, Wymondham,
Norfolk. NR18 0NY.

No. 9   (The official organ of THE CUTTERS ASSOCIATION)   JUNE, 1993

SHIPMATE GUESTS BOARD COAST GUARD CUTTER

In such a momentous event as the commemoration in Liverpool most certainly was, attracting thousands of ex-servicemen and women from both home and abroad, as well as ships from more than a dozen countries, it is fitting from our point of view that the US Coast Guard was represented by the USCGC 'Gallatin'. It was equally appropriate that members of the Cutters Association should be represented also. A party of six, comprising Russell Linsell (Gorleston), Jim Nesbitt (Banff), D. Studholme and J. Morgan (Sennen), Vic Harland (Totland) and Fred Wallace (Lulworth) not only attended the Cathedral service and participated in the Marchpast, but were honoured guests at a specially arranged reception and lunch aboard the Coast Guard cutter. Russell Linsell was accompanied by his wife, whilst J. Morgan was accompanied by his daughter.

Fred Wallace said of the visit:
'The Captain of the 'Gallatin' made us most welcome and he and his staff really put themselves out to make us feel at ease during both the reception and the tour of the ship. We had an excellent lunch and I was most impressed by it all. I was also impressed by the fact that the Commander USCG Europe, after arranging the visit, journeyed up from London to be there for the Reception. He remained for the whole of our stay before dashing back to keep an appointment in the City!'

During the visit to the 'Gallatin' there was an exchange of goodwill gifts. Russell Linsell presented Captain Paul Regan with a framed photograph of 'Gorleston', and in return accepted, on behalf of the Cutters Association, a plaque featuring the 'Gallatin' and inscribed with the following message:

The US Coast Cutter 'Gallatin' was originally commissioned in December 1968. In 1989 she commenced a two year refit and was recommissioned in 1991. With a range of 14,000 miles and speeds of up to 29 knots, she is fitted with the most modern weapons available.

Her dimensions are: length 115.2 metres with a beam of 13.1 metres. She is the sixth Coast Guard cutter to be named after Albert Gallatin who served as Secretary to the Treasury under US Presidents Jefferson and Madison.

To the Cutters Association
'A grateful Nation
Remembers your efforts',
USCGC 'Gallatin' (WHEC - 721)
28th May, 1993

Each of the visitors were also given a USCG cap with the ship's name emblazoned on the front, together with histories of the US Coast Guard and their peacetime and wartime activities.

Of the Marchpast, Russell Linsell said: 'I was surprised that the crowd lining the barriers clapped and cheered us all the

Copy of Cutters Association Newsletter

say 'What's that', so he must have absorbed his brief and remembered the picture of 'Fishguard' in the commemoration brochure. The Cathedral Service on the Sunday was most impressive and very moving'.

Our senior member, Captain Joe Baker-Cresswell, together with his wife, lunched aboard H.M. Yacht 'Brittania' with HRH Prince of Wales and were presented to the Princess Diana.

SHIPMATES VISIT NEW WALNEY

Three members of the Association Russell Linsell and two ex-Walney shipmates Harry Finch and Pat Patrick were guests aboard the new Walney Pompey dockyard. Pat Patrick reports:

"After coffee in the wardroom our group was treated to a talk (with slides) on how the new MCMV ship is equipped to deal with modern mine counter measures. Then followed a stem to stern tour of the ship and a chance to chat with many of the ship's 35 complement. There followed a brief 'stand easy' for lunch and refreshments, during which I presented the Captain with a model of the old Walney and Harry Finch handed over a framed photograph of the old 'Walnut' all her finery. In return we were each presented with mounted ship's crests.

LOUGHRAN REPORT

In a recent letter from 'our man in Chesterfield', ex-Lulworth crew member John (Paddy) Loughran, we have received news of other Lulworth shipmates, all whom have had to endure long periods of illness. Thanks to John maintaining contact with his old shipmates we are able to report that Les Kennett still battles on after eighteen months of ageing problems. Ron Coulson, who so bravely made the journey to Peterborough a couple of years ago after his stroke is making a courageous effort to cope with his disability, whilst his wife Rita still shows great fortitude after a by-pass operation. Tom Hackett is doing quite well and happily is able to resume driving. A line from old shipmates would doubtless do much to cheer them up at this time.

EDITORIAL

I feel apologies are due to all shipmates for the absence of NEWS over the past months. This unsatisfactory situation is not due to any lack of enthusiasm, or neglect of duty on the part of the editorial staff (yours truly). The simple facts are that there has been an acute shortage of news from you, the Association members, on whom I have to depend in order to keep the publication topical. It has always been my wish that the NEWS should be a sort of 'chatting old ships' by post. This can only be achieved with your help. All we old seadogs have left in our declining years is our memories, and my own view is that it can be a source of pleasure to share with them with shipmates with whom we shared a common experience half a century ago. What about it!

HMS TOTLAND — FIRST CARIBBEAN CONVOY

Prior to departing South Africa's favourite city, 'Totland' acquired a new crew member — a small dog. The newcomer became a familiar figure around the upper deck and the friend of almost everyone on board. John Dexter recalls:

"Able Seaman Gainty was given the dog by friends in Durban. We got the captain's permission to keep him on board and he was soon adopted as the ship's mascot. We named him 'Bob' and he quickly gained his sea legs. Regrettably his stay was short-lived. One day he was playing around the quarter-deck where the shipwright was carrying out repairs to the gangway, which was propped up on its side. The ship gave a sudden lurch and the heavy gangway fell on the dog. The crew were most upset by his demise. We put the little chap in a weighted sack and gave him a send-off over the stern."

By the 29th May 1945, 'Totland' was based at Colombo, in readiness for operations 'Dracula' and 'Zipper' — the relief of Burma and Malaya. However, in spite of her extensive overhaul in Durban, she was continually plagued by mechanical faults, which raised doubts about her suitability for inclusion in the pending operations. It was finally decided to send her home. She sailed on her last voyage in the service of the Royal Navy on 26th June 1945.

Chapter Eleven
HMS Gorleston — Errands of Mercy

Within little more than a week of being commissioned into the Royal Navy, the cutter *'Gorleston'*, with Cdr. P.G.L. Cazlett DSC., RN., in command, got her first taste of action against U-boats, and a face-to-face encounter with the dramatic consequences of it. When barely half-way across the Atlantic, on the voyage from Halifax to the U.K., in company with sister ship *'Landguard"*, she was despatched to the assistance of the merchantman *'Empire Drew'*, which had been torpedoed in the early hours of 12th June 1941. This was only the first of a number of rescue operations which were to highlight her activities as a convoy escort during the following months. But first, there was much to be done to prepare her for the testing times ahead. She was sent to the Clyde on her arrival from Halifax where she underwent a boiler clean, some modification to her equipment, and was fitted with Type 286M RDF. It was during this period that her passage crew was replaced, and Cdr. R.W. Keymer RN., installed as Captain. An ex-submarine officer, he was to remain with the ship for two and a half years.

'Gorleston' sailed on 24th August to join up with convoy OS4, bound for Bathurst. The escort, designated Force 'J' comprised the destroyer *'Walker'* (Senior Officer); together with *'Fara'*, *'Islay'*, *'Bideford'* and the cutter *'Lulworth'*.

When only two days out, there was an urgent call for medical assistance from the Dutch merchantman *'Meermirk'*, indicating that a passenger on the ship had sustained serious injuries in an accidental explosion. The nature of the accident is described by Arthur Ottaway, Sick Berth Attendant in *'Gorleston'* at the time:

"The incident involved a Glaswegian named Gabriel MacDonald, a civilian radio operator, en route for Bombay, where he was to take up a new post. In spite of heavy seas running at the time, he and his fellow passengers were taking the sun on the boat-deck. A crew member, who was bending signal flags to the halyards, failed to notice that the halyards had become entangled with the firing lanyard of a distress rocket, which was not in its customary upright position. As the crewman hoisted the flags, the rocket was accidentally discharged and sped along the boat-deck, stopping at the feet of Gabriel MacDonald, where it exploded."

In answer to the call for assistance, *'Gorleston'* sent away her medical officer, Surgeon Lt. James C. Gray RNCR., together with his assistant, Arthur Ottaway. Heavy seas made things difficult for both launching the boat and making the hair-raising passage between the two ships.

"Once we got the boat into the water, it seemed an eternity of being tossed around like a cork in the boiling sea," said Arthur Ottaway. "Several attempts were made to manoeuvre the boat alongside the *'Meermirk'*. One minute we were looking up at the screw, and the next minute, looking down at her deck. However, good seamanship prevailed and the boat's crew finally got us into a position where we would make the hazardous leap to the merchantman's ladder.

"By the time we got on board, more time had elapsed than was good for the patient. A careful examination of his injuries, established that one foot was beyond repair and amputation was the only course to take. The surgeon was optimistic about the other foot. The patient had been moved to the smoke saloon, just beneath the bridge, and the only lighting was from that inserted in the deck-head. Our operating table was a camp bed.

"Sterilization of instruments, as we did it that day, was never taught in Haslar, and we had to make do with well-scrubbed curry pots in the ship's galley, watched over by a wide-eyed Hindustani cook. All the utensils were boiled up on an old coal-burning stove, along with soup tureens and salad bowls. One of the hardest tasks, was to break the news of our intentions to our suffering patient. We need not have worried. The brave little Scot did not turn a hair, though it was probably a mixture of shock and morphine helped him to tell us to get on with it.

"The operation took place on the camp bed, the only good light being provided by the ship's Aldis lamp, held in the steady hands of the First Mate, who stood up to things very well. Our patient was a little man with a lot of guts!"

The medical team spent four days aboard the *'Meermirk'*, returning to *'Gorleston'* on the 30th. Three days after their return to their ship, Gabriel MacDonald was successfully transfered to the *'Fara'* for landing at Horta.

For the happy sequel to this story, we must leap forward to 1989, when after repeated attempts to trace his wartime patient, Arthur Ottaway's search reached a conclusion. In a letter to him, dated 14th April 1989, Gabriel MacDonald recounts the events which brought him and Arthur Ottaway together:

"I well remember that afternoon when the rocket exploded and I took the brunt of it. I recall sitting on the deck looking at my shattered legs, and my first thought was that I would never walk again. I also recall you and your surgeon coming on board, when he told me that I would have a fifty-fifty chance of surviving and that I would have to fight like hell to pull through. They eventually took me to a hospital in Horta, in the Azores, where I stayed for five months, before being flown to Lisbon. From there, I was flown to Bristol, where I was met by a member of the Marconi staff, who accompanied me by train to Glasgow and then home. The doctor in Horta did not do a very good job on my right foot, and I had to undergo another operation at Killean Hospital to rectify the problem. I am glad to say that I am mobile, though my walking is limited. After I recovered from my injuries, I worked in the office of the Marconi Company in Glasgow, where I remained until I retired."

At the time of getting in touch with Arthur Ottaway, Gabriel MacDonald was 81 years old.

Some hours after *'Gorleston's* medical team had been safely installed in the *'Meermirk'*, U-boats launched an attack on the convoy, about 240 miles west of Slyne Head, Ireland. Like ghosts in the night, they claimed four ships from the convoy; the 6,303 tons *'Saugor'*, bound for Freetown with general cargo and aircraft; the 4,736 tons *'Tremoda'*; the 4,954 tons *'Embassage'*; and the Norwegian vessel *'Segundo'*. The following day, U-boats breached the defences again and sank the 16,298 tons *'Otaio'*. Rescue ships picked up 142 survivors.

Throughout the passage of convoy OS4, *'Gorleston's* boat's crews were continually active. Apart from going to the assistance of the *'Meermirk'*, Leading Seaman W.J. Kendall RANR, was transferred to *'Lulworth'* where he successfully carried out repairs to her Type 141; an Elecrical Artificer was ferried across to the *'Fara'* to assist with multiple electrical defects; and the Medical Officer answered a call for assistance from the merchantman *'Fidelity'*.

In the case of the latter, things turned out to be not quite what they seemed. In his report Cdr. Keymer wrote:

"At 1735 on the 3rd, received a signal that *'Fidelity'* required medical assistance. This ship, which had joined the convoy early on, and unannounced to me, had changed in appearance and moved about in the rear of the convoy, so much, that despite the inability of myself and other adjacent escorts to find out anything about her by speaking to her, she was obviously something of a hush-hush nature. We closed, and after a series of unintelligable signals, decided to send the Medical Officer on board as requested.

"From his report on return, it appears that there had been some sort of dispute between the senior officers, who were French speaking, resulting in one of them, allegedly anti-British, being found dead from a gunshot wound. My Medical Officer was unable to say whether the wound was self-inflicted or not. The *'Fidelity'* left the convoy at dusk under orders for Gibraltar."

There were no further attacks on Convoy OS4 and the surviving ships were handed over to *'Vansittart'* at 1600 on 9th September. The escorts continued to Bathurst, where their crews made the best of an all too brief stay before being sent back into the fray.

On the 16th September convoy SL87, comprising eleven ships, sailed from Bathurst. Cdr. A. MacRae DSO., RNR., was installed in the *'John Holt'*.

The escort comprised *'Gorleston'* (Senior Officer); *'Lulworth'* and *'Bideford'*. They were later joined by the corvette *'Gardenia'* and the Free French destroyer *'Commandant Duboc'*. During the early hours of the 22nd, the leading ship of the fourth column of the convoy, the 5,302 tons *'Silverbelle'*, was hit by a torpedo in an attack from her starboard side. In spite of her damage and the fact that her screw was immobilised, she remained afloat.

Recognising the possibility of salvage, Cdr. Keymer decided to attempt towing the ship. *'Gorleston'* arrived on the scene at about 1005, where *'Gardenia'* and *'Commandant Duboc'* were screening the vessel. Cdr. Keymer straightaway communicated his intentions to the Master of the *'Silverbelle'* by loud hailer, learning at the same time that some of the merchantsman's officers and crew had been taken aboard the French destroyer.

At the same time, he was informed of the extent of the damage and the ship's general condition. No. 5 hatch cover had been blown off by the explosion and the steering gear and screw rendered inoperable. There was also flooding in the poop. With this information, he informed *'Commandant Duboc'* of his intentions to tow and ordered that the *'Silverbelle's* crew should be returned to their ship. In the meantime *'Gardenia'* signalled that she was low on fuel, and it was decided that she return to the convoy with the object of arriving before dusk. Because of the possibility of there still being a U-boat in the vicinity, it was deemed necessary for *'Gorleston'* to escort the corvette back, leaving the French ship to screen the merchantman in their absence.

'Gorleston' returned at 1230, when Cdr. Keymer signalled to the French ship:

'When executive signal is made please carry out high speed zig-zag around us while we attempt to get the ship in tow. Drop depth-charges occasionally, if you have plenty, to scare the sod!"

By 1305, the cutter had *'Silverbelle'* in tow and was proceeding at 5 knots. It was fortunate that whilst the steamer's steering gear was out of action, her rudder was in a midship position. Within little more than an hour of commencing the tow, there was deep concern for the damaged vessel's deteriorating condition. She was taking water in her No. 4 hold and the crew were working frantically to shift the cargo. There was further concern on board, when 'Gorleston' commencing firing at a suspicious patch of water about 2000 yards off her port quarter. This new development prompted Cdr. Keymer to send to the *'Commandant Duroc':* "Close and attack with depth-charges area covered by my fall of shot." The Frenchman duly obliged and Keymer responded with another signal — 'Thank you. That will make him keep his head down. Resume your station.' A message was then sent to *'Silverbelle'* to put their minds at rest about the sudden activity.

At 1532, just when things appeared to be proceeding nicely, there came a despairing call from the damaged merchantman: "My ship has gone down two feet since commencing tow due to water pouring in No. 4 hold. Afraid I must abandon ship." Cdr. Keymer's response to the message was: 'I do not intend to abandon tow till ship sinks. You can come aboard here if you must."

Not being satisfied that the *'Silverbelle'* was in any different state to when towing started, he then despatched his First Lieutenant and Engineer Officer, together with a Signal rating, to investigate the situation, after informing the ship's Master of his intentions. A party of volunteers was also put on board with collision mats and a portable pump.

During all this activity, there were warnings from Admiralty of possible further U-boat activity in the vicinity of the convoy. Since this sudden turn of events could necessitate *'Gorleston'* having to rejoin the convoy, Cdr. Keymer decided to hand over the tow to the *'Commandant Duboc',* and signalled the destroyer accordingly. The passing of the tow was a masterly feat of seamanship in the light of the prevailing sea conditions and the fact that the exchange took place with the ships still underway. The Master of the *'Silverbelle'* was then instructed to tow his boats astern, if the situation became critical. With the *'Commandant Duboc'* well in control of the tow, *'Gorleston'* took on the role of mother hen, screening the two ships from possible U-boat attack.

THE HAND - ME - DOWN SHIPS

At 2035, Cdr. Keymer was informed, via a signal from the French destroyer, that *'Silverbelle'* had requested he stop. Keymer replied:
"You are in charge of the tow and should, I think, keep moving slowly. The golden opportunity of saving this ship is being lost. I am taking my men off so I want you to ease down. I will send some of the crew of the *'Silverbelle'* that I have on board this ship."

That manoeuvre was successfully carried out and the towing operation continued through the night. The cutter continued to screen the two ships until the early hours of the 23rd, but at 0137, the anticipated order for her to rejoin the convoy, prompted Cdr. Keymer to signal to the *'Commandant Duboc'*:

"Proceed to Ponta Delgarda. I will report your position, course and speed to Admiralty. Tugs have been ordered from Ponta Delgarda. Have Captain's briefcase — will take it to Londonderry, where I want my rope and pump set. Goodbye and Good Luck."

During the ensuing six days, in worsening weather the stricken merchantman was pulled at a painstakingly slow pace towards safety, while her crew laboured incessantly shifting cargo and trying to make the vessel watertight. The drama heightened on the 28th, when the *'Commandant Duboc'*, her fuel situation critical, was forced to abandon the tow and return to Freetown to replenish her tanks. An attempt to refuel from the *'Silverbelle'* had to be aborted because of worsening weather. In her absence, conditions in the merchantman became so perilous that it was decided to abandon the ship.

Unwilling as the master was to surrender his vessel to the sea, it was inevitably necessary for him to do so, but before leaving, he managed to dismantle the Bofors gun and put it in the sole remaining lifeboat. Commendable though his actions were in saving his crew and the gun and getting them safely to Freetown, it might be considered an amusing climax, that he was later criticised for having lost the spanners which had been issued with it.

A total of eleven ships were lost during the passage of convoy SL87, including the *'Silverbelle'*. The 3,753 tons *'St. Clair II'* was torpedoed on the night of the 23rd and sank in less than ten minutes, whilst the *'Niceto de Larrinaga'* of 5,591 tons sank almost immediately after two explosions. The latter was carrying a cargo of manganese, RAF packing cases and had an aeroplane on deck. The cutter 'Lulworth' rescued 32 survivors from the ship. The 5,000 tons 'Edward Blyden' sank within fifteen minutes after being torpedoed on the night of the 22nd. Her Master reported:

"The ship was struck by a torpedo on the port side No. 3 hatch at 2152. She veered heavily to port. I then straightened the ship up to clear other ships in the convoy. At about 2154, another torpedo struck the ship under the bridge on the starboard side. Engines stopped and orders were given to abandon ship. At 2200 she was awash and at 2204 she broke amidships and disappeared."

Three more ships were torpedoed and sunk within a few minutes of one another in the early hours of the 24th. They were the 3,790 tons 'Dixcove', the 4,876 tons 'Lafian', and the Commodore ship 'John Holt' of 4,795 tons. It is remarkable that the crew losses were so light. In all, 322 were rescued from a total of 340. The only man lost in the 'John Holt', was a crew member of the Bofors gun. He had tried to get into a lifeboat, but fell into the water between the boat and the ship's side and was never seen again.

'Gorleston' played a major part in the rescue. She landed a total of 104 survivors at Ponta Delgarda and a further 65 on her arrival at Londonderry. Less than a month later, Cdr. Keymer received a letter from one of the survivors of the 'John Holt', dated 21st October 1941, and signed E.L. Browne, Captain R.E. The contents echo the feelings of all who are plucked from the sea after traumatic experiences:

"I would like to thank you and your wardroom of **HMS Gorleston** for your kind hospitality whilst aboard your ship, following your picking us up from the 'J.H.' on your last voyage. More important, you and your ship's company certainly saved my life and that is something mere words cannot repay."

Chapter Twelve

HMS Gorleston
— Leads Last Assault of the War

In August 1942, *'Gorleston'* was once again involved in an attempt to salvage a damaged merchant ship, this time the *'City of Manila'*. She sailed from Freetown on the 4th, in company with the armed merchant cruiser *'Cheshire'*, *'Folkestone'* (Senior Officer), *'Pentstemon'* and *'Wellington'* and was later joined by the destroyer, *'Zetland'*. The convoy comprised 33 ships.

As was usually the case, the convoy's passage was comparatively incident free for the first few days, but on the 16th, U-boat activity began and by 2240 both *'Folkestone'* and *'Gorleston'* made their first attacks. During the early hours of the following day, it was estimated that at least three U-boats were in touch with the convoy. These were later known to be U333, U214 and U406. The customary pattern of daytime shadowing of the convoy persisted as the enemy manouvred for attacking positions, whilst the escorts dashed hither and thither in attempts to spoil the U-boats' intentions.

Despite their vigilance and tenacity in pursuit, U214 managed to penetrate the defences and, at 1559, fired two torpedoes into the SS *'Triton'*, as a result of which, the steamer sank within eight minutes.

The battle continued into the following day with constant U-boat sightings followed by unsuccessful depth-charge attacks, often leaving the convoy with only one escort to protect it. During the afternoon of the 18th, U214 once again managed to elude her pursuers and within the space of five minutes, claimed three more shots on ships in the convoy. At 1645, she torpedoed the *'Hatarana'*, which was so badly damaged that she had to be sunk by gunfire. A minute later the *'Cheshire'* took a hit, but managed to stay with the convoy. The third victim, the *'Balingkar'*, sank within half an hour of being torpedoed at 1658.

HMS GORLESTON – LEADS LAST ASSAULT OF THE WAR

In the afternoon of the following day, U-406 got in his first shot of the action, seriously damaging the *'City of Manila'*. Throughout the three-day battle U-333, commanded by one of Germany's most experienced submariners Peter Cremer, did not fire a shot. His boat had suffered severe damage from a series of depth-charge attacks and was in no fit condition to participate. Although *'Gorleston'* played an important part in the cat and mouse game with the enemy, she had an additional and not unfamiliar role to play. At 1445 on the 19th she was despatched to stand by the badly damaged *'City of Manila'*, which was by then some twenty-five miles astern of the convoy. Although the convoy was, by this time, enjoying the added protection of aircraft cover, the hazards of standing by a disabled merchantman, somewhere in the 31,350,000 square miles of the Atlantic, for whatever purpose, with U-boats active in the vicinity, was a thankless task.

By the time *'Gorleston'* arrived at the scene, the rescue ship *'Empire Voice'* had already taken on board forty-six members of the crew. A further forty-nine survivors were taken aboard *'Gorleston'*, among them one cat. A second cat was not accounted for. Having assisted in the rescue, Cdr. Keymer's next task was to determine the extent of the damage to the ship. Since he could get no useful information from the survivors, he decided to send away a boarding party to carry out an inspection and, at the same time, recover any secret papers which might still be on board. One boat, in the charge of Lt.Cdr. Pat Smythe RNR., who was gaining experience in the cutter, prior to taking command of the River Class Corvette *'Cam'*, was despatched at 1640. The boarding party comprised Lt. (E) Russell Linsell RN., additional personnel from *'Gorleston'* and a small group of officers from the *'City of Manila'*. About an hour later, the party returned to report that the steamer had been torpedoed on the starboard side below the bridge, and that her No. 2 hold was flooded, and she was listing about 5° and down by the head. The starboard side of the fore-deck was awash. Lt. Linsell reported that the engine-room and boiler-room bilges were dry and main engines and auxiliaries were apparently undamaged. He reported also, that there was 150 lbs of steam in the boilers and all watertight doors below the upper deck were closed.

With this encouraging information to hand, Cdr. Keymer decided to put a steaming party on board, with hopes of salvaging the ship. However, he was fully aware that in spite of the inspection report, the general state of the ship would remain suspect and the success of a salvage operation would depend largely on there being no adverse changes in the weather. He conveyed his intentions to Senior Officer in *'Folkestone'*, adding that he hoped to man the merchantman with uninjured survivors of her crew, together with a party from *'Gorleston'*.

Upon receipt of the reply — 'Carry out proposals', the first members of the steaming part were sent away by boat, the remainder to follow as quickly as boatwork would allow. This activity was also largely dependent on there being no worsening of the weather.

The first task of the steaming party was to carry out a further inspection of the damaged ship. The results were far from promising. Things had deteriorated since the first visit. She was further down by the head and the list to starboard had increased. Steam pressure had dropped to 45 lbs. and water was finding its way into No. 3 hold. To add to the problems there were distinct signs of freshening weather. The work of the steaming party was impeded by approaching darkness and by 2115, with no artificial lighting aboard, it was decided to abandon the operation until the following morning. The steaming party returned to *'Gorleston'*.

The dawn of a new day saw the boat once again embarked on the hairy passage between the two ships. Any hopes of continuing with salvage were dashed when, after a further inspection, so extensive was the deterioration in the ship's condition, that steaming her was considered out of the question. The full extent of the increased problems in the *'City of Manila'* was explained in detail when the boarding party returned to their ship. The alternative to steaming the merchantman was to tow her stern first, but this idea was eventually discounted in the light of gathering heavy seas. It was considered that the ship would not survive much longer. All that

HMS GORLESTON — LEADS LAST ASSAULT OF THE WAR

remained to be done, was to remove all salvable items.

At 0740, *'Gorleston's* boat was despatched, to return four hours later with all stores, fittings and articles useful to the war effort on board. The most unpleasant task to fall to the boarding party was to humanely slaughter all livestock before leaving the ship. Lt. Linsell's party had, in the meantime, made a last minute inspection to determine whether there was anything left undone to preserve the existing bouyancy of the vessel. He concluded that the situation was hopeless.

In his report on the incident, Cdr. Keymer wrote:- "At 1130, all stores immediately available having been transferred, and the question of safe boatwork becoming a problem, the ship was abandoned finally, and although no material changes in her condition up to the moment of sinking were observed, she took a sudden plunge and disappeared within ten seconds at 1406. The operation was considerably hampered by the necessity of continuous anti-submarine patrol, and the danger of stopping ship for longer than it takes to hook on a seaboat.

"There is strong reason to believe that a U-boat actually witnessed the foundering of the *'City of Manila'*."

That U-boat could have been U333, which had remained in the vicinity though unable to carry out an attack. *'Gorleston'* had been attendant upon the stricken ship for 23 hours with the constant threat of attack by submarines. Throughout all this activity, the convoy had sailed on with no further losses.

Three months later, in November 1942, the cutter's Sick Berth Attendant, Arthur Ottaway; was involved in a story of camaraderie concerning a German prisoner of war. The story, enacted in the Mediterranean, culminated in a reunion nearly half a century later. Arthur Ottaway and Gerhard Schwenk, were of the same age, and had enlisted roughly about the same time. Neither of them could have anticipated that their paths would cross in war-related circumstances. Whilst Gerhard had spent his early days with the Luftwaffe, based on a German airfield in Northern Norway, from where he flew as a Radio Operator in attacks against convoys out of Reykjevik, Arthur was occupied with convoy escort duties to and from the west coast of Africa.

In November 1942, both *'Gorleston'* and Gerhard's Groupe were active in the Mediterranean, the cutter being one of the support ships active off Algiers, whilst the German's Groupe was harassing shipping in the same area out of Sicily. *'Gorleston'* had assumed the role of Senior Officer of the harbour anti-submarine patrol at 1400 on the 23rd and remained so until relieved by *'Folkestone'* at 2200.

During the hours of darkness of 22nd/23rd, almost continuous attacks were carried out by enemy Dornier and Heinkel bombers on the harbour and ships of the A/S patrol, at both high and low level. So hot was the activity that the cutter's captain manned one pair of Lewis guns, mounted on the starboard side of the bridge. Gerhard Schwenk was a wireless operator in one of the Heinkel 111 aircraft which made a low level attack around midnight. It was to be his last mission of the war. His aircraft flew into a hail of fire from five ships, sustaining several hits before crashing into the sea. Gerhard was the only crew member to survive.

"We were flying towards the first ship," he said: "and had to swerve to avoid it. We were then fired at from the other side. We received several hits from tracer and came down in a steep dive. The plane went under, but I managed to get out with another member of the crew. He had the rubber boat and tried to inflate it, but the pressure flask did not work. I saw him go under and did not see him again. I swam around in my full flying kit, not making much progress because of the strong currents. I was very tired, having been through almost eight days with hardly any sleep. Every day we must fly. About two hours later, I accepted that my life was at an end."

Fortunately for Gerhard, he had been spotted from *'Gorleston'* and a scrambling net was placed over the side of the ship. Gerhard clambered aboard in a state of near exhaustion and was taken to the sick-bay, where Arthur Ottaway assisted in giving him medical aid for his injuries.

"I had swallowed a lot of sea water," said Gerhard. "Arthur took good care of me whilst I was in the ship and we got along well together."

The friendship between the two young men had taken root. When *'Gorleston'* reached Gibraltar, Gerhard was put ashore, headed for internment, the beginning of four years in prisoner of war camps in Canada and England. Before leaving the cutter he and Arthur exchanged addresses. After the war both made attempts to contact one another. Arthur's address had been taken from Gerhard during his incarceration, as had the manuscript of a book he was writing about his wartime experiences. He had no idea of Arthur's whereabouts. Meanwhile, the Sick Berth attendant had written to the German's Galsenkirchen address, but received no response. He was unaware that his old adversary had returned from the war to find his home in ashes, and moved elsewhere. Finally a letter to the Burgermeister of Walthrop, a town twinned with Herne Bay, brought the response for which Arthur had waited over forty years. Gerhard had been traced to Delmenhorst, and a chain of correspondence and telephone conversations began, coupled with an invitation to visit. The reunion of the two war-time friends took place at Gerhard's Delmenhorst home in June 1989.

In May 1943, *'Gorleston'*, together with sister ship *'Totland,* was in the thick of the action during the passage of convoy UCI. Her role during repeated attacks by U-boats, was to give the accompanying escorts valuable data from HF/DF plots for their interception and attack on enemy submarines.

Arthur Ottaway recalls the ship's arrival in Curacao and subsequent events:

"Thanks to the Salvation Army, Curacao was one of the better runs ashore in tropical climes. They would send a small bus down to the jetty each day at noon, to pick up those of us who wished to explore the other side of the island, where the *'Sally Anne'* had a wonderful lake at their disposal, with all the facilities one needed for an afternoon's relaxation. Their canteen was excellent and their charges reasonable. However, it was not all play for me as L/SBA. I was often required to exchange and co-operate with the Pharmacists Mate from one of the US Vessels present. He was a red-haired Texan, whose every word was a sentence. Instead of a simple no, he would drawl — 'guess I cain't rightly approve of that fella'.

"Evening duty meant sharing the 'pro wagon' with my American counterparts, when we set up for business at the rear of the hotel Cracao, where there was a large chalk pit. The 'modus operandi' was to park our five ton truck in the entrance to the chalk pit and wait for the 'silly sailors' of both ships who, when loaded with inexpensive rum, came staggering towards us with their floozies. Before they could pass the pro-wagon, they had to accept the issue of condoms and prophylactic cream. Refusal meant that they had to abandon the operation or get carted off by the US Patrol.

"The 'pro-wagon' consisted of six forty gallon drums, three on each side of the truck. Two of the drums contained Condies Fluid, the remainder water. There were a number of wash bowls on portable stands, and the tables were loaded with soap and disposable towels. Each returning sailor could have a good wash down before returning to his ship, after giving name of ship and official number to the duty medical ratings. This precautionary exercise saved the errant lads a visit to the sick-bay ten days later."

Within fourteen days of her return from the Caribbean, 'Gorleston' was assigned to KMF/MKF convoys between the U.K. and Algiers, the purpose of which was to sustain forces in North Africa. By the end of June 1943, she had joined 'Totland' in West Africa Command. While she was on that station, she was delegated the task of escorting a floating dock on the 1600 miles passage from Dakar to Gibraltar. On this occasion she was Senior Officer Escorts, with never less than five trawlers under her command. They were 'Birdlip', 'Butser', 'Inkpen', 'Fandango', 'Duncton', 'Yestor' and 'St. Wistan', from Freetown Escort Force, with 'Lord Hotham, and 'Imperialist' from Gibraltar Escort Force.

The dock sailed in two halves, named 'Regusci' and 'Voulminot' respectively. Two Dutch tugs, the "Zwarte Zee' and 'Roode Zee' were charged with the towing duties. The voyage took twenty-two days, at an average speed of 3/4 knots, with the tows stretched over some five-hundred yards, putting severe restrictions on manoeuvrability.

HMS GORLESTON – LEADS LAST ASSAULT OF THE WAR

The course taken was a fair weather coastal route, owing to the structural state of the docks. Hugging the coastline helped to dispel the fears of the tug Masters, that should the tow part in deep water, they would be unable to recover it, unless some of the weight was on the bottom. Whilst there were some advantages in staying in the soundings, it was considered advisable to avoid being sighted from the Spanish coast. This was achieved in spite of an unexpected tidal set combined with rapid movements in visibility off Cape Juby, which took the convoy to within ten miles of the fort, situated on a small islands off the point.

On the face of it, the operation would appear to have been pretty monotonous, what with the snails' pace and the length of time taken to complete the passage. However, whilst the tugs and their charges plodded steadily on, the escorts were kept busy on zig-zag patrols and continual visual and listening watch for enemy submarines and aircraft.

Humdrum as it might appear, the complexities of such a long towing operation, demanded round the clock vigilance. It was particularly demanding on the tug Masters.

In her capacity as Senior Officer, *'Gorleston'* had the added responsibility of tending the sick. There were several cases of minor illnesses among the crews of the escorts, which were prescribed for by signal. Two more serious cases necessitated the despatch of her medical officer to provide treatment. The more serious of the two, a case of malaria and pneumonia, could have proved fatal without skilled attention, and caused the MO to remain in the trawler *'Yestor'* for three days.

Being the only escort fitted with Radar, the cutter was required to carry out a number of night interceptions of unlit fishing vessels, as well as the collection of two trawlers from Gibraltar. She subsequently arrived on completion of the voyage from Dakar with barely 15% of her fuel remaining. Whilst the distance travelled 'over the ground' by the docks, whilst under escort, was 1,575 miles, *'Gorleston'* recorded 4,344 miles during the same period. Her many responsibilities included the supply of water to the trawlers. This was achieved with hose and tow over her stern. In his report on the operation, Cdr. Keymer paid tribute to those who participated in what was assuredly a delicate and trying exercise:

"The intelligent co-operation of both tug and dock Masters, was of such a high order that not only was station kept by one tow on the other, without any noticeable deviation, both by day and night, but the signalled course was so accurately made good throughout, that the majority of the trawler escorts were able to keep station within very small limits on the darkest nights without the use of Radar. This was achieved in winds of average strength 4, and tows of estimated sail area of over 6,000 square feet each, and drawing only four feet of water, without telephone communication and with only one naval signal rating, who was installed in the Commodore tug. The greatest deviation in calculation of geographical position between the Senior Officer Escort and the Commodore, was five miles."

This was *'Gorleston's'* last task whilst with West Africa Command. Consistent with the movements of her sister ships, she was assigned to the East Indies Fleet. It was at that time that her Captain, Cdr. Keymer, was succeeded by Lt.Cdr. W.A.C. Leonard RNZNVR. In a letter to his replacement, Cdr. Keymer wrote:

"I am sorry in many ways not to be able to turn *Gorleston'* over to you in person, especially as I have been in command of her for the whole of her operational life under the White Ensign. Please do not hestitate to drop me a line if you think I can help at all, as this is a rest cure, and I have plenty of time for correspondence, which is a pleasant change from the past four years. I shall always be interested to hear of the 'Old Lady's doings and to know what part of the world she is in, so that I can keep an eye open for her. As I expect you know, these are lovely little ships and carry everything that opens and shuts. My regards to those I know and the best of luck."

Cdr. Keymer was highly thought of by his officers and crew. His engineering Officer, now Lt.Cdr. (E) Russell Linsell RN (Rtd.), said of him:- "I was lucky to have a good Commanding Officer in Cdr. Keymer, and I look back on my two-and-a-half years in *'Gorleston'*

HMS GORLESTON — LEADS LAST ASSAULT OF THE WAR

as the best time of my life."

"Commander Keymer had been C.O. of a submarine before W.W.2, and he had a good appreciation of technical matters. If anything broke down, he would say "If a chinaman can carve a ball inside a ball inside another ball, I am sure we can put this right." This remark could be very galling to a technical officer who had just finished explaining what had gone wrong and why he was unable to put it right.

"In Western Approaches escort vessels there were many occasions when things went wrong. So the Captain's Chinaman became a by-word in the wardroom, and whenever we were in trouble, the cry would go up "Send for the Captain's Chinaman." One such occasion was when the radar set broke down.

"We were outward bound from Londonderry to Freetown in March 1942. Our Escort Group (42nd) had a radar officer in the Senior Officer's ship, *HMS Wellington* (Commander L.F. Durnford-Slater RN), but the sea was too rough to launch the sea boat. So the captain appointed a committee of talent to try to deal with the fault. There was the P.O. Telegraphist, the Electrical Artificer, the Gunner (T) and the narrator, a young Temporary Lieutenant (E) RN, who had an electrical degree.

After much poring over the circuit diagram and prodding with the Megger, the trouble was traced to a large condenser in the high voltage supply to the transmitting valve. Now any schoolboy knows that you can rewind a coil, but once the insulation of a condenser has broken down, you've had it. This was reported to the Captain who accepted the explanation with his usual remark but said "Show me where it has failed. The thing is useless anyway, let me see inside the box." The box was about 3 inches high and 4 inches by 3 inches across the top from which protruded three insulated terminals. The Electrical Artificer got busy with his soldering iron and when the lid was unsweated it revealed four condenser units immersed in oil. Each unit was about 2 inches long and 1¼ inches in diameter, and only one had broken down. It looked as if a small bullet had been fired at it making a hole slightly charred at the edges. The exhibit was taken up to the bridge and the Captain agreed that the diagnosis had been correct. Chinaman could do no more! After I had left the bridge, the Captain gave the damaged unit to the Doctor who happened to be taking the air in the Dog Watches. It must have reminded him of a bandage. A couple of days later the Doc came down to tea in the wardroom and said nonchalently "Here's your condenser, Chief. I've repaired it for you." Sure enough, he had carefully unwound the roll of paper and tin foil until the puncture marks disappeared, then he had cut off the damaged end with his surgical scissors and rolled it up again. Megger tests showed that the insulation had been restored, and, what is more, we could charge it up and get a spark from it. By this time we had reached Freetown and the Group Radar Officer visited us to help with the problem. He, at once, suggested that we put the repaired unit back in the box and see if the set would work. To everyone's great surprise, it did.

The Captain was delighted to have his radar set in action again, and we promoted the Doctor to Leading Chinaman. There was also another twisty to the story.

While we were examining the connections inside the condenser, we noticed that two units had been wrongly connected so that they were subjected to twice the intended voltage. It was one of this pair which had broken down. The fault was easily corrected.

Other ships in our Escort Group had suffered the same trouble, and we learned later that a total of some seventy radar sets in the Western Approaches command had the same fault. It might not have been discovered but for Commander Keymer's Chinaman."

En-route for the Indian Ocean, *'Gorleston'* was assigned to another towing operation, sailing from Alexandria on 27th March 1944. Although far less intricate than the Dakar/Gibraltar convoy, an incident in the Red Sea, had almost disastrous results. F. Plowman, who joined the cutter as an Ordinary Seaman on 22nd February 1944, recalls:

"It was in the early house of the morning of 18th April, that we rammed the American Liberty ship, the *'Mark Anna'*, making a sizeable hole in her hull and causing some damage to our bows".

Jack Waterman, another *'Gorleston'* crew member, was on Watch at the time:-

"I was in the OA's caboose, below the bridge, at the time, when I heard this whirring sound. Suddenly a beam of light appeared. I went out onto the deck and saw this large shape across our bows. It was like watching Cinerama, because I couldn't believe what was happening. Suddenly there was a bang and things fell off the bulkheads. The rest of the lads dashed out of the caboose with all speed. As we struck, a seaman on his way to the wheelhouse, was thrown to the deck with the impact.

"I remember there was an exchange of words between our skipper and the Master of the *'Mark Anna'*, then our skipper went on board for a parley."

Tom Hebden has this recollection:

"I was in the stokers' mess, near the boiler-room, in my hammock when I heard the bang. Everyone in the mess leapt from their hammocks and dashed through the boiler-room flat to the upper deck. I don't recall anyone being injured, but we certainly made a large hole in the merchantman. I think our ice-breaker bows spared us more serious damage."

Philip Myers, Sick Berth Attendant in the cutter at that time said:

"Although I was SBA, I did extra duties as a Radar Watch-keeper. I was on duty at the time of the collision with the American ship, and reported her for the first time when she was about seven miles distant. I kept the Officer of the Watch informed right up to the time of the impact."

Sid Viccars, Yeoman of Signals in *'Gorleston'* said: "I remember that one of our signalmen, Charlie Wyatt was drafted to the towing tug for communication purposes. He came from Hull and claimed that he first went to sea in a fish box. Charlie was some time later, returned to us after a spell of sunning it up in some camp with air conditioning."

The damage to *'Gorleston's* bow was sufficiently serious for her to be detained in Port Said for about two weeks whilst repairs were carried out.

During that period of inactivity, the cutter's crew were given leave

THE HAND - ME - DOWN SHIPS

and the opportunity to stay at rest camps at HMS *Stag* and Lake Timsah. As welcome as this respite from sea duty was, it did have some disadvantages, as F. Plowman explains:

"From what I can recall, *'Stag'* was on the outskirts of Port Said, near the entrance to the Canal, and on the East Bank. It appeared to be run by a Chief Petty Officer, a well-built man, clad in immaculate tropical whites and wearing a pith helmet, with a CPO's badge displayed on the front. I think the camp comprised a couple of Nissen huts and about three rows of tents. The camp at Timsah was situated on the west bank, about half-way down the Canal. It was run by army personnel but was used by the three services.

"The brick-built administration, catering and sanitation blocks faced a sandy beach, complete with palm trees, that would have been a delight to any travel agent. The visitors' quarters were tents, without any furnishings, standing in a wooded area of fir trees. We spent one night sleeping on the ground fighting a losing battle against hordes of insects. After this unpleasant experience, we slung our hammocks between the trees and thereafter had undisturbed nights under the stars."

On completion of her repairs *'Gorleston'* returned to escort duties which took her to Haifa, Cyprus, Aden, Kilindini and Madagascar. She was by that time, attached to the Kilindini Escort Force. Four years of arduous sea duties were now taking their toll on the cutters, and all of them, at one time or another, towards the end of the war, were despatched to Durban for major refit.

In March 1945, *'Gorleston'*, unaware of the impact she was to make on the city, steamed in to the welcoming voice of Durban's 'Lady in White', the legendary Peria Siedle Gibson, who will never be forgotten by the thousands of servicemen who visited South Africa's favourite city during World War II. A classical pianist and international concert artiste, the 'Lady in White' sang in her rich soprano voice, to all ships entering the harbour. She died in 1971 at the age of 82.

What endeared *'Gorleston'* to the hearts of Durban's people, was the charitable performances given by the ship's very talented concert party. During the cutter's long stay, the concert party's non-stop

HMS GORLESTON – LEADS LAST ASSAULT OF THE WAR

Revue, 'Round the Bend' provided as much enjoyment for the residents, as did their generosity to the members.

On the 6th April 1945, the Concert Party performed under the auspices of the South African Legion of the BESL., at Durban's City Hall, to raise funds for London's bombed out victims of the war. On the 22nd, at the Metro Theatre, they staged a concert in aid of the Merchant Navy's Officers Memorial Club and Nautical School, by arrangement with the Institute of Estate Agents and Auctioneers, Natal Branch.

Both shows were produced by Sid Viccars, John Wettern and Tommy Fields, the latter, a well-known professional saxophonist, who had played with nationally well-known British dance bands, including the Joe Loss orchestra.

The producers also appeared in the show, and it will come as no surprise that Tommy Fields was the star attraction. The cast comprised 'Stripey' Talbot, 'Butch' Nettleton, Jimmy Kerr, Spearing, Norman McDonald, Olney, V. Walker, G. Cooper, J. MacIntosh, Bobby Morris, Douglas Cook, Jack Richmond, C. Dashwood and G.E. Head. Jack Leibermann was the party's accomplished accompanist at the piano. *'Gorleston'* had not only an abundance of talent, but also a willing band of behind-the-scenes helpers, including Ernest Marling, John Ransley, Norman Sparney, George Morrice, George Daley, 'Bunny' Austin and Peter Ferguson. Jack Leibermann, who served in *'Gorleston'* from January 1944 to January 1946, recalls:-

"In recognition of the proceeds gained from our concerts, the equivalent of our WVS, organised a trip up country for us, when we did a series of 'whistle stop shows'. They were so pleased with our efforts, that they offered us a choice of pianos from a Durban music shop, and I had the enviable task of choosing it. Our carpenter, Norman Sparney, made a wooden case for it, and it was stowed in the vicinity of a hatch, so that it was easily accessible to the upper deck for concerts, etc."

After a memorable stay in Durban, *'Gorleston'* steamed for Colombo. The crew were not to know the importance of the role the cutter was to play in the last operations of the war, 'Dracula' and

'Zipper'. The implications of that role are explained by Captain Joe Baker-Cresswell RN:

"I was very fond of *'Gorleston'*, and this is how I came to know her. Towards the end of 1943, I was given command of all escorts in the Indian Ocean. I had been Chief of Staff to the C in C Western Approaches, having before that founded the Training Service for all escorts in the Atlantic, and ran the show for a year from the yacht 'Philante'. U-boat activity was hotting up in the Indian Ocean with the long-range German U-boats being especially active off the East African coast as far north as Aden. The Japanese were also a considerable nuisance on the Australian trade. My base in 1943 was Colombo. There I held office in the C in C's Headquarters and also the Command of the Cruiser 'Caradoc', which was unseaworthy.

"I immediately set about training my motley command, which consisted of the entire Indian Navy, some escorts from home and some from Australia and South Africa. I used to embark in various of these ships and take them out on exercises, but this was not altogether satisfactory, and I looked for a suitable Headquarters ship. *'Gorleston'* was the answer. She was fitted out as an escort and had ample accommodation for my considerable staff. I conducted all exercises from her, and also took her out on various anti-submarine operations.

"Mine was a totally separate command, the rest of the Eastern Fleet being based at Trincomalee, on the other side of Ceylon. The final operation of the war was the invasion of Malaya. A large armada was concentrated at Madras with all the East Indies Fleet and transports. I undertook the escort myself in *'Gorleston'* with most of the 206 ships in my command present. So *'Gorleston'* had the honour of leading the vast armada.

"We left Madras and settled down nicely to an efficient routine when, on the second day out, peace was declared. It was impossible to stop such a huge organisation at a moment's notice and the whole thing just went rolling on while the Supremo and C in C decided what to do next. I had no doubts. I sent my two little MTB's up to Port Swettenham to take the Japanese surrender. This they did and settled down for the night, the Japanese being only too glad to hand over

HMS GORLESTON — LEADS LAST ASSAULT OF THE WAR

their army.

"Towards dawn, the army turned up with amphibious tanks and the whole panoply of war with tremendous noise. They were staggered to see the White Ensign at the masthead. We finally arrived at Singapore where I attended the Surrender Ceremony. My force then became a mine-sweeping force, and I sent those ships not so fitted back home, except for my picked Frigate, which I sent to take the surrender at Bali. I applied to go home and took *'Gorleston'* with me, calling at Colombo to wind up my organisation, and Bombay to say goodbye to the C in C India, who had been so good to me providing all I needed for the Colombo base. So I took *'Gorleston'* alongside the South Railway Jetty at Portsmouth and said goodbye to her. She had done me proud in a job the like of which will never be seen again."

The honour Captain Baker-Cresswell bestowed on *'Gorleston'* is dwarfed by that he so rightly deserved for his achievement on 9th May 1941, when as Captain of the *'Bulldog'*, and in company with *'Aubretia'* and *'Broadway'*, he recovered a German Enigma coding machine from the captured U-110. Ending the career of the U-boat's Captain Fritz Lemp, one of the enemy's U-boat Aces who, on the same day that war was declared, sunk the first British maritime casualty of the war, the liner *'Athenia'* whilst in Command of U30, proved an added bonus.

Although many historians claim that the capture of the Enigma machine shortened the war by two years, it is interesting to note that had it not been for a sudden inspiration on the part of Captain Joe Baker-Cresswell, the outcome could have been very different. Commenting on the incident, he said:

"Historians do not appear to have estimated what the consequences would have been had I not had the inspiration to take the submarine intact, but had carried out my original intention, which was to ram and sink the U-boat. At that time the Boffins at Bletchley had not broken into the secret cipher and could not de-code the messages which passed between Grand Admiral Doenitz and his U-boats. This only came after the capture of the Enigma and the keys and documents that went with it. Later when the Germans modified the machine, the Boffins solved the modifications. They could not have done so without the machine itself, and Doenitz was probably right in being confident that messages enciphered by the Enigma could not be broken.

"The great importance of its capture was its timing. Our losses at sea in the first half of 1941 were such that if they had continued we might not have been able to continue the war. The capture of the Enigma gave us that precious breathing space till the end of the year when the Americans joined us in the battle. The Enigma keys were recovered in a sealed envelope from Lemp's cabin. When I handed over the Enigma to Lt. Bacon in my cabin in the *'Bulldog'* he said: "This is what we have been hoping for since the beginning of the war".

Chapter Thirteen
HMS Sennen

Prior to the United States of America taking up arms against the Axis powers in World War II, a number of her citizens volunteered for and were accepted to serve in the British Armed Forces. Some fought as pilots and air crews with the Royal Air Force, whilst others were given commissions in the Royal Navy.

Whether their reasons for joining in the fight prematurely were out of a strong desire to suppress the forces of oppression, or perhaps, a deep-rooted ancestral link with Britain, is neither here nor there. Some certainly went to great lengths to get to the United Kingdom and volunteer, irrespective of what the implications were as far as the United States was concerned.

When the United States did join in the battle in December 1941, many of the willing volunteers transferred to US Forces, but there were many who elected to soldier on under the British flag until the end of hostilities.

One of the countless puzzling events of World War II, is the enlistment in the Royal Navy of three Americans, who made their way to Britain in 1941. Their arrival and enlistment is commemorated in a small plaque in the floor of The Painted Hall at Royal Navy College, Greenwich. The inscription reads:

15th June 1941
On this day came three citizens of
THE UNITED STATES OF AMERICA,
the first of their countrymen to become
sea officers of THE ROYAL NAVY.

No names are given, and one can reasonably assume that the reason for this omission, was the uncertainty as to what the reaction of the United States Government would be since she was not then officially at war. The question of who the three volunteers were, is posed in an article by Lt. Eric T. Perryman USNR, which appeared in Naval Institute 'Proceedings' in June 1977. Then, and ever since, there has been specualation as to their identity and, to the best of the authors knowledge, the question remains unanswered.

However, the answer to who at least two of the mysterious Americans were, could very well lie in a number of clues and coincidences connected with the cutter *'Sennen'*, which sailed from Halifax on 20th May 1941, with Lt.Cdr. D.C. Kinloch RN., in command.

The first clue is provided by 'Joc' Willson, who joined the ship at the time of her commissioning.

"When we sailed from Halifax, we had two American civilians on board who were seeking passage to the U.K. to volunteer for enlistment in the Royal Navy. Their names were Edward Mortimer Ferris and George Hague. I am not sure of the spelling of the latter. I believe they both had yachting experience."

Les Suffolk, another *'Sennen'* crew member, confirms the presence of the two passengers:

"There was much speculation among the crew as to who the civilians were. We often saw them relaxing in the wardroom or taking exercise on the upper deck."

The most significant coincidence is that *'Sennen'* arrived in the United Kingdom on the 5th June, which would make Ferris and Hague eligible to be among the three Americans who enlisted ten days later. Mortimer Ferris's enlistment was the subject of a newspaper article of that time, in which he is claimed to have said that he had earlier volunteered for service in the US Navy, but had been turned down on the grounds that he was considered too old. However, there could have been no doubt as to his qualifications. On completion of his time at Royal Naval College Greenwich, he was commissioned Lieutenant RNVR. The newspaper also reported that Ferris later married a British WRNS Officer whom he met whilst at the College.

The interesting twist to this story is, that Lt. Ferris, was drafted

HMS SENNEN

to the *'Sennen'*, the very ship on which he had hitched a ride, and later became her First Lieutenant. A *'Sennen'* crew member who got to know him well, is Bill Dawes, now living in California, who joined the cutter in January 1942 as an Ordnance Mechanic:

"Edward Mortimer Ferris was a most interesting person — very fair and very intelligent. We used to have long talks at Dawn Action stations in my workshop, which was his DA station. Shortly after joining us, the ship took him as its First Lieutenant, and what a joy it was to have a 'Jimmy the One' with feelings of compassion towards his shipmates."

'Joc' Willson said of him:

"The US Navy's loss was the Royal Navy's gain. I suspected at the time that he was destined for promotion and possibly his own command."

That early assessment of Lt. Ferris, later proved correct. He did get his own command in the *'Byard'* and from then on reached the highest rank possible in his chosen 'foreign' service. The Navy List 1946, lists him as T/Commander RNVR and a Staff Officer with the British Admiralty Delegation Joint Staff Mission in Washington.

George Hague's career after reaching the United Kingdom remains a mystery, but it is the author's opinion that Edward Mortimer Ferris was one of the 'first three' referred to on the plaque at Royal Naval College Greenwich.

'Joc' Willson recalls *'Sennen'* taking on board another 'foreign passenger':

"We called at the neutral port of Las Palmas, where we disgraced ourselves by entering harbour with our log line trailing astern. I remember there was a German merchant ship tied up there, which had probably been interned. Our visit caused much speculation among the crew, but the apparent purpose of it was soon explained. During the evening, a young merchant seaman was slipped aboard, who had apparently escaped from internment. We sailed immediately after."

'Sennen's passage crew after her commissioning in the USA, comprised mainly men from the Battleship *'Malaya'*, but some, like Mortimer Ferris, reached her by round about routes. 'Joc' Willson

was one of them.

"I received instructions by telegram, to report to the Station Master at Perth. The train North from King's Cross was crowded with naval personnel, and talking with other junior naval officers, it soon became evident that many of them had received a similar telegram. In fact, we were bound for Scapa Flow, but the line north of Perth was blocked by snow. However, the line had been cleared by the time we got there, so there was no undue delay, though the whole of Scotland appeared to be under snow. When we halted at quite small railway stations, kindly ladies had hot tea ready to refresh the Naval drafts. On arrival at Scapa, I joined a contingent of officers and some Senior Ratings, embarked in the Battleship *'Queen Elizabeth'* for passage to Canada. There were about twenty-five of us altogether.

"We were soon steaming westward and were well out into the Atlantic, when it was rumoured that a German heavy cruiser had broken out. The *'Queen Elizabeth'* was diverted towards the Bay of Biscay. It was lucky for us that the rumoured break-out did not materialise. However, the diversion left the 'Q.E.' with insufficient fuel to make the Canada crossing, and she was ordered south to Gibraltar. We were put ashore there and I was billeted at the Rock Hotel, not so luxurious as it might sound, where the food consisted mainly of sardines and lettuce."

The *'Queen Elizabeth'* later joined up with Force 'H' in the Mediterranean and, in December 1941 was badly damaged by charges placed under her by Italian 'Chariots', causing her to settle on the bottom of Alexandria harbour.

Ten days elapsed before 'Joc' Willson and his colleagues were able to resume their passage to Canada:

"Our chance came in the sloop *'Aberdeen'*," he said. "She had been modified by the addition of extra cabins for her auxilliary role as the C in C's yacht, so she had spare accommodation. During the passage to Halifax, unaccompanied, an attempt was made to supplement the onboard diet by doing a bit of fishing, navy style. We dropped a depth charge on the Grand Banks, but brought up no fish. On arrival in Halifax, we boarded a train which took us to Boston and, as the United

HMS SENNEN

States was still neutral, it was arranged for us to travel in locked carriages. However, we had to change trains and were spotted by the press. On reaching our destination, I was billeted in the battleship *'Malaya'*, where I remained until being assigned to *'Sennen'*. On joining the cutter, I took charge of the office, which included the ship's safe. My opposite number during the shake-down period was Lt. Pheiffer of the US Coast Guard.

"Among my duties I was Cipher Officer and responsible for all incoming and outgoing ciphered signals. I liaised with the PO Telegraphist. Two signals I shall always remember deciphering. One devastatingly simply read — 'HOOD BLOWN UP'. The other — COMMENCE HOSTILITIES AGAINST JAPAN."

Another member of the passage crew was Les Suffolk. Of the voyage home in the company of sisterships *'Walney'* and *'Totland'*, he recalls:

"We obtained an Asdic contact and ran in for an attack with depth-charges. Our only reward for our efforts was to see hundreds of sacks of Canadian flour pop to the surface. One can only assume that our contact was the hull of a sunken merchant ship."

Following a turn of duty as part of the local escort for convoy HX139, and a three-week refit on the Thames, *'Sennen'* had a change in her command, when Lt.Cdr. R.S. Abram RN., replaced Lt.Cdr. D.C. Kinloch. By this time, and up to the latter part of 1942, she was engaged mainly on the U.K. to Freetown run. It was during one of these convoys that Les Suffolk was temporarily incapacitated:

"I went down with quinsy. The 'Doc' put me in quarantine which resulted in me being isolated in the Engineer's Office. I was put on wardroom victuals, which would have been very nice if I had been able to eat them. I could only manage the M & B tablets — plus, of course, my daily tot. I believe my recovery was hastened by the latter."

Prior to, and following the North Africa landings, on 8th November 1942, *'Sennen'* was engaged on KMF/MKF convoys to and from Algiers. These were largely uneventful compared with actions in which she was involved barely six months later. On the 12th February

THE HAND - ME - DOWN SHIPS

1943, her captain was succeeded by Lt.Cdr. F.H. Thornton OBE., DSC., RNR.

Twice within the month of May 1943, whilst with the 1st Escort Group, she found herself in the thick of the action against German U-boats. The first was during the passage of the slow westbound convoy ONS5, when mountainous seas were almost as threatening as the enemy submarines. It proved a most uncomfortable experience in the light of the cutters' reputation for rolling, and often in extremely poor visibility.

The convoy was contacted by a group of U-boats off the southern tip of Greenland on 28th April, but it was not until the following day that they made their presence felt, when one of them, in a head-on attack, claimed one merchant ship. That attack could not have come at a worse time for the escorts, some of which were running dangerously low on fuel. With forty ships in their charge, an assault by U-boats in force, would have entailed a great deal of fuel-consuming chases, and given the enemy an advantage. Similarly, it would have been just as much an advantage to the U-boats for the escorts to break off for re-fuelling. However, the fuel shortage in some of the escorts was so critical that they, including their Senior Officer *'Duncan'* were left with no alternative but to speed on to St. John's to replenish their tanks. Under normal sea conditions, refuelling would have been carried out at sea, but the prevailing abnormal circumstances made this impossible. The heavy responsibility of Senior Officer, in the absence of *'Duncan'* was passed to Lt.Cdr. R.E. Sherwood RNR, in the Frigate *'Tay'*.

With the escort now depleted, and at a disadvantage in the heavy weather, it was fortuitous that two of the U-boats in touch with the convoy, U-439 and U-659, were sunk in a collision with one another. Surprising as this incident might be considered, it was not an isolated occurrence. In spite of the vastness of the Atlantic, there were other occasions when U-boats suffered the same fate. However, in this instance, the scales were tipped, if only slightly, in favour of the convoy.

The following day, 4th May, saw the beginning of an engagement between escorts and U-boats, which was to last throughout the ensuing twenty-four hours, when, despite the vigilance of the escorts, the U-Boats, employing 'Pack' tactics, despatched eleven ships. In spite of fog adding to the atrocious sea conditions, the escorts claimed two submaries. U-192 fell victim to *'Pink'* whilst *'Loosestrife'* claimed U-638.

The enemy was to pay dearly for his successes. The same day, the 1st Escort Group, which included the cutter *'Sennen'*, arrived on the scene, and almost straightway, *'Pelican'* claimed U-483. In the continuing action, *'Sennen'* came out of the fray with the credit for having damaged U-267. Although the U-boat survived the attack and the remainder of the war, her crew scuttled her in May 1945, after the German surrender.

Hit hard as they were, the enemy persisted in their harassment of the convoy, only to meet equally strong resistance from the ever vigilant escorts. The price they paid for their boldness and audacity was to lose U-531 to the *'Oribi'* and U-125 to the 'V' Class Destroyer *'Vidette'*. When the smoke had cleared, the total casualties to the convoy were twelve merchant ships sunk. The enemy had lost six U-boats, plus the two which brought about their own destruction in collision. A flying boat from RCAF 5 Squadron claimed the destruction of U-630.

Although the enemy had destroyed about a third of the merchant ships during their assault on convoy ONS5, their U-boat losses brought the total (329 up to May 1943) to an intolerable level. Forty-one submarines sunk during the month of May 1943, was the highest recorded monthly figure throughout the course of the war. One of the contributory factors for this upsurge in success against U-boats, was the extension of air cover on the convoy routes. The enemy had previously enjoyed the advantage of the 'Black Gap', an area in the North Atlantic with poor air cover, which consequently became the burial ground for a large number of merchant ships. The growing success of HF/DF, in both ships and aircraft, also played a major role in switching the advantage from the U-boats to the convoy escorts.

The loss of five more submarines during the passage of *'Sennen's* next convoy, SC130, was largely responsible for Grand Admiral Doenitz calling off the North Atlantic Battle. The losses of both boats and men had reached such an intolerable level, that he was faced with no other alternative.

Convoy SC130 sailed from Halifax on 11th May with thirty-eight ships. It was met on the 14th by B7 Group, again with *'Duncan'* as Senior Officer. The following day brought a succession of attacks by U-boats. For four more days, the escorts, aided by increased air cover, did an excellent job in keeping the enemy at bay. On the 19th, the 1st Escort Group, which included *'Sennen'*, met the convoy, having been despatched from St. John's. In company were *'Pelican'*, *'Spey'*, *'Jed'* and *'Wear'*. Their arrival coincided with a concerted attack by U-boats, in which *'Sennen'* was to play a significant part.

In one action, *'Jed'* had already contacted a submarine and made attacks with depth-charges and 'Hedgehog'. Although this produced no convincing evidence of a kill, an oil patch suggested that she might have inflicted some damage. By the time *'Sennen'* joined in the chase, *'Jed'* had lost contact with the target. Shortly after, *'Sennen'* obtained a strong echo, which was confirmed as a submarine, and an attack with depth-charges followed. This was followed by a barely audible underwater explosion, but this could not necessarily, have come from the target, which continued to move slowly on an evasive course. After running on for some distance, *'Sennen'* altered course for another depth-charge attack, but the contact was lost. When she arrived at the oil patch, which had appeared following *'Jed's* 'attack, it was discovered to have become considerably larger and there was an abundance of wreckage, which included splintered timber. Much of it was difficult to identify because of the increasing amount of oil, which by then, was spread over an area of about fourteen hundred square feet. A final effort by the two escorts was made to try and regain contact with the submarine. This not only proved fruitless, but the presence of other U-boats and the fact that the convoy was now some thirty miles distance, prompted *'Sennen'* to return to her station. *'Jed'* followed later.

Although official sources credited both *'Sennen'* and *'Jed'* with having sunk U-209, post-war research and analysis revealed that they had, in fact, sunk U-954 with the loss of all hands. The loss of this particular submarine was a great personal blow to Grand Admiral Doenitz. His son Peter was amongst those lost in U-954.

With the dying light of the 20th, five enemy submarines had been sunk, two to the escorts and three to the air patrols. *'Duncan'* and *'Snowflake'* accounted for U-381; a Liberator aircraft of 120 Squadron claimed U-209 and U-258; whilst a Hudson of 269 Squadron destroyed U-273. Not one merchant ship was lost in what was *'Sennen's* last spell of action in the North Atlantic.

On her return to the United Kingdom, she went into Grimsby for refit. Refurbished, she was assigned to the East Indies Fleet, arriving Kilindini, 28th October 1943.

George Rixon, who joined her at Greenock in June 1941, recalls one of the many incident's in the ship's career with the Royal Navy:

'We once went to the rescue of a group of Malaysian seamen who, with their captain, had been adrift for sixteen days. I believe their ship had been sunk by a Japanese submarine. Because of the possibility of the enemy wanting to take their British captain, the Malaysians concealed him with their bodies. We were told that the Japanese had attacked their raft by turning the submarine's screws on to it. When we picked them up they were in urgent need of medical attention for their injuries, salt water boils, etc."

Jack Woodhams joined *'Sennen'* in Capetown on 20th February 1945, and remained with her until she was de-commissioned in January a year later:

"*'Sennen'* was undergoing a lengthy refit when I joined her. We sailed on 23rd February for Mombasa, from whence, after a brief stay, we were despatched to Colombo as escort to four motor launches. We suffered one small mishap when one of them broke down and we had to tow it into Seychelles. We finally reached our destination without further incidents, where we hung about for some days before being sent off to Akyab. Within twenty-four hours of our arrival, we were despatched to Kyaukpyu, a mere eighty miles south of Akyab on the Burma coast, to pick up a troopship and escort it to where we had just come from. For the next few weeks, we were in and out of Rangoon on a variety of tasks which comprised escorting small convoys or patrols of one sort or another, then on to Madras where the 'Zipper' convoy was assembling for the relief of Malaya and Burma.

"There were few incidents as I recall, though we had to sink the occasional drifting mine by rifle fire, and stand by one landing craft which had broken down. The most traumatic incident occurred during our passage to Malaya, resulting from an object sighted floating some distance from the ship. We sent a boat away to investigate. One can imagine the feelings of the boat's crew when they discovered that the object was the headless body of a sergeant of the Royal Marines. The remains were brought alongside. Later with the Rev. Truelove on board, the boat pulled away to a short distance from the ship where, after a brief service, the weighted body was returned to the sea.

"It was about this time that we discovered that water was entering the stern gland of the ship. We sailed to Singapore, where we went into dry dock for repairs to be carried out. Whilst there, we entertained a number of rescued prisoners of war on board. We were in Singapore when Lord Mountbatten took the Japanese surrender."

It was during this period with the East Indies Fleet that Lt.Cdr. B.M. Skinner RN, took over command in the cutter, having concluded a year's service as captain of the cutter *'Landguard'*. The activities of the previous months might appear mundane by comparison with *'Sennen's* exploits in the North Atlantic, but there was, until the Japanese surrender, quite a bit of submarine activity in that theatre of the war.

On the 6th December 1945, *'Sennen'* sailed from Aden on her last voyage in the service of the Royal Navy. Like her sister ships, she had perpetuated the good name of the cutters, and survived numerous encounters with the enemy.

She arrived in the United Kingdom on 16th January 1946, where she was destored at Chatham, prior to being returned to the United States. Lt.Cdr. Skinner said goodbye to her on 16th February and Lt.Cdr. F.H. Sherwood DSC., RCNVR took over command for her homeward passage.

Chapter Fourteen
HMS Banff & HMS Fishguard

From the time of their commissioning into the Royal Navy in May 1941, and up to August 1943, the cutters, *'Banff'* (Lt.Cdr. C.P.S. Evans RN), and *'Fishguard'* (Lt.Cdr. H.L. Pryse RNR) were almost constant companions or, as the Navy would say, 'Chummy Ships'. Their first convoy, HX125 out of Halifax, with ill-fated sister ships *'Hartland'* and *'Culver'* in company, was the beginning of a relationship which was to take them on more than a dozen voyages to and from the west coast of Africa. These were code-named OS (outward bound to Freetown), and SL (Freetown to the United Kingdom), respectively. On average they took about 18/19 days over a route that was almost constantly patrolled by marauding U-boats. Many merchant ships were lost between Freetown and Cape Verde Islands, and the southern approaches to the Bay of Biscay.

After a conversion refit on the Thames in August, both cutters were allocated to Special Escort Group 'H', Western Approaches Command, with the destroyer *'Egret'* and resumed their duties as escorts operating between the U.K., Bathurst and Freetown. In the main, these voyages were very much 'run of the mill' and apart from the by now customary attention of shadowing U-boats, no outstanding incidents of note are recorded in the ships' activities.

Two members of *'Banff'*'s crew, Reg Stanley and Edward Boyd, consider their draft to the cutter to have been fortuitous. Both had been destined to join the former American destroyer *'Campbeltown'*, which earned a place in history, when she was packed with explosive and used to blow up the dock at St. Nazaire on 28th March 1942.

Reg Stanley recalls: "I had completed my LTO's course at *'Vernon'* and was enjoying a nice soft number as despatch rider, complete with motorcycle, when my draft came through. I reported to the drafting office and collected the necessary documents. Twenty-four hours later I was informed that I was the wrong Stanley. However, any hopes I might have had about returning to my 'DR' job, were quickly dashed when along comes a draft to *'Banff'*. I was provided with a rail warrant to London and on arrival, was met at the station and whipped across town by a 'Wren' driver to a large office block. I had the strange feeling that I was embarked on some urgent and very secret mission! Fortunately, that was not the case. I was then sent by taxi via the East End, to the docks, where *'Banff'* was undergoing refit. We sailed from the Thames for Londonderry, arriving there on 19th May 1941."

Edward Boyd said: "I was a young Leading Seaman in the Torpedo Branch, when I got my draft to join the *'Campbeltown'* in Londonderry. How I came to be diverted to *'Banff'* I cannot remember. However, I have one favourite memory of those Freetown convoys. I used to bring home stalks of bananas, which I took to the Childrens' Hospital in Belfast. What a joy it was to see the youngsters faces light up!"

For the latter part of 1942 until March 1943, *'Banff'* and *'Fishguard'* were fully occupied with convoy escort duties to and from the Mediterranean. These convoys were of vital importance to Allied forces then established in North Africa, following the landings of 8th November. A constant flow of men, supplies and equipment was sustained in spite of frequent enemy intervention.

On 5th May 1943, both cutters, then attached to the 44th Escort Group made a return voyage across the Atlantic to St. John's, Newfoundland, with convoy ON182. The convoy, comprising 56 ships, with Commodore W.E.B. Magee DSO, RNR, installed in the *MV 'Westland'*, sailed from Liverpool at 1030 on Thursday, 6th May. *'Banff'* and *'Fishguard'* departed Londonderry on the 2nd to join up with the escort. In *'Banff'* Lt. Peter Brett RNR, had replaced Lt.Cdr. Evans as Captain. Richard 'Dickey' Hawkey, who had joined her as a midshipman in the Spring of 1943, had a special memory of that convoy:

"In spite of the fact that both outward and homeward passages were not without incidents, what I remember most about it was the icebergs. We sighted them on the 12th, south of Greenland, and it was necessary for the convoy to make a change of course to avoid them. We were all over-awed by their magnificence."

During the night of the 15th, the convoy was enveloped in dense fog. It was a particularly demanding time for the look-outs with icebergs in the vicinity and the ever present threat from prowling U-boats. In the darkness and the swirling fog there was a tendency for ships to loom up, leaving only seconds in which to avoid disaster. Both the fog and icebergs took their toll of convoy ON128. The *'Athel Duchess'*, the *'British Statesman'* and the US *'Alfred Moore,* each reported collisions with other ships, whilst the rescue ship *'Gothland'* struck an iceberg and damaged her bows. Miraculously, the casualties were light in the appalling conditions.

The invasion of Sicily was the next major Allied offensive in the Mediterranean. Described by Admiral Cunningham as the most momentous enterprise of World War II, Operation 'Husky' was enormous in every respect. The maritime aspect of it alone involved some two-and-a-half thousand ships. Surprisingly, the gathering together of such an armada was achieved with minimal interference from the enemy. Up to the time of the invasion, which commenced on 10th July 1943, and during the early stages, the worst enemy was the weather. Gale force winds and high seas complicated the task of landing the large military force and thousands of tons of equipment and supplies to sustain it. There was no let-up for the Allied troops, nor was there any respite for the merchant ships and escorts in the ongoing task of replenishing ammunition, food and equipment. The task of ensuring the safe passage of these convoys from both Britain and the United States, fell to escorts and air forces.

'Banff' and *'Fishguard'* shared in that responsibility. Dickey Hawkey recalls:

"We were despatched to the Mediterranean on 24th June with a small convoy, arriving Gibraltar on 2nd July, where we waited for a convoy from the United States. Destined for the invasion, this turned up on schedule, and it was our task to shepherd it from Gibraltar to as far as Malta. The American escort comprised destroyers and I think their Commander had some misgivings about handing over his charge to a couple of cutters and diverse other small vessels from the Royal Navy. Nonetheless, we delivered the convoy to British Fleet destroyers off Malta, then turned round for Gibraltar, via a couple of days in Algiers, to await the empties. We did not have long to wait. On the 28th, we were headed for Norfolk, Virginia, where our arrival coincided with a desperate need for repairs. It was during this passage that I celebrated my 20th birthday, coupled with my promotion to Sub.Lieutenant."

Donald Hopewell, Chief Yeoman of Signals in *'Banff'*, from joining the ship in April 1942, said:

"Prior to docking in the United States, there was a meeting of heads of departments, when the Captain and Engineer Officer suggested that we make the best of the dock facilities, to get as many modifications and repairs done as we possibly could. We each contributed a lengthy list of defects, including a boiler clean, which would not only be beneficial for the ship, but would help to prolong our stay in the States.

"Refit in America was a revelation; ramps from the side of the dock, spray-painting of ship's side, and a boiler clean by chemicals. A bonus was a luxury diet of steaks and choice meats, fresh vegetables, eggs and the daily dollop of ice-cream. We also had the run of the PX, which meant we could buy anything as long as it did not have 'US' stamped on it. Naturally, there had to be a catch in all this high living. Ours was the limitation of eleven dollars for the week, which severely restricted our spending. However, we had an excellent Canteen Manager who, by his enterprise, managed to acquire loads of samples and Lend-Lease stores."

Derek Blake had joined *'Banff'* from the Flower Class Corvette *'Carnation'* early in 1943. He recalls the return passage from the States:

"We sailed up the coast with a mixed bag of USN, RCN and RN ships. Just prior to the Americans leaving us, we had warnings of a U-boat on the prowl. There were several Asdic contacts and we were closed up at 'action stations'. The OC Quarterdeck was Gunner (T)

HMS BANFF & HMS FISHGUARD

Eric Thorman RN, who always seemed to have difficulty in maintaining silence. It was very dark, and there was a certain tenseness among the depth-charge crews. Suddenly, a searchlight from one of the American ships, pierced the darkness, no doubt sweeping the sea for a suspected surfaced submarine. In the hubbub which followed, our captain ordered the light to be doused. As its beam swept towards us, Able Seaman Tommy Gordon, a member of the after gun's crew, shouted — duck! or they'll see you. The Gunnery Officer, whilst trying to maintain silence, ducked with the rest of us. The light was duly extinguished and whilst we were all embarassed at being suckered by Tommy Gordon, I think the Gunnery Officer was the most embarrassed of us all. Come daybreak, the American ships had broken away from the convoy and were nowhere to be seen."

James Byrne, who joined 'Fishguard' in 1942, tends to remember most the effects of bad weather on the ship:

"I recall that in late 1942, somewhere off the west coast of Ireland, we encountered the most attrocious weather. I was on the bridge, when I am sure that at one time, we registered a 53° roll. So violent was it that we lost one of our boats and also the starboard 3" gun platform, amongst other bits and pieces. In a further gale in 1943, we had steamed out with the 44th E.G. to join up with an incoming convoy. The seas were so bad that we were unable to turn about to take up the escort, and were 'hove to' when the convoy passed us. We had a couple of days of that before we could turn around and take up our station."

Although 'Fishguard' was engaged in her fair share of action against U-boats, James Byrne has a memory of one in particular:

"We had been despatched from a convoy to screen a merchant ship whose engines had broken down. These lone vigils were always a nerve-racking experience, with the ever-present threat of a U-boat turning up. However, all went well until we were eventually required to return to our station with the convoy. As we steamed at full speed, our Radar picked up a submarine on the surface. Our attention was immediately turned towards it and we managed to get off three rounds from our 5" gun before the U-boat dived. He was no doubt shadowing

THE HAND - ME - DOWN SHIPS

our convoy, but the gunfire served to make him keep his head down. We spent the following three hours in hot pursuit and dropped a few depth-charges, but without apparent success."

By the end of 1943, both cutters were embarked for service with the East Indies Fleet. *'Fishguard'* had by this time had a change in Command, when Lt.Cdr. C. Donovan Smith DSC, RD, RNR, replaced Lt.Cdr. Pryse. *'Banff'* had a change in Engineering Officer, when Lt. (E) Harry Duckett RN, joined the ship.

"Within days of sailing for the Mediterranean we were sent to give assistance to the French submarine *'Minerie"*, said Dickey Hawkey. "She had been damaged by depth-charges dropped by aircraft. When we met up with her about 180 miles off Brest, we discovered that she was able to proceed on her own. We promptly rejoined the convoy. Apart from an attack by three enemy aircraft during that afternoon, little else happened to cause us concern and we arrived in Gibraltar during the morning of the 20th."

The stay in Gibraltar was brief. *'Banff'* contined her passage through the Mediterranean and although there were constant threats of attack by enemy aircraft no action resulted. However, there was much evidence that others had not been so fortunate. Wreckage was sighted off Algiers, and on the 28th when barely out of sight of Malta, the cutter went to the rescue of four South African airmen who were adrift in their dinghy.

An interesting twist to the latter incident, is provided by Donald Hopewell: "When we got the airmen safely on board, we discovered to our surprise, that the pilot was one of a group of RAF personnel to whom we had given passage to Gibraltar. The sequel is that during a leave in Durban in 1944, one of the families who offered their hospitality to members of our ship's company, turned out to be that of the same pilot."

By 11th November, *'Banff'* had passed through the Suez Canal and arrived at Port Taufique. Within twenty-four hours of her arrival, she was embarked to the Red Sea as escort to a number of motor launches. What should have been a straightforward operation, turned out to be a near disaster, due largely to one of those freak changes in the weather, which are not uncommon in tropical climes.

Donald Hopewell recalls: "We were hit by a violent tropical storm. The heavens were lit by lightning and torrential rain reduced visibility to a minimum. The sea was whipped up into a frenzy and we on the bridge were heavily drenched. In these appalling conditions, the convoy was scattered wide and starshell was fired in an attempt to keep the motor launches in sight. Unfortunately, the first three starshell failed to illuminate, much to the concern of our captain.

"Leaning over the bridge, he shouted to the gun's crew — why haven't the stars come out? Such an enquiry to a thoroughly soaked and impatient Petty Officer in charge, was bound to provoke a typically naval-type response. Which it did. The Petty Officer was heard to mutter, in reply — how should I know, I don't make the bloody things — I only fire 'em! The storm subsided almost as quickly as it had begun and the scattered convoy was quickly rounded up. What surprised me was the cold. Not what I expected. The next day, we were despatched to search for a reported Japanese submarine, but after much dashing about, the fruitless search was finally broken off."

From then on, until March 1944, both *'Banff'* and *'Fishguard'* were assigned to escort duties on the Kilindini/Aden passage. However, due to recurring mechanical faults, *'Banff'* was ordered to Durban for refit. On the same day of her arrival, 13th March 1944, *'Fishguard'* proceeded from Kilindini with convoy DKA14, bound for Aden, just another of the 'local' voyages which were, by then, all too familiar to the cutters on the East African Station.

Coincidentally, in the early evening of that day, on the opposite side of Africa, in the Gulf of Guinea, nearly three thousand miles distant, the German submarine U852, captained by Heinz Eck, was stalking the Greek steamer *'Peleus'*. Whilst *'Fishguard'* was quietly going about her business of protecting her charges, U852 was preparing to send another merchant ship to the bottom. Ironically, the paths of *'Fishguard'* and the U852 were to cross about six weeks later.

U852 had left Kiel on 18th January, embarked on her first patrol and was headed for the Indian Ocean. It was 28 years old Eck's first operational command. At 1757 on the 13th March, Eck sighted the *'Peleus'*, which was in British service and had a crew of thirty-five, some of them British. At a range of little more than 600 yards U852 loosed two torpedoes which, thirty-two seconds later, ploughed into the unsuspecting ship. Following the crippling explosions, the surviving members of the steamer's crew took to the water. Eck, meanwhile dived his boat to reload torpedo tubes.

When he surfaced about an hour later, he spotted the remnants of the *'Peleus'* crew adrift on rafts. U852 intercepted the survivors and took three of them on board for interrogation. The unfortunate seamen were later thrown back to the sea. Any hopes they might have had of survival, disappeared when the U-boat Commander ordered members of his crew to turn their machine-guns on to the rafts. Hand grenades were also hurled at the hapless survivors. When U852 departed the scene, just four of the crew of the *'Peleus'* were left alive. One of them, the Third Officer, died twenty-five days later of his wounds. Thirty-eight days of exposure to the harshness of the Atlantic passed before, on 20th April, the three survivors were sighted and picked up by the Portugese vessel *'Alexandre Silva'*, about 500 miles from the position where the *'Peleus'* had been taken by the sea. They were eventually landed in Capetown from whence two of them were despatched to London.

By the 3rd May, *'Fishguard'* was back in Kilindini, after two outward and homeward voyages between her base and Aden. The day before her arrival, U852 had reached the Indian Ocean and was active off the coast of Somaliland, south west of Socotra. During the early hours of the 2nd, the submarine was sighted on the surface by Wellington aircraft of Aden Command. Thus began a twelve-hour running battle in which U852 was so badly damaged that she was unable to submerge. Seven of her crew, including the First Lieutenant, were killed in the action. As nightfall approached, Eck, with little or no chance to escape, managed to get his boat into a small bay, where she grounded, and subsequent attempts were made to carry out repairs, but so extensive was the damage that it was finally decided to scuttle. Whilst the crew set about placing explosive charges, the fifteen wounded members were put ashore, and all classified documents destroyed.

Unfortunately for Eck and his crew, the detonation of the scuttling charges was observed in the British sloop *'Falmouth'*, then two miles distant and already speeding towards the U-boat's position. On arrival, it was discovered that the submarine lay close inshore, with a 30° list to port. Most of the bow and stern sections had been blown off, but the midship section, though flooded, was largely intact. *'Falmouth'* sent away an armed party to round up the survivors of U852, who had fled inland. By the 4th, from the submarine's crew of sixty-six, she had on board the Captain, five other officers and thirty ratings. Two other British ships *'Parrett'* and *'Raider'* also had prisoners on board. A close guard was put on the wreck and work began almost immediately on recovering gear, instruments and documents. Most of this was later despatched to the United Kingdom. An order from Admiralty called for the U-boat's captain, together with nine other members of the crew, to be flown to the U.K. at the earliest possible moment. There can be no doubt that Eck's treatment of the *'Peleus'* survivors had already been reported to London.

On the 11th May, *'Fishguard'* was despatched from Kilindini to join in the complex salvage operation. James Byrne, in the cutter at the time recalls:

"We anchored off the U-boat for about ten days, whilst the boffins who we had brought with us, set about examining the wreck, which although beached, had its conning tower above water, even at half tide. We were later relieved by sister ship *'Sennen'*, but returned again on the 30th. Our stay had seen our diet reduced to corned beef and biscuits, so our relief from the operation, if only temporary, was especially welcomed."

Alan Groves, another *'Fishguard'* crew member, added: "We started the salvage job with pumps and compressors. We had divers at work and interpreters to mark everything that was taken from the submarine. This was littered over our deck like a 'car boot' sale. During all this we were under strict orders not to touch anything. During the hours of darkness we took a break from the salvage work to patrol the area."

On the 12th *'Fishguard'* reported that the U-boat was now opened from end to end, but pumping was ineffective, and that two, and possibly four torpedoes were stored in upper deck storage. The following day, the cutter was asked when it would be possible to have the torpedoes ready for removal, so that a suitable vessel could be arranged to hoist them in and transport them for expert examination. The painstaking removal and recording of components and gear, kept *'Fishguard'* fully occupied until her relief. On the 20th, she reported that the submarine's list had increased and in anticipation of it possibly capsizing, top weight was cut away and a wire led from the conning tower to the shore. The control room had been pumped out to the floorboards and a major leak stopped by Sub.Lt. (E) Butler of the *'Prudent'*, and Diver French. However, the water levels rose quickly when the pumps stopped.

The salvage operations were concluded on 6th June and the salvage party returned to Kilindini. The cutter *'Sennen'* arrived on the 11th, having recovered a considerable amount of equipment from the U-boat. Both *'Fishguard'* and *'Sennen'* then returned to their escort duties.

In October 1945, whilst *'Fishguard'* was still operating in the Indian Ocean, the captain of U852 was called to account for the killing of survivors from the *'Peleus'*. At a British Military Court in Hamburg, he, together with crew members Hoffman, Weispfennig, Lenze and Schwender, were charged with having participated in the killing of crew members of the *'Peleus'* against the Articles of War, by shooting and throwing hand grenades at them. The court found them guilty as charged. Eck, Hoffman and Weispfennig were executed on 30th November 1945. Schwender was sentenced to fifteen years imprisonment, whilst Lenze was committed to prison for life.

When *'Banff'* arrived at Durban on 13th March, 1944, she found that there were no berths available to her. She was sent on to Port Elizabeth, where she was under refit until 29th May. Eddie Ivison, serving in *'Banff'* at the time, recalls a visit up country:

"Some of the crew were sent to farms in the area of Cape Province.

The leave was, I believe, financed mainly by farmers who contributed funds to the Navy League. At the conclusion of one of these visits, some of us mustered at the railway station together with our hosts, who had come along to see us off. The day after our return to the ship, lower deck was cleared and the skipper gave us a good lambasting for alleged misconduct at the railway station. Two ladies of the Navy League were present. Being the Leading Hand and in defence of my colleagues, I suggested that the two representatives contact our hosts who, having been present at the time of our departure, would surely discount the story as rubbish. The outcome of their enquiries was to lay the blame squarely on the shoulders of Nazi-sympathisers, who had phoned in the mis-information to the Navy League."

On 26th July, *Banff* arrived at her base in Kilindini, when Lt.Cdr. James D'arcy Nesbitt RNR, was appointed Captain, after two years in the battleship *Duke of York*. Between that date and early November, the cutter was engaged on a number of small convoys in and around the Indian Ocean, interspersed with 'exercises', one of them in company with *Totland* and the submarine *Truculent*.

It was during November that she was despatched on what can be best described as a 'Flag Waving' operation in Zanzibar. Dickey Hawkey said of it: "We were detailed to take the U.S. Consul in Nairobi to Zanzibar for the Bi-Centenary Celebrations of the Al Besaid Dynasty of Sultans. What a fascinating place it was. A Commemorative set of stamps was issued for the occasion, of which I bought a set, convinced that it would rocket in value. Alas, that was not the case."

In his recollections of the visit, Donald Hopewell said: "The officers were sent ashore for the formal celebrations. We on board were asked to provide illuminated ship, with fireworks, after sunset. There followed a frantic search for cables and light bulbs and we finally managed to get a lit cable from stem to stern — all remniscent of the pre-war Spithead Reviews. The four members of the Signals Staff were responsible for the pyrotechnics which comprised 'starshell' and the ship's total stock of red and white rockets and 'snowflake'."

The celebrations over, *Banff* returned to more familiar activities.

THE HAND - ME - DOWN SHIPS

Among her single-ship convoys, was the passage of the U.K. bound Polish Liner *'Batory'*, from Mombasa. It was *'Banff's* task to escort her safely through the Gulf of Aden and the Red Sea as far as Suez. The cutter's Captain Lt.Cdr. Nesbitt recalls an incident during that voyage:

"The *'Batory'* was very slow as she had quite a dirty bottom. When we were about to enter the gulf, we experienced quite heavy weather. Our engineers had a salt water hose running onto one of the main engine bearings which was running very hot. As though that was not enough, our Surgeon Lt. Robin Taggart, reported to me that one of the young ratings had severe peritonitis and had to be operated on as soon as possible. I told him that we could'nt stop just then in a dangerous place and that the nearest place was Djibouti at the western end of the Gulf.

"In any event, operating would have been near impossible with *'Banff'* jumping all over the place, so in view of the urgency of the matter, I sent a signal to the Captain of the Polish ship, who was most helpful. We stopped and he made a wonderful lee for us whilst the patient was transferred to his ship. We built a platform on the thwarts of the whaler as a sort of stretcher. All went well until our doctor signalled that he would be staying on the *'Batory'* and would carry out the operation himself. The two ships then proceeded through the Gulf and the Red Sea. When we got our doctor back, he brought with him a letter from the Polish Master, which contained a report of what happened aboard his ship.

"Our doctor reported that when he boarded the *'Batory'*, he found she was full of pregnant service women from Mombasa, on their way home presumably for their confinement, and the ship had a good hospital, together with a number of young army doctors. Apparently they had little to do all day but lounge about drinking. Our doctor picked out the most sober looking candidate to act as his anaesthetist, because the rest of them were in no condition to assist. In the middle of the operation, the acting anaesthetist said he would have to 'empty ballast', but Taggart forbade him and told him, if necessary, to do it down his leg. Which he did, and all was well!

"The Master of the ship said that he was going to take the patient back to England, as he was very young and would like to see him in the bosom of his family. Having got our charge safely to her destination, we returned to Mombasa with one doctor back, minus one young rating."

With the end of the war looming up, *'Banff'* and *'Fishguard'*, were engaged on what might be termed a period of odd jobs, during which *'Fishguard'* took her turn for refit in Durban, before being assigned as escort to the first convoy into Singapore on 7th September 1945. She was present when the Japanese surrender was taken on the 11th.

'Banff' was assigned to collect a convoy of eight ships from Chittagong and escort them to Rangoon, via Akyab.

"There is not much water along that coast," said Lt.Cdr. Nesbitt. "I only had an American type fathometer, which passed as an echo sounder, and that was broken anyway. As we were Senior Officer of escorts, it was quite a responsibility. The convoy was one of the first of the slow ones into Rangoon, just as the Japanese were moving out, and the fast convoy was ahead of us. All went well, except that we had a large steam yacht in company with an Indian CO. The ship would keep cutting corners and making a lot of smoke. He could not do our convoy speed of 9 knots.

"We arrived at the mouth of the Rangoon river, where the Japanese had moved all lightships and bouys, added to which I had never been to Rangoon in my seagoing life. My pre-war days had been with Blue Funnel on the China and Japan run. However, the Commodore of the convoy, in the *'Itria'* had a pilot on board who knew the Rangoon river well, so he was all right. As for the rest of us, there was a large motor launch putting pilots aboard the other ships. I was quick to spot that the pilot flag was upside down. Well, as Senior Officer Escorts, and having delivered my charge safely, I was feeling skittish, so I asked my Chief Yeoman of Signals, Donald Hopewell, to make to the M.L. the following signal — 'do your pilots stand on their heads? Apparently, the message was not understood aboard the M.L., so she came alongside to find out what it meant. I went to the wing of the bridge, expecting to see a very young Sub.Lt. RNVR, instead of which

THE HAND-ME-DOWN SHIPS

a very irate and red-faced Rear Admiral stuck his head out of the wheelhouse and roared — 'what a bloody stupid time to make a signal like that! The Chief Yeoman smiled and disappeared to the opposite wing of the bridge, and I carried on up river, right under the stern of the nearest ship in the convoy, as they had run out of pilots when it came to our turn. We made our way successfully up river to our allotted berth and I heard nothing more about my contretemps."

The problem of *'Banff's* broken fathometer was later resolved by an unexpected source, as Cdr. Nesbitt explains: "A few weeks after the Rangoon river convoy, I was at a cocktail party in Durban, where I met a Director of the South African Telephone Company, who was interested to hear that I had signalled Admiralty for a certain sort of button microphone to mend my fathometer. Unfortunately, someone in the U.K. had put it on a plane for Delhi, Bombay, or somewhere else, and we did not receive it. However, this nice Telephone Company Director, sent out a technician to *'Banff'* and he managed to fix the offending fathometer with a small button microphone which, he explained, they used in their telephones. We had no further problems. If I remember rightly, I paid something like a couple of shillings for it, apart of course from a few drinks to celebrate."

The latter part of *'Banff's* foreign commission, was spent scurrying between Seychelles, Madagascar and Diego Suarez. Her trip to the latter was as escort to two large, brand new motor launches, via Tulear on the south west coast of Madagascar, Majunga to the north west, then round the top of the island to Diego Suarez. The brief stay there was an experience the crew of *'Banff'* could well have done without.

"We had been there a day or two," said Cdr. Nesbitt, "when a number of the ship's company went down with bacillary dysentry, including myself. When the doctor saw us, he said we were lucky, since he had just received a supply of a suitable drug with which to remedy our unpleasant condition. It certainly did the trick."

The end of the war came for *'Banff'* and *'Fishguard'* in November 1945. Both had survived the rigors of escort duties in the North and

South Atlantic, and the often monotonous activity of two years in eastern waters. The thoughts of their crews were now centred on the prospect of being home for Christmas. They were not to be disappointed. *'Fishguard'* arrived Portsmouth on 1st December, whilst *'Banff'* arrived on the 16th.

Chapter Fifteen
Author's conclusions

With hostilities grinding to a halt in the Far East, and *'Totland'* having been spared the final mopping up operation, my thoughts were synonymous with all who had endured the war; to return home to the family I had not seen for the best part of three years. My two younger brothers, one in the Royal Navy, the other with 6th Commando, had both grown into their manhood in my absence, and my two little sisters had reached their teens. I had missed those important years in the relationship with my father, a veteran of The Great War of 1914—1918, and most of all I was acutely aware of the great relief my return would bring to my dear long-suffering mother.

True, there was some disappointment in being excluded from the last operation of the war, an anti-climax to what had been an eventful commission. The fact that I was about to sever relationships which had endured for three years in *'Totland'* had not yet sunk in, but I was never to forget 'Scouse' Martin, 'Bombhead' Merton, 'Lofty' Dexter, 'Old Mo' Cooper, 'Freezer' Frost, 'Horse' Langdon, 'Jock' Brogan, 'Bungy' Williams, 'Happy' Day, 'Doc' Burgess, 'Bunny' Austin, 'Whacker' Payne, 'Lofty' Hillier, 'Taff' Williams, 'Shorty' Burroughes, 'Pat' O'Mahoney, 'Kiwi' Marr, 'Tubby' Maynard, Charlie Coombes and Geoff George, to mention but a few with whom I had shared so many happy and memorable experiences.

I spent the last few months of my service with the Royal Navy as 'care and maintenance' crew member of a Frigate. I did not see *'Totland'* again. She sailed for the United States, with a passage crew, on 26th March 1946. On her arrival, she was handed back to the U.S. Coast Guard and returned to service with the name *'Mocoma'*. In 1950, she seriously damaged her bottom off Star Reef, Florida, and was taken out of service. She was eventually sold off on 15th July

AUTHOR'S CONCLUSIONS

1955.

'Gorleston' returned home, 23rd April 1946, and with her original name *'Itasca'* went back into Coast Guard service. E.R. Carley, took passage to the United States aboard her:

"Having been called up in October 1945, and allocated to the Writers' Branch of the Royal Navy, I was fortunate enough, after completing my initial training at Wetherby, Yorkshire, to be assigned a drafting to the U.S.A. (Saker 2), employed with the British Admiralty Delegation in Washington D.C. I made the voyage in *'Gorleston'*. We had also two Ministers of Religion on board, who were returning home after spending a holiday in the U.K. I particularly remember that they were confined to their quarters for most of the voyage, because of sea-sickness."

Four years later, on 4th October 1950, the cutter was decommissioned by the Coast Guard and sold off.

'Banff' was returned, with her named changed to *'Sebec'*, on 27th February 1946. Just over a year later, she was recommissioned and re-named *'Tampa'*. She remained operational until August 1954.

'Lulworth's renewed service with the Coast Guard was short-lived. She was finally paid off and sold on 23rd October 1947, just twenty-two months after her return on 12th February 1946.

John Loughran said of her: "We were indeed fortunate to have served in *'Lulworth'*, in spite of the thousands of gallons of paint we lavished on her. 'Journey's End' was a moving experience for us all."

Arnold Sayers enjoys a permanent reminder of his time in the ship, to add to his happy memories: "Three of the wardroom officers were given the task of sailing the ship back to the United States. It was a trip we all enjoyed. On arrival in Boston, we had to oversee the unloading of the remaining stores, and then came the question of wardroom effects. Most were straightforward, but when it came to the oil painting of *'Lulworth'* on escort duty, by Lt.Cdr. E.G. Dalison, Captain of *'Londonderry'*, neither of the two surviving members of the wardroom were interested, so I paid them £5 each, which left £5 for my share, since the wardroom had paid Dalison £15 for it in 1943. I believe it to be an excellent painting which I am proud to have

THE HAND - ME - DOWN SHIPS

hanging in my study."

'Landguard' did not make the return voyage home. Just eleven months short of a score of years as a sea-going vessel, she was sold off to the Madrigal Company of Manila as scrap. She was towed round to Singapore by the *'Brown Ranger'* early in September 1949.

'Hartland', in spite of the heavy damage inflicted on her at Oran on 8th November 1942, was eventually salvaged and scrapped in 1949. Both she and sister ship *'Walney'* found a distinguished place in the annals of Naval History.

'Culver' too made the supreme sacrifice. She, together with the members of her crew who went down with her, like those who gave their lives in *'Hartland'* and *'Walney'* have a special place in the memories of all surviving cuttermen.

The cutters may not have been 'proper warships', as they were once so mistakenly described, but they gave an excellent and most commendable account of themselves, and gained the life-long affection of all who served in them.

The ships have long since gone, and the surviving crew members are diminishing in numbers. If you should meet one of them, don't be surprised to find him reluctant to talk about the cutters' exploits. It is more than likely, that he will ramble on about some hilarious, or even outrageous escapade ashore in some foreign port. But then, that is how old sailors are!

On the 17th April 1991, some forty or so survivors of the ships, together with their wives, and now members of the Cutters' Association, were re-united at a special get-together at the Bull Hotel in Peterborough. The occasion was the 50th Anniversary of the ships being handed over by the United States Coast Guard to the Royal Navy. For many, it was their first reunion with old shipmates in nearly half a century. Mostly in their seventies, and some in their eighties, they relived the good times of that dramatic period in our history, yet never forgetting the shipmates who were lost.

In a special tribute to the cutters and their crews, the then Commandant of the United States Coast Guard, Admiral J.W. Kime, said in a message handed to Lt.Cdr. Peter Dixon (ex-Lulworth) and

AUTHOR'S CONCLUSIONS

Chairman of the Cutters Association, by Commander O. Coy USCG:

"Greetings and congratulations from the United States Coast Guard. Fifty years ago, the first 'White Ensign' cutters were transferred from the United States Coast Guard to join His Majesty's Royal Navy in the fight for freedom. The origins of your proud organisation, The Cutters Association, flow from the historic transfer under the now famous Lend-Lease effort. Indeed, it also marks one of the memorable occasions in the history of the U.S. Coast Guard.

"Thank you for your service in a noble cause during a dark hours in the World's history. It was your valour and determination that helped achieve victory in those troubled times. Today, you have good reason to look with pride on the professionalism of the young sailors, in both the Royal Navy and the U.S. Coast Guard, who are serving shoulder to shoulder in the Persian Gulf in the cause for Freedom. You helped to establish the standards and traditions that have become our guide. For this, and your continued interest in our service, I thank you, one and all.

"The 38,000 men and women of the U.S. Coast Guard join me in saluting you and wishing you a very, very Happy Anniversary."

The words of Admiral Kime are directed at all men who served in the cutters, whether they be members of the Cutters Association or not. Having shared in the common experience of service in those grand old ships, a cutterman can always look back on them with pride and affection with the gratifying knowledge that they have now been lifted from the depths of anonymity.

End Piece

The picture of *'Banff'* which appears in the photograph section, was supplied by one of her captains, Lt.Cdr. James D'Darcy Nesbitt RNR. (Rtd), with the following comment:

"The photograph was taken on the very day I joined the ship in Kilindini. The very first thing I had to do was to shift her from Kilindini to an anchorage right alongside the Naval offices in Mombasa, as I had to be captain of the Admiral's flagship for the day. The resident Admiral (East Africa) was being relieved that day by another. When I heard this, I asked for a photograph to be taken of the ship for their benefit and of course, for mine, and I told them I wanted a bugler, having just come from a very pusser flag ship. They were flabergasted at my request, but I insisted.

"Believe it or not, they dug up a very young sailor, Kenya RNVR., out of jail for the day, where the poor lad had been incarcerated for stealing a chicken. He played the bugle beautifully, so the next day, as the two Admirals, sitting in the stern sheets of their barge and passing *Banff's* stern on their way to Kilindini to see the new Admiral's domain, I ordered our young bugler to sound the 'alert', which he did most admirably and then the 'carry on', also beautifully. It was something to see the two Admirals nudging one another as they heard the bugle. They just didn't believe that such a sound could have come from an escort! Do note the Admiral's flag at *Banff's* masthead."

During the compilation of this book, some of the contributors have, regrettably, 'crossed the bar'. They are Donald Hopewell, Chief Yeoman of Signals in *'Banff';* Richard (Dickey) Hawkey, Sub.Lt.RNVR., in *'Banff';* William (Bill) Dawes, Ordnance Mechanic in *'Sennen';* (Lofty) Johnson of *'Landguard';* Charlie Anderson, ERA., in *'Landguard';* G. Jackman *'Lulworth'* and H.V. Emmins *'Totland'*.

CUTTERS' CAPTAINS

Commanding Officers in the ten cutters, during their service with the Royal Navy, were as follows:-

'BANFF' Lt.Cdr. P.S. Evans RN (May 1941)
Lt. Peter Brett RNR (February 1943)
Lt.Cdr. J. D'Arcy Nesbitt RNR (August 1944)
Lt. J.N. Coombs RNVR (December 1945)

'CULVER' Lt.Cdr. R.T. Gordon-Duff RN

'FISHGUARD' Lt.Cdr. H.L. Pryse RD, RNR (June 1941)
Lt.Cdr. C.D. Smith DSC, RD, RNR (October 1943)
Lt.Cdr. C.A. Woods RNZNR (June 1945)
Lt.Cdr. C.G. Scott RNVR (July 1945)

'GORLESTON' Cdr. P.G.L. Cazlett DSC, RN (May 1941)
Cdr. R.W. Keymer RN (July 1941)
Lt.Cdr. W.H.C. Wood-Roe RNR (November 1943)
Lt.Cdr. W.A.C. Leonard RNZNVR (December 1943)
Lt. G.M. Berlyn SANF (V) (January 1945)
Lt.Cdr. P.E.C. Pickles, MBE, RNVR (September 1945)
Cdr. S.M. Booker RNVR (February 1946)

'HARTLAND' Lt.Cdr. G.P. Billot DSO, RNR

'LANDGUARD' Lt. G.C. Gladstone RNVR (June 1941)
Lt.Cdr. R.E.S. Hugonin RN (February 1942)
Cdr. T.S.L. Fox-Pitt RN (October 1942)
Lt. Cdr. B.M. Skinner RN (January 1945)
Lt. R.N. Kinder RN (January 1945)
Lt. H. Crawshaw RNVR (April 1946)
Lt. L.E. Smythe RN (September 1946)

CUTTER'S CAPTAINS

'LULWORTH'
Lt.Cdr. C. Gwinner DSO, RN (June 1941)
Cdr. R.C.S. Woolley RD, RNR (February 1943)
Lt. D. Bowie RNVR (December 1945)

'SENNEN'
Lt.Cdr. D.C. Kinloch RN (June 1941)
Lt.Cdr. R.S. Abram RN (November 1941)
Lt.Cdr. F.H. Thornton OBE, DSC, RNR (February 1943)
Lt.Cdr. B.M. Skinner RN (May 1945)
Lt.Cdr. F.H. Sherwood DSC, RCNVR (February 1946)

'TOTLAND'
Lt.Cdr. S.G.C. Rawson RN (June 1941)
Lt.Cdr. L.E. Woodhouse RN (June 1941)
Lt.Cdr. F.A. Ramsay DSO, DSC, RN (October 1942)
Lt.Cdr. H.E. Tourtel RNR (July 1943)
Lt.Cdr. G.D. Davies DSC, RNR (October 1944)
Lt. C.R. Speak RNVR (February 1945)
Cdr.Mech. A. Healey (November 1945)

'WALNEY'
Lt.Cdr. Peter Meyrick RN

250 FOOT CUTTERS ("LAKE" CLASS)
(Pre - Transfer 1941)

Cost
  $900,000 each (hull and machinery

Hull
Displacement (tons)	1,662 trial (1929); 2,075 fl (1929)
Length	250' oa; 239' wl; 236' bp
Beam	42' mb
Draft	12'11" mean (1929); 16' max (1929)
Block Coefficient	.490

Machinery
Main Engines	1 General Electric motor driven by generator driven by a turbine
Main Boilers	2 Babcock & Wilcox watertube boilers. 250 psi, 250° superheat
SHP	3,350
Propellers	Single, 4 blades

Performance
Max Speed	17.3 kts (trials, 1929)

Logistics
Fuel Oil (95%)	90,000 gal
Complement	8 officers, 4 warrants, 85 men (1940)

Electronics
Detection Radar	Not fitted (1941)

Armament
1929	1 5"/51; 1 3"/50; 2 6 pdrs.
1941	2 3"/50 (single); 1 Y-gun; dc tracks

Index

Aberdeen 148.
Abram, Lt.Cdr. R.S. 149.
Agnew, Capt. W.G. 33.
Alexander Hamiltom 3.
Alexandre Silva 162.
Ambrose, T. 24.,25.,27.,29.,311.
Alguada Lighthouse 91.
Allen, Rear Adml. E.C. (Junr) USCG 3.
Andrews, Adml. A. USN 12.
Anderson, Charlie 71.
Ashanti 78.
Athel Duchess 157.
Athel Regent 108.
Athel Princess 108.
Atherbaskan 66.,69.
Aubretia 143.
Auricula 24.
Aurania 107.
Aurora 33.,40.

Baker-Cresswell, Capt. J. 88.,142.
Balingkar 128.
Banff 16.,70.,155.,168.
Barbarigo 21.
Barber, Capt. Robert F. (Rtd.) USCG 10.
Bate, R. 106.,107.
Batory 166.
Baton Rouge 108.,109.
Bennekom 21.
Bennett, Rear Adml. A.C. USN 35.
Berwick 24.
Bevan, Sub.Lt. M. 83.
Bideford 24.,29.,55.,58.,60.,67.,74., 120.
Billot, Lt.Cdr. G. 39.,40.,48.,49.
Birdlip 134.
Bismarck 104.
Blake, D. 158.
Bold 70
Boyd, E. 155.,156.
Boyle Capt. G. 57.
Brett, Lt.P. 156.
Brilliant 45.
British Fortitude 108.
British Statesman 157.
Broadway 143.
Brooks, A. 68.
Brown, Heber.
Bulldog 143.
Butser 134.
Byard 147.
Byrne, James 159.

California 104.
Cam 129.
Cape Clear 104.
Carley, E.R.
Carnation 158.
Carlow Lt. 26.,28.
Cayuga 2.,7.,9.
Cazlett, Cdr. P.G.L. 120.
Chalk, Sub.Lt. W.R. 74.
Challenger 24.
Champlain 2.
Charybdis 66.
Cheerly 70.
Chelan 2.
Cheshire 128.
Chitral 88.
City of Manila 128 - 131.
Coulson, R. 74.
Colorado 7.
Convoys: CU1 . . . 108.
   DKA14: HX125: . . . 19.
   HX128: . . . 105.
   HX139: . . . 106.
   KMS50: . . . 113.
   MC13: . . . 117.
   MKF13: OB34: . . . 106.
   ON182: . . . 156.
   ONS5: . . . 150.
   OS4: . 106.,120.,123.
   OS10: . . . 21.
   OS15: . . . 24.
   SC130: . . . 152.
   SL87: . 124 - 127.
   SL89: . . . 24.,107.
   SL109: . . . 58.
   SL115: . . . 81.
Cooke, Gordon 72.
Coombes, S., 113.,116.
Commandant Duboc 124 - 126.
Costello, 'Lou'. 113.,116.
Cossack 12.
Costick, Walter 24.,28.,31.
C.P. Hughes 108.
Cremer, Peter 30.
Culver 19—32.
Cunningham, Adml. Sir Andrew 33.,157.

Danae 88.
Dawes, W. 147.
Dempwolf, Capt. R.W. USCG 11.
Deutschland 8.
Denpark 61.
Dexter, J. 98.,113.,114.,119.
Dexterous 55.

178

INDEX

Dickey, Lt.Cdr. G.D. USN 49.
Dixcove 127.
Dixon, Lt.Cdr. P. RN 88.
Duff, Lt.Cdr. R.T. Gordon RN 20.
Duke of York 165.
Duncan 150.,153.
Duckett Lt., (E) H. 160
Duncton 134.
Dunn, A. 109.

Edinburgh Castle 112,
Egret 69.
Eisenhower Lt. Gen. D 42
Elder L. 39.,42.,50.
Edward Blyden 127.
Elles, General Sir Charles 67.
Embassage 123.
Emmins, H.V. 12.
Empire Bombadier 89.
Empire Drew 120.
Empire Norseman 108.,109.
Empire Storm 106.
Empire Tarpon 54 - 57.
Empire Voice 124.
Engenio di Savioa
Epervier 44.,45.,51.
Escapade 17.
Evans, Lt.Cdr. C.P.S. 155.
Evans, Lt. J.E. RNVR 50.
Exe 99.,108.

Falmouth 163.
Fandango 134.
Fara 120.
Ferris, Lt. E.M. RNVR 140.
Fidelity 123.
Fields, T. 141.
Finch, J.H. 39.,40.
Fishguard 54.,155 - 168.
Folkstone 108.,128.,132.
Fox-Pitt, Cdr. T.S. RN 65.
Freetown 111.
Fritillary 24.

Ganges 94.
Gardenia 124.
George, G. 13.,100.
German, Lt. J.P. USCG 11.
Gorleston 22.,84.,99.,120 - 144.,128 - 144
Gossamer 16.
Gothland 157.
Gray, Surg. Lt. C. 121.
Grenville 66.,69.
Grogan, Lt.Cdr. H.E. USCG 11.
Groves, A.
Gwinner, Cdr. Clive RN 74 - 82.

Hartland 33 - 55.
Hartland Honours 52.
Hartingdon 108.
Hastings 58 - 60.,63.,74.,80.
Hatarana 128.
Hawkey, Lt. Richard RNVR 156.
Hazard CPO., L 50.
Hebden, T. 139.
Hedgehog 17.
HF/DF 201
Hickson Lt. V.A. RN 48.
Hood 104.
Hopewell, D. 158.,165.
H.P. Jones 108
HS 293 Bomb 65.
Hugonin, Lt.Cdr. R.E.S. 21.,59.,64.
Hunter, Lt. I.H. RNVR 41.

Illustrious 11.
Ingria 63.
Inkpen 134.
International Ice Patrol 5.
Imperialist 134.
Islay 120.
Isola, Agastino 81.
Itasca 2.,5.,6.
Ivison, E. 165.

Jackman, G. 86.
Jed 152.
Johnson, Hallett 8.
John Holt 123.,127.
Johnson, Hon. William R. 13.
Jubb Lt. A.H. RNR. 27.
Jurgen, Nissen

Kendall, W.J. 123.
Kennett, L. 78.,80.
Keymer, Lt.Cdr. R.W. RN 124 - 126.
Kinder, Lt. R.N. 125.
King George V 104.
King Tom 111.
Kinloch, Lt.Cdr. D.C. 149.
Kipling, Lt. R.F. RN. 26.
Krestchmer 0 - 75.

Laconia 104.
Lady in White 140.
Lafian 127.
Lancaster, C.J.S. 85.
Landguard 14.,15.,21.,54 - 73.
Langdon, H. 106.
Langletarne 24.
Lansdale 108.
Law, Lt. P.R. RNVR 78.
Leonard, Lt.Cdr. W.A.C., RNZNVR 136.

179

INDEX

Lever, F.E. 16.
Liebermann, J. 141.
Linsell, Lt.Cdr. (E) RN 13.,129.,136.
Londonderry 24.,28.,33.
Longobardo, Primo 74 - 82.
Lord Hotham 134.
Loughran, J. 77.,79.,87.,90.
Lulworth 21.,58.,59.,62.,74 - 93.,120.

MacDonald, Gabriel 120.,122.
McKittrick, Capt. H.V. USN 12.
Macleod, Lt. (E) K.M. 14.,18.
MacRae, Commdr. A. 123.
Madison 108.
Magee, Commdr. W.E.B. 156.
Malaya 11.
Maritima 108.
Mark Anna 138
Marshall, Col. G.C.W. 40.
Massawa 116.
Masterful 89.
Masterson, S.H. 45.
Meermirk 120 - 122.
Mendota 1.
Meteor 38.
Meyrick, Lt.Cdr. P., RN 38.,44.
Miller, Don 98.
ML's. (Motor Launches) 483 & 480,43
Morgan, Lt. J.H., RNVR 41.
Mohawk 88.
Moose Jaw 85.
Moseley, Lt. W. RN 46.,47.,49.
Mount Felton 108.
Myers, P. 139.

Nesbitt, Lt.Cdr. J.D'arcy, RNR 70.,72.,165.
Ness 99.,108.
Newcastle 88.
Newman, Capt. Q.B. USCG 3
Niceto de Larrinaga 126.
Nicholson, Capt. B.W.L. 108.
Nordlys 62.
Norfolk 104.
North, Lt. (E) 78.,80.
Nurterton 25.

Obelkevitch, Gunner USN 50.
Ocean Salvor 89.
Oklahoma 7.
Oran 34.
Orchis 24.
Orkan 102.
Otaio 123.
Ottaway, A. 120.,131 - 134.
Operation Dracula 142.

Operation Husky 157.
" Musketry 66 - 69.
" Reservist 33.,35.
" Torch 33 - 53.
" Zipper 142.

Palliser, Capt. A.F.E., RN 11.
Parrett 163.
Pathenon 108.
Patrick, (Pat) 17.
Pattinson, Sub.Lt. G., RNVR 29.,31.
Payne, F. 118.
Peleus 161.
Pelican 152.
Pembroke 94.
Pentstemon 128.
Peters, Capt. F.T., RN 38.,44.,51.
Phillips, Lt. A.L., RNVR 45.
Phoebe 88.
Pietro Calvi 74 - 82.
Pink 151.
Plowman, F. 138.,140.
Pontchartrain 11.
Prince of Wales 104.
Prinz Eugen 104.
Prudent 164.
Pryse, Lt.Cdr. H.L. 155.
Pye, J. 68.

Queen Charlotte 94.
Queen Elizabeth 148.
Queenworth 39.

Raider 163.
Ramillies 88.
Ramsey, Lt.Cdr. F.A., RN 99.
Regusci 134.
Renown 105.
Repulse 104.
'Reservist' 33.
Resolution 11.,104.
Revenge 105.
Rixon, G. 153.
Roberts, C. 71.
Roberts, M. 12.
Robins, M. 15
Robert F. Hoke 89.
Rodney 105.
Roode Zee 134.
Roosevelt, A.D. 42.
Royal Star 59.
Ryan, P.C. 31.

Sandar 106.
Saranac 2.
Sargent, Vice Adm. R. USCG (Rtd). 4

INDEX

Satellite 57.
Saugor 122.
Sayers, A., CBE 85.,87.,88.
Schneider, H. 108.
Schewe, G. 25.
Schuch, H. 25.
Schwenk, G. 131 - 134.
Sebago 2.
Segundo 123.
Sennen 104.,106.,147 - 154.,163.
Sheffield 105.
Sherwood, Lt.Cdr. F.H. 154.
Sherwood, Lt.Cdr. R.E. RNR 150.
Shoshone 2.
Sicily 157.
Silverbelle 124 - 126.
Simkins, S. 65 - 67.
Skinner, Lt.Cdr. B.M., RN 70.,154.
Slater, K. 12.
Smith, Lt. A.M., RNR 73.
Smith, Lt.Cdr. C. Donovan 160.
Smythe, W. Cdr.P. RNR 129.
Snowflake 153.
Somerville, Adm. Sir James 107.
Spey 152.
Spreewald 30.
Stanley 21
Stanley, R. 155
St. Clair 11 126.
St. Wistan 134.
Stark, Adm. H., USN 2.
Stephenson, S. 16.
Suffolk 104.
Suffolk, L. 149.

Tahoe 2.
Tay 150.
Thilmere 38.
Thomas Holt 63.
Thorman, E. 159.
Thornton, Lt.Cdr. F.H. 150.
Ticehurst, A. 50.
Totland 94 - 103.,104 - 119.,134.,170.
Tourtel, Lt.Cdr. H.E., RNR 110.
Tremoda 123.
Triton 128.
Tromontane 51.
Trucco, Emelio 81.
Typhon 47.,51.

U 96 21.,22.
U 99 75.
U 105 30.
U 125 151.
U 156 104.
U 192 151.

U 209 152.
U 214 128.
U 267 151.
U 273 153.
U 333 30.,128.,131.
U 381 153.
U 406 128.,129.
U 439 150.
U 483 151.
U 522 108.
U 531 151.
U 630 151.
U 659 150.
U 852 161 - 162.
U 954 153.
Ital. *Barbarigo* 21.
Ital. *Pietro Calvi* 74 - 82.

Valiant 88.
Vanjar 106.
Vansittart 123.
Verbena 21.
Veteran 8.
Viccars, S. 141.
Victorious 104.
Vidette
Voulminot 134

Waesche, Adm. R.R., USCG 2.
Walker, Capt. F.J., RN 83.
Walmer Castle 20.
Walney 17.,33 - 53.
Walney Honours 52.
Ward, Sub. Lt. Peter RNVR 53.
Waterman, J. 138.
Wear 152.
Westland 156.
Wellington 99.,128.,137.
Weston 99.,108.
Wettern, J. 141.
Wild Swan 24.
Willenbrok, H.L. 21.
Wilson, P. 72.
Willson, J.O.C. 13.,147
Wolverine 74.
Woodhams, J. 153.
Woolley, Lt.Cdr. R.C.S., RNR 86.
Woolwich 88.
Wyoming 8.

Yestor 134.

Zwarte Zee 134.

181